Down from Bureaucracy

———————————————

Down from Bureaucracy

THE AMBIGUITY OF
PRIVATIZATION AND
EMPOWERMENT

Joel F. Handler

PRINCETON UNIVERSITY PRESS

PRINCETON, NEW JERSEY

Copyright © 1996 by Princeton University Press
Published by Princeton University Press, 41 William Street,
Princeton, New Jersey 08540
In the United Kingdom: Princeton University Press,
Chichester, West Sussex

Library of Congress Cataloging-in-Publication Data

Handler, Joel F.
Down from bureaucracy : the ambiguity of privatization and
empowerment / Joel F. Handler.
   p. cm.
Includes bibliographical references and index.
ISBN 0-691-04461-9 (cl : alk. paper)
1. Decentralization in government—United States.   2. Community
power—United States.   3. Power (Social sciences)—United States.
4. Privatization—United States.   5. United States—Politics and
government—20th century.   6. Decentralization in government.
7. Welfare state.   8. Schools—Decentralization—Illinois—Chicago.
I. Title.
JS341.H275   1996   350′.000973—dc20   95-37270

This book has been composed in Sabon

Princeton University Press books are printed
on acid-free paper and meet the guidelines
for permanence and durability of the Committee
on Production Guidelines for Book Longevity
of the Council on Library Resources

Printed in the United States of America
by Princeton Academic Press

1   3   5   7   9   10   8   6   4   2

For Betsy, and Alina, Kate, Jeffrey, and Lane

———————————————

CONTENTS

ACKNOWLEDGMENTS

I THANK Stuart Biegel, William Clune, G. Alfred Hess, Jr., and Austin Sarat for their valuable comments. My colleague, Yeheskel Hasenfeld, has taught me most of what I know about organizations. The reference librarians at UCLA Law School provided invaluable help for which I am deeply grateful. Part of the writing was done at the Rockefeller Foundation Bellagio Study and Conference Center. I thank the Foundation for that opportunity.

Down from Bureaucracy

————————————

Chapter 1

INTRODUCTION

IT IS BY NOW commonplace to note that "decentralization" and "privatization" are worldwide movements. Not only in Western Europe and the United States, but also in the Third World, governments are trying to lessen their presence (at least in the economy), unload state enterprises, and rely more on private markets. At least in the Western democracies, common themes are reducing the role of national government, lowering public spending, reducing the direct provision of services, and intervening less in the lives of citizens. In each society, however, these ideas have different meanings and policies and raise different issues. In the United States, decentralization, deregulation, and privatization are usually thought of along two historic dimensions: the allocation of authority between units of government and between state and market. Within organizations, whether public or private, decentralization refers to the process of assigning more responsibilities to lower organizational units.

The allocations and reallocations of organizational authority are conscious activities. What drives them? In the United States, there are two strands that are mutually reinforcing. The first is the taxpayer's revolt, which began in 1978 when California voters passed a referendum sharply reducing the local property taxes. The antitax movement spread quickly to the other states as well as the national government. Not only is it exceedingly difficult to raise taxes, but there is also strong support to reduce taxes. The taxpayer's revolt—which shows no signs of abating soon—plus national and state deficits have resulted in a significant downward flow of governmental authority. As will be discussed more fully in subsequent chapters, the federal government continues to mandate state programs, and states continue to mandate county and local programs, but neither provide sufficient funding. Despite recently enacted legislation purporting to check federally imposed unfunded mandates, it is unlikely that this situation will substantially change in the near future. This tactic serves the interests of national and state politicians, but increases the responsibilities at state and local levels. More and more public activities are being carried out at the local level, and indeed, local taxes are increasing.

Another consequence of the taxpayer revolt and the resulting squeeze at the local level is the increasing use of the private sector. Here, we speak primarily of contracting public services to private for-profit or not-for-profit organizations in order to save money. Again, we will have a lot to say about privatization and contracting out in subsequent chapters.

At the same time, there is a strong ideological component to the tax-payer revolt and consequent devolution to the local and private sectors. For a variety of reasons—perhaps stemming from the Vietnam War—there developed a profound distrust of government. To a considerable extent, the antigovernment, antibureaucracy mood is directed at Washington. This was certainly a theme that the Reagan presidency stressed. But the mood extends to the local level as well. For the first time in our history, school bonds are routinely rejected by the voters. No doubt part of this mood can be attributed to the greed of the 1980s "me" generation, but, again, there is more to the story. There is the view that public agencies—from the largest national bureaucracies to local school districts—are corrupt and inefficient, and that there are ways that government can do more with less if only they would change their ways. Government agencies will change their ways, the argument goes, if they have fewer resources, if they are more under the control of ordinary citizens at the local level, and if they are forced to adopt the incentive systems of the private sector. Government bureaucracy should be decentralized to the local level and, preferably, taken over by the private sector. The allocations of public authority are defended on grounds of freedom, efficiency, and accountability. The decentralization and privatization movement combine powerful symbols with saving money. Virtue is rewarded.

While virtue is (or may be) rewarded at the symbolic level, decentralization and privatization is often warfare in the trenches. The allocations of public authority involve intense power struggles by the relevant stakeholders. The voters may be interested in symbols and services. The stakeholders are interested in power and resources as well as symbols. The struggle for power includes not only the *definition of values* but also the *arenas* and *procedures* of conflict. At certain periods, and for certain issues, victors seek national definitions and authority; their influence is greatest at that level of government. Opponents will argue states' rights or the traditions of local government. Victors will favor efficient administration; opponents will emphasize "objective" criteria and due process.[1] The struggle for power is continuous; it extends throughout the life of the organization. In government, the interaction between federal, state, and local units of government—or more precisely, units *within* those units of government—is constant and dynamic; sometimes it takes the form of mutual alliances, and at other times, of conflict. The same is true with the relationship between the state and private organizations. Privatization, although justified in terms of efficiency, is the reallocation of power and resources between various interest groups or stakeholders.

A common theme throughout the decentralization debates concerns

[1] Moe 1989.

the role of the ordinary citizen. Local control, as well as the market, is justified in terms of enhancing the power of the citizenry—they are closest to the elected official or administrator or they can vote with their feet. The contrast is the helpless number manipulated by the faceless bureaucrat or the corporate boss. (On the other hand, centralization is also justified in terms of the ordinary person. It is through centralization that society can replace parochialism with norms of equality.)

Decentralization, deregulation, and privatization are moves toward local control. This book asks the question: What are the consequences of these moves for citizen empowerment? Will ordinary citizens—clients, patients, teachers, students, parents, tenants, neighbors—have more or fewer opportunities to exercise control over decisions that affect their lives?

The empowerment of client groups has been a stated aim of a long series of social policies, starting with the War On Poverty, through the era of mandated citizen groups in scores of programs during the 1970s, to the most recent structural innovations in school reform. Initially, citizen empowerment was the program of the traditional or liberal Left, but that is no longer true. For a long time, conservatives have talked of empowering "mediating institutions" and of market-based incentives as a way of achieving citizen autonomy and bureaucratic accountability. A prominent example is the sale of public housing to tenants by the Thatcher government. Citizen or community empowerment is also urged by minorities who champion the preservation of cultural diversity, by activists and academics who celebrate the victories of the subordinate against systems of social control, and by a wide range of "new" social-movement or postmodern groups under the broad labels of feminism, environmentalism, and peace. School reform at the local level is urged by religious fundamentalists, African American nationalists, or parents fed up with incompetent, politically corrupt bureaucracies. In short, citizen empowerment is very diverse, very broadly scattered, and means very different things; it is not simply an issue of Right versus Left, state versus market.

Citizens are treated in this book as one of the stakeholders in the modern social welfare state. In many situations, public agencies are captured by citizens—the rich and the powerful as well as various special-interest groups. The emphasis, here, however is on subordinate groups, people who are ordinarily relatively powerless in dealing with public and private agencies. Deregulation and privatization is often justified as representing the removal of burdensome and oppressive state control, but for subordinate groups, it might only mean re-regulation under another master. However, this conclusion is not foreordained. Decentralization involves shifts in power relations. Is there now more space for subordinated individuals and groups? The ideologies of the "new" social or postmodern movements rest in part on the "legitimation crisis" of the modern welfare state; translated, this means that the dominating, bureaucratic, top-down regulatory state can no longer fulfill its promise of emancipation. At least for these new social movements—and others as well—decentralization, broadly conceived, presents opportunities for struggle from below.

· · ·

In this introduction, I will give a rough approximation of key terms. As will be seen, there is a lot of overlap in the definitions. Subsequent chapters will provide more detail in the context of numerous examples. Following the definitions, I describe the plan of the book.

DEFINITION OF KEY TERMS

Broadly speaking, state functions include: (1) the direct provision of services; (2) the subsidization of services administered by private (nongovernment) agencies or individuals; or (3) the regulation of services that are both financed and provided by nongovernment sources. *Decentralization* of state functions has at least three meanings. It can refer to the sale of government assets. In Europe and the Third World, there are many more state-owned assets than in the United States; therefore, selling these assets is a more significant policy initiative than in the United States.[2]

Decentralization can refer to the *delegation* of authority within the public sector. Many public social protection systems in the United States are partially financed and administered by state and local units of government under more or less federal supervision. Decentralization, here, means a further reallocation of authority from the federal government to lower units of government. In this context, decentralization is part of the continuing history of federalism—the allocation and reallocation of authority between the states and the federal government.

Decentralization also refers to *deregulation*, a broad movement in the United States that started initially as an anti-inflation policy during the Carter administration. Deregulation can mean the reduction or loosening or elimination of regulatory controls. Decentralization can also include *privatization*—the delegation of regulatory control from the public to the private sector, which, in turn, can be for profit or nonprofit.

Privatization can mean reducing the collective domain, or providing the same level of public services but more efficiently by using the private sector.[3] Most often it means retaining responsibility for collective financing, but delegating authority to the private sector—called *contracting* or

[2] Donahue 1989, 5.   [3] Donahue 1989.

contracting out. This is a very familiar practice in the United States; perhaps our most prominent example is defense contracting. But a great many other services are contracted out. In fact, more than half of all government spending on goods and services is publicly financed but privately produced.

Privatization can be *demand driven*—examples are the nonpublic provision of education, health, and retirement. In these circumstances, there is not necessarily a reduction in publicly provided services; rather, the increase in services comes about through private markets.[4] When privatization is *policy driven*, it can result in "load shedding" in that government reduces or eliminates its role in particular areas, for example, the sale of assets. As noted above, most common, in the United States at least, are various forms of contracting that involve government retaining its fiscal responsibilities but delegating the production of goods or services. Privatization can also come about through deregulation; regulatory responsibility is shifted in varying amounts to private regulation.[5] Thus, the implications of privatization will vary depending on both the form and the degree that it takes. Contracting, for example, may dilute government control and accountability but may increase services.

In the developed welfare state, it is commonly assumed that the social protection system is state-centered. And, indeed, that is an accurate description of major parts of the system—various kinds of income support, health care (in developed countries other than the United States), a good deal of housing, a great many social or human services. But social protection is a much broader concept. It includes the private sector—for example, employment-based health care and pensions—as well as the nonprofits, which, at least in the United States, are extremely important. And, in all societies, it includes the household or families. Families have always been considered crucial in procreation, child development, and socialization. They have always played an important role in health care and general social support. And, there has been a re-emergence of interest in issues related to families, especially single-parent families, adult roles, and the socialization of children.

The three large systems—government, the private sector (both for-profit and not-for-profit), and family—interact. Families have always been influenced by public programs, whether by subsidy or regulation. There is public regulation of employment-based protections. Most of the revenue of the not-for-profits now comes from government sources in the form of contracting for services or user charges. Thus, even within the not-for-profit sector, there are market mechanisms. It is misleading to look at social protection systems in dichotomous terms—public versus

---

[4] Starr 1988. [5] Nader and Nader 1982; Starr 1988.

private; formal versus informal. Instead there is overlap and blurring, a continuum.[6] With the predominantly public social services, such as education, social security, personal social services, and health care (Europe), there are residual private sector services. In the predominantly private sector, such as housing, employment, and health (the United States), there is a residual public sector. And throughout there is the so-called informal or family support system.

Decentralization and privatization affect the system of social protection in both symbolic and real terms.[7] There are shifts in moral definitions and values as well as in the allocations of power, responsibility, and resources. At the most basic, or microlevel, support can materially affect the family protection system. A familiar example is the effect of child care or home-based health care on the life of the single mother. The degree and kind of subsidy or regulation may either enhance or diminish the quality or availability of child or health care or make it impossible to obtain. Similar kinds of effects may be produced by school-lunch programs, substance-abuse clinics, counseling, health care programs, and other kinds of social services. Decentralization and privatization reallocates power and authority to lower units of government or to the private sector. In both decentralization and privatization, especially when government ceases production but retains financial responsibility, various units of government, service providers, contractors, and community organizations ("mediating institutions") have expanded authority, with important consequences for clients and consumers.[8]

The debates about decentralization and privatization are usually cast at a more macro or symbolic level. The contemporary versions of decentralization, deregulation, and privatization started with the Thatcher government in Great Britain and then spread to Western Europe. In the United States, the anti–big government movement came into its own, at least symbolically, in the Reagan administration.[9] In any event, it is safe to say that today it represents a worldwide general attack on collectivism and a renewed emphasis on private property and freedom of contract.[10] While often cast in terms of costs and benefits, efficiency, and budget management, it is really a debate about governance, the allocation of power in society, and the management of public problems. The "old style" provision of services—tax financed and provided by public sector employees with tenure—now seems a remote choice. More likely are various mixtures of public and private financing and delivery.[11]

In a wide-ranging essay, called *The Meaning of Privatization*, Paul Starr argues that, however varied the meaning of privatization, it is unambiguously a serious political countermovement against the growth of

---

[6] Rein 1989.   [7] O'Higgins 1989.   [8] Bendick 1989; Starr 1991.
[9] MacLennan 1985.   [10] Sunstein 1990.   [11] Bosanquet 1984.

big government. It should be viewed as a conservative attempt to reconstitute the major institutional domains of society, to roll back state activities in the name of efficiency, effectiveness, and freedom of choice.[12] Whatever its various meanings, privatization involves a shift from public action to private concerns, from the public to the private sphere. It is a signal about the competence and integrity of the public sector; it calls into question the need or the capacity for collective action. Privatization shifts power to those who can more readily exercise power in the market.

Starr's interpretation is not the only one; there is a literature that takes a different view of the possibilities of decentralization and privatization. One interpretation comes out of the social movement literature. Both in the United States and on the Continent, scholars have claimed that there are "new" social movements[13] or a new populism[14] or postmodernism that is antimaterialist, antigrowth, anti-industrialization and antibureaucratization.[15] These movements prefer small-scale, decentralized, antihierarchical, direct democracy to conventional politics. Whatever the various strands, they call into question the promise of the modern, liberal, capitalist welfare state. One of the essential common themes is participatory, grass-roots democracy. The new movements do not view decentralization and privatization in Thatcherite terms; rather, they see them as opportunities for democratic politics.

Thus, whether from the Right or from the Left, a key aspect of decentralization and privatization is *empowerment. Power* and *empowerment*—as with the other key terms—are much used and abused words, sometimes slogans but at other times imbued with important meanings. As will be discussed more fully, with appropriate illustrations, in subsequent chapters, power and empowerment involve material or objective behaviors but also have deep psychological aspects. Feelings of powerlessness or lack of control are significant issues for subordinate people.

Empowerment varies in context. Conservatives (and others) emphasize the consumer choice through market mechanisms. Entrepreneurs, whether businesses, not-for-profits, or lower units of government, compete for customers who can vote with their feet. Consumers (clients) are empowered in that they have something that the entrepreneurs need and want. As we shall see, it is argued by many thoughtful commentators, that consumer choice is the single most powerful engine for the reform of government. Liberals, too, question large, centralized bureaucratic institutions in education, social welfare, and local government services; they seek much more local control. And more radical communitarians want face-to-face citizen-government.

Empowerment—of governments, contractors, businesses, providers,

[12] See also Walker 1984.
[13] Tarrow 1989.
[14] Boggs 1986; Boyte 1980.
[15] Handler 1992.

clients, patients, parents, consumers, tenants, neighbors—demonstrates not only the complexity of decentralization and privatization, but also the fact that despite its political heritage, it is not necessarily conservative or a counterattack on the progressive, welfare state. The move away from big, regulatory government and toward private enterprise is without doubt a major impetus, but it would be a mistake to ignore the progressive, communitarian implications.

PLAN OF THE BOOK

The book is divided into two parts: "The Organization of the Welfare State: Public and Private" and "The View from Below: Empowerment by Invitation, Empowerment through Conflict."

In part I, chapter 2, we ask: What accounts for decentralization between units of government? What are the particular forces that construct and shape the allocation of public authority? The thesis of this book is that decentralization—the deliberate allocation of authority to lower bureaucratic units, whether public or private—is a major technique for managing conflict. In the programs that we are concerned with, there are serious, recurring conflicts. Although the different levels of government and interest groups have different interests and concerns, decentralization often works to the advantage of most of the important stakeholders. For this reason, decentralization is ubiquitous throughout public programs.

Public and private agencies are "organizations." The first step in developing the thesis, then, is an analysis of what organizations are. We are particularly concerned with how organizations respond to internal and environmental incentives. We next turn to the politics of regulatory design. This section describes how the various stakeholders—both internal and external to the organization—struggle to shape the design of the organization and the regulatory program both to try to further their ends and to neutralize their opponents. Various design features further certain interests and thwart others; it is no accident, for example, that agencies are "inefficient" or "rule-bound" and bureaucratic. The final point made in this section is that the politics or struggle over regulatory design continues through the life of the regulatory program. The next two sections apply the general theories of organizations and administrative politics to the special characteristics of government agencies and the implementation of public programs. These two sections develop the concepts of both top-down and bottom-up implementation. They demonstrate the importance of local context on the actual delivery of public policy.

The material in chapter 2 is foundational in the sense that organizations—both public and private—are crucial factors in the development and evolution of public policy. At the same time, the theories that are discussed in this chapter are well-known, and the specialist may want to skip immediately to the next chapter.

The next chapter presents four case studies that illustrate the thesis developed in chapter 2. All of the case studies involve major, multidimensional conflicts in American society—work and welfare, race, gender, family, bureaucracy, state and local power, and public education. The quick historical survey of social welfare programs provides a snapshot view of the various ways that decentralization is used to manage conflict as political, social, and economic forces change. The second example deals with decentralization changes that are going on with command-and-control economic regulation—principally the introduction of market incentives and formal cooperative regulation. The Reagan administration's program of devolution marked a major reversal in federal-state relations; the energy and action for a large variety of domestic programs is now at the state and local level. The third example is the response of a conservative state—Arizona—to the demands of expanding social needs during the Reagan Era. This example illustrates how the characteristics of decentralization are played out at the state level. The final case study—local control of education financing and exclusionary zoning—shows the power and tenacity local governments can bring to bear when protecting their interests against upper-level reforms in two of the major domestic issues in America—race and redistribution.

These two chapters present the theory of public agencies and some of the flavor of the politics of bureaucratic or program design. The case studies are not representative; rather, they are illustrative of the variety and context of decentralization.

Chapter 4 describes the next step on the decentralization continuum—*privatization*. It discusses the theory of privatization and reviews the empirical literature on the movements' extent and variety. The chapter views privatization in terms of the two themes—the management of conflict and the implications for client empowerment—and concentrates on contracting—by far the most popular form of privatization. The consensus seems to be that both theoretically and empirically, contracting fulfills the stated goals of efficiency and accountability only when there is competition, which can occur in both public and private organizations. The chapter then reviews the experience of competition in contracting with the New Jersey state government and Massachusetts mental health services. The conclusion, supported by other empirical studies as well, is that while there are important examples of competition in public service contracting achieving its goals, these are limiting situations. By and large, competition is hard to initiate or maintain.

The chapter then turns to the impact of public contracting on the not-for-profit sector. Here, there have been major organizational transformations. In short, as mutual dependency between government and non-profits thickens, charities have become bureaucratized and increasingly resemble public agencies. We see an extension of government through the private sector. The chapter concludes with an examination of the literature on what difference this makes for the client.

Part II changes the focus. It is the view from below, and addresses the conditions of empowerment—how it can get started, and how it can be maintained.

Chapter 5 starts with a close look at the concepts of power and empowerment. The manifestation of power, at first blush, is relatively straightforward, but quickly gets complex and subtle, especially when one considers the various ways dependent people are socialized and manipulated. Similarly, empowerment also becomes subtle and complex. Power and empowerment involve both material and psychological factors. The argument is made that empowerment is a dynamic, reflexive developmental process, deeply dependent on context. A major issue, both analytically and empirically, is quiescence in hierarchical relationships. The chapter then goes on to analyze the many faces of power and empowerment in human service agencies.

Chapter 6 explains how the regulated citizen—whether client, recipient, patient, parent, student, suspect, or victim—is invited to share in the exercise of public authority. Most often, as we shall see, the sharing is done informally. A familiar, but little-talked-about example, is street-level law enforcement. However, formally structured sharing is quite common—an old example is professional self-regulation—and is increasingly used as an alternative to command-and-control regulation. Many alternatives are now being experimented with; these include market-based incentives, as well as many forms of privatization. The principal alternative discussed, a case study dealing with the delegation of enforcement authority in worker safety, is an example of cooperative, flexible regulation. I use this example because its success depends on the empowerment of lower-level stakeholders—in this case, construction workers. This case study is used to develop the theoretical conditions necessary for the empowerment of dependent people, whether they are employees, clients, patients, parents, or students. The worker-safety case study shows the interconnections between ideologies or professional norms; technology, that is, the methods of getting the work done; and the importance of reciprocal incentives, that is, how relationships must be structured so that all parties gain in material ways from cooperation. This last point—the importance of incentives—brings us back to the initial discussion of the theory of organizations in chapter 2. The worker-safety case study also returns us to the re-examination of privatization. In this example, public authority for enforcement has been delegated to special committees.

The chapter then turns to cooperative regulation in human service agencies. The examples here deal with special education, home-based care for the frail, elderly poor, and nursing home residents. There are cases in which empowerment is possible, but, not unexpectedly, the conditions are fragile. I argue that much depends on whether the power holders can benefit materially from the exchange. The analogy is to the worker-safety example in the previous section.

The chapter concludes by examining empowerment in more political contexts. The two examples are the experience of tenants assuming control over public housing, and neighborhood political organizations in five cities. Again, we see the importance of reciprocal material benefits.

Chapters 7 and 8 examine empowerment in adversarial relationships. The example used for both chapters is school reform. Schools, along with family, but often in opposition to family, are considered our most important socializing agencies. It is no wonder, then, that disputes involving schools have always been among the most contested. These disputes, often intense, and always enduring, range from the mundane—relating to patronage, jobs, resources—to those pertaining to our most cherished symbols. Schools involve family values, patriotism, and community as well as the perennial flashpoints of American politics—race and redistribution.

For the past several decades, schools have been a major battle ground for reform. Substantively, it is charged that schools are failing; that they are to blame for the decline in values; and that they are not producing a sufficiently educated, productive citizenry. A large part of the blame is focused on the education bureaucracy. It is felt that the large school district is remote, bureaucratic, unresponsive, and corrupt; and that teachers, and their unions, are more interested in job protection than in education.

School reform is proceeding basically along two tracks. One emphasizes uniform, standardized, minimum-quality performance rules—competency training and performance for teachers, standardized tests for students, specified curricula, minimum requirements for graduation. The other reform initiative is the opposite—radical decentralization to the level of the schoolhouse, emphasizing significant teacher, parent, and community resident involvement. Both approaches are susceptible to myth and ceremony—symbolic reassurance that reforms are being implemented, while the status quo continues behind the scenes: for example, exemptions and excuses for performance standards, or no real power to parent groups. On the other hand, genuine reforms raise important questions of individualized treatment versus uniformity and equity and the empowerment of previously subordinated or excluded groups versus societal or legal standards and community preferences. Familiar examples include constitutional prohibitions on discrimination and religious instruction, but there are many such conflicts ranging throughout the curriculum: standards for teachers, school discipline, school health, extracurricular activities—in short, just about everything connected with schools. Moreover, these problems are increasing as schools are being called upon more and more to assume the burdens of other support systems for children and youth—families, neighborhoods, health care, recreation, employment preparation.

Chapter 7 examines how these issues are being fought out in education reform. The chapter returns to theories developed in Part I as it describes schools as organizations and discusses the politics of structural reform. It asks: What are the sources of authority and control in public education? The chapter then turns to the various examples of restructuring now going on around the country—teacher empowerment, choice, controlled choice, vouchers, magnet schools, alternative schools (e.g., Comer, Accelerated Schools, described in chap. 7), and site-based management. Major attention is devoted to the most radical reform now under way—democratic localism for the Chicago public school system—in which every public school is to be governed, at the local level, by a board comprised mainly of elected parents and community residents. The history, current experience, and evaluations of the Chicago reform are described in detail.

Chapter 8 continues the discussion of the Chicago reform. It probes more deeply the question of how one assesses empowerment, especially empowerment in continual struggle in the context of strongly hierarchical bureaucratic relations, a multilayered bureaucratic and political environment, entrenched interests, and racial and ethnic politics. Chicago represents a most difficult but important case.

Can we generalize from the Chicago experience to the larger questions of participatory democracy? Decentralization and privatization are manifestations of broader movements that reject statism. Large public bureaucracies, whether state capitalism, corporatism, social welfare, or socialism—for good or evil—are the dinosaurs of the twentieth century, it is said. While the theoretical and organizational approach of the twenty-first century may be characterized as "without statism," for subordinate citizens, there will always be a state, though perhaps in different locations. Whether subordinate citizens will be more or less empowered under a decentralized regime will vary with context. There are many examples of empowerment as well as of domination. Much depends on the position of the power holders; cooperative regimes can work, especially when material benefits can be exchanged. Relationships, then, have more of a chance of renewal. And there is continuing, widespread interest in cooperative, flexible styles of regulation. In situations of conflict, the outcomes are more uncertain. Subordinate people need outside resources and steadfast allies.

PART I

The Organization of the Welfare State: Public and Private

Chapter 2

THE CONTEXT OF DECENTRALIZATION

DECENTRALIZATION is the *allocation of authority*. In the public sector, decentralization is an aspect of federalism—the continuous, dynamic process of adjusting relations between federal, state, and local government, as well as special-purpose governments, such as school districts, port authorities, sanitation districts, and so forth. Decentralization also involves internal *bureaucratic* relations, or the allocation of responsibility between various levels or units of organizations. Decentralization can also mean *privatization*—the allocation of authority between government and the private sector (both profit and not-for-profit). The three dimensions, of course, are not separate. One of our major points is that "governments," while many other things in addition, are primarily organizations, collections of organizations, and relations between organizations. The line between public and private is not distinct. Government agencies contract with each other and with nongovernment organizations to carry out public business. While the three aspects of decentralization will be analyzed separately, their connections will also be discussed.

In the programs that we are concerned with—economic regulation, work, welfare, health care, education—there are serious, recurring conflicts. Although the different levels of government and interest groups have different interests and concerns, decentralization often works to the advantage of most of the important stakeholders. For this reason, decentralization is ubiquitous throughout public programs.

WHAT ARE ORGANIZATIONS?

Empowerment is a relationship. An individual can be empowered vis-à-vis another individual. Groups can be empowered politically. Here, we are concerned with the empowerment of subordinate people in public programs or services—with the relationship between clients, patients, workers, students, and parents with agencies, usually but not always public. We ask: How do agencies respond to clients, and why? How do clients respond to agencies? If we can answer these questions, we will be in a better position to address the possibilities for restructuring client-agency relations.

The first task is to find out what organizations are like. When people think about organizations, they usually think of the *rational-legal* model.

Political leaders design an organization to carry out agreed-upon, specific policy goals. The structure of the organization—the allocation of authority, labor, and resources—is designed for particular purposes. It is rational.[1] It is legal because the structural components are governed by impersonal, universally applied formally adopted rules. This model, of course, rarely applies. Organizations are structured for a variety of reasons, only one of which may be to achieve some of the goals of some of the actors.

There are a variety of theories to explain organizations. The one used here combines political economy and the new institutionalism.[2] The rational-legal model looks at organizations as self-contained structures. The political economy perspective looks at the relation of an organization with its environment and the effects of that relationship on the internal processes of the organization. Organizations depend on the environment for two types of resources: (1) legitimacy and power; and (2) productive resources. An organization gains legitimacy by conforming to the dominant cultural and belief systems in its environment. Power refers to the authority and influence within the organization. Production resources—money, personnel, clients—are required for the organization's delivery and incentive system.[3]

The task of the organization is to insure a stable flow of resources from its environment. The environment consists of other organizations and interest groups. To the extent that an organization or interest group controls a critical resource, that external group will control the organization. A well-known example is the hospital. Until recently, legitimacy and the flow of production resources depended almost exclusively on the medical profession, which, in turn, controlled the hospital. Hospitals now are increasingly controlled by the principal payers—insurance companies and government.[4]

Organizations use a variety of strategies to cope with the environment. Some organizations are powerful enough to command sufficient resources, but this is rare, especially in the areas of our concern. Most organizations either compete, or, more usually, negotiate and cooperate. An important strategy, for our purposes, is the recruitment and processing of clients. As long as organizations have a choice (and most do), they will favor those clients that will enhance legitimacy and garner or preserve resources and avoid or somehow marginalize "undesirable" clients.

---

[1] This is the key assumption of the "rational-choice" approach to public institutions—"that individuals are rational in the sense of choosing the best available course of action and that individuals take account of the foreseeable consequences of their actions" (Spiller and Ferejohn 1992, 2).

[2] Hasenfeld 1992a, 24–44; Powell and DiMaggio 1991.

[3] Hasenfeld 1992a.   [4] Hasenfeld 1992a, 31.

Schools track minority students; hospitals and doctors avoid Medicaid patients; employment services deflect the less employable. The interests of the organization do not necessarily coincide with the interests of the clients they are supposed to serve.[5]

The political economy perspective draws attention to the need for the organization to conform to cultural and belief systems of the environment to gain legitimacy. This is the focus of the institutional perspective. Organizational legitimacy is based on *institutional rules and practices*. The sources of legitimacy of schools are based on curriculum requirements, the adoption of national standards, and the credentialing of teachers and students. Health care institutions adopt national standards for the credentialing of staff, for diagnosis, and treatment.

Institutional rules and practices come from a number of sources— laws, professional organizations, national standards, public opinion. An important source is imitative—organizations imitate other, successful organizations, what DiMaggio and Powell call "institutional isomorphism."[6] Institutional isomorphism draws attention to the idea that organizations function within networks or sectors. Often there are competing organizations, as well as suppliers, regulators, interest groups, political leaders, and so forth.[7] But the network or organizational field is much broader. Industries, professionals, associations are national, even international. The institutionalists argue that these belief systems and cultural symbols are of the essence of organizations.[8] The development of rules and values, that is, the institutionalization of organizations, is a key part of managing the organizational environment.

Organizational rules are not necessarily related to the *work* of the organization; in fact, quite often they are *decoupled*. For example, the institutional rules of schools (curriculum requirements, student and teacher certification) may bear little relationship to what actually goes on in the classroom. Decoupling introduces Meyer and Rowan's important concept of "myth and ceremony."[9] The institutional rules are the "myth"— the unproven belief system that the organization is rationally related to the social goals (e.g., students are learning the required curriculum; teachers are teaching in a professional manner). The "ceremony" is the symbolic acts—for example, certification, graduation. Decoupling, or myth and ceremony is analogous to decentralization; it is an important organizational technique for managing conflict with the environment.

What is the process of institutionalization? What determines the structure and content of organizational rules? Political economy theory implies rational actors calculating costs and benefits; the emphasis is on

---

[5] Hasenfeld 1992a, 32.   [6] DiMaggio and Powell 1991.
[7] Hasenfeld 1992a, 36.   [8] DiMaggio and Powell 1991, 13.
[9] Meyer and Rowan 1991.

change—organizations trying to cope with unstable environments. The institutionalists favor cognitive or cultural explanations—the practices and habits of the historical frameworks within which the actors are imbedded. "Institutionalized arrangements are reproduced because individuals often cannot even conceive of appropriate alternatives (or because they regard as unrealistic the alternatives they can imagine). Institutions do not just constrain options; they establish the very criteria by which people discover their preferences."[10] In other words, environments are not necessarily co-opted by organizations; rather, environments penetrate the organizations, they create "the lenses through with actors view the world and the very categories of structure, action, and thought."[11] Thus, rather than intentionality, institutionalists see actors functioning on the basis of "taken-for-granted scripts, rules, and classifications, . . . shared 'typifications,' where actors infer motives post hoc from menus of legitimate accounts."[12] "For highly institutionalized acts, it is sufficient for one person simply to tell another that this is how things are done."[13]

Institutionalists emphasize homogeneity across organizations and stability rather than change and adaptation.[14] "[I]nstitutionalization [is seen] as the diffusion of standard rules and structures rather than the adaptive custom-fitting of particular organizations to specific setting."[15] Organizations cope with uncertainty through routine and rules rather than calculation. Norms are important, but actors use them "flexibly and reflexively to assure themselves and those around them that their behavior is reasonable."[16]

This is a passive view of organizational behavior, and it has been challenged by those who see contradictions and conflict not only between organizations and institutions but within organizations themselves. Organizations both shape and are constrained by the relational frameworks within their environments.[17] Change can come from environmental actors. States exercise coercive power (law) or authority, such as the diffusion of reforms. One example would be due process for employees, sometimes imposed by law but other times, adopted as "the thing to do";[18] another example is the spread of procedures to deal with sexual harassment issues. Organizations can voluntarily seek the approval of authorizing agents—an example would be an agency seeking accreditation from a national organization. Incentives may be offered to organizations willing to conform. Or, as noted, organizational actors, on their own, may copy institutional designs that they think more appropriate. Sometimes

---

[10] DiMaggio and Powell 1991, 13.
[11] DiMaggio and Powell 1991.
[12] DiMaggio and Powell 1991, 15.
[13] Zucker 1991.
[14] Powell 1991.
[15] DiMaggio and Powell 1991, 27.
[16] DiMaggio and Powell 1991, 21.
[17] Scott 1991.
[18] Edelman 1990.

mimetic behavior happens consciously; other times, it is more subtle, episodic, indirect, even unplanned. Whatever the sources, "most types of organizations confront multiple sources and types of symbolic or cultural systems and . . . they exercise some choice in selecting the systems with which to connect."[19] In any event, scholars note that over time organizations will mirror salient aspects of their environments.[20]

Powell argues that contrary to what institutionalists imply, organizational change is not necessarily a passive or a constraining process. Indeed, the use of legitimating rules and symbols may enhance prestige and power. Organizational fields are not static; they produce conflicting demands. Organizations attempt to alter or resist demands made upon them. In many situations, organizations are proactive, strengthening or expanding their power by strengthening or expanding the power of the interest groups they regulate.[21] In the face of threatening changes, existing organizations will try to protect their interests and preserve the status quo, but newcomers may challenge the incumbents. Multiple and conflicting pressures provide space for organizational actors to maneuver. According to this view, there is agreement with political economy theorists that sources of change and innovation usually come from outside the organization.[22]

Sources of change are themselves institutionally shaped by culture, symbols, and meaning. "The deployment of material resources not only involves real material relations; it also communicates meanings."[23] Friedland and Alford argue that social theory "must be reconstructed by asserting the centrality of the symbolic in the organization of social life."[24] "The central institutions of contemporary Western societies—capitalism, family, bureaucratic state, democracy, and Christianity—are simultaneously symbolic systems and material practices."[25] Individuals and organizations pursue their ends, but these ends become meaningful through symbolic systems. Social relations are both instrumental and ritualistic.

> The meaning and relevance of symbols may be contested, even as they are shared. Individual, groups, and organizations struggle to change social relations both within and between institutions. As they do so, they produce new truths, new models by which to understand themselves and their societies, as well as new forms of behavior and material practices.[26]

In short, individuals or organizations may be "institutionally constrained, but they are not determined."[27]

---

[19] Scott 1991, 181.
[20] Scott 1991, 179.
[21] Farber 1992; Macey 1992.
[22] Jepperson and Meyer 1991; Powell 1991.
[23] Friedland and Alford 1991, 246.
[24] Friedland and Alford 1991, 247.
[25] Friedland and Alford 1991.
[26] Friedland and Alford 1991, 254.
[27] Friedland and Alford 1991, 256.

   While there is interdependence between institutions, there is also contradiction. Friedland and Alford argue that "institutional contradictions
are the bases of the most important political conflicts in our society [and]
it is through these politics that the institutional structure of society is
transformed."[28] Political struggles are often over the appropriate relationships between institutions—for example, the conflicts between family,
religion, and the state over education; or between democratic principles
of citizenship and due process and labor relations. Groups appropriate
the logic of some institutions to press for changes in other institutions.
The modern, bureaucratic state depends on democracy for legitimation; yet, democracy undermines bureaucratic rationality. Friedland and
Alford insist that these conflicts and contradictions are almost always
multidimensional—between democracy, capitalism, state, family, and
religion.[29]
   When we think about the conflicts in major public programs, such as
deregulation of the airlines and communications, environmental protection, occupational health and safety, school reform, social welfare systems, the privatization of services, or the many other examples that we
will discuss, we tend to focus on the practical, regulatory interests of the
state and the impact on businesses, workers, teachers, parents, students,
clients, and recipients. Significant changes seem to be happening in the
reallocations of public authority, the regulation of significant parts of the
economy, and in social welfare programs. These are battles over material
interests—with interest groups for tangible advantages, with constituents
for benefits, with presidents for control over administrative behavior. But
policies perform other functions as well. The institutional theorists emphasize the importance of symbolic systems as part of the salient environments of organizations. Policies not only grant or deny material benefits,
they also define values and confirm status; they are expressive and symbolic.
   Social problems are constructed to serve both tangible and intangible
interests. Problems such as "worker safety," "inefficiency," "oppressive
government," "local control," "empowerment," "the market," or "educational performance" do not arise on their own. Conditions do not become social problems and enter political language because they suddenly
materialize or change in character; usually they have always been present.
Rather, conditions become social problems for ideological purposes.
They serve the interests of those who define the social problem. "They
signify who are virtuous and useful and who are dangerous or inadequate, which actions will be rewarded and which penalized."[30]
   The definition of problems creates authority and status; it allocates re-

---

[28] Friedland and Alford 1991, 256.   [29] Friedland and Alford 1991, 257–58.
[30] Edelman 1988, 17.

sources and rewards. Explanations rationalize particular actions and justify authority in people who claim competence in dealing with particular causes. The ascribed meaning to events is thus reciprocal; observers construct themselves by constructing others. "There is an important sense in which language constructs the people who use it, a view manifestly in contrast with the commonsensical assumption that people construct the language they use."[31] Explanations of problems and solutions will endure if they comport with dominant ideologies.[32]

The various theories of organizations have direct relevance to the story of this book. We are concerned with the competition among organizations—both public and private—to acquire or maintain authority and control resources. How do organizations respond to these incentives? As we shall see, of particular importance are the changing characteristics of the private nonprofit sector as it increases its role in providing publicly financed services. The language used to describe the policies and programs discussed in this book—*decentralization, deregulation, federalism, local control, states' rights, community, accountability, privatization, the free market,* and *empowerment*—are highly charged symbols. They have importance in themselves; as we shall see, a great many "victories" are the symbolic affirmation of status. They are sources of legitimacy and the mobilization of support. At times, there are only symbolic changes with little change in regulatory behaviors. We shall also see the opposite— symbols are also used to camouflage allocations of power. Stakeholders within the organization and in the organizational environment struggle over both material and symbolic interests.[33]

The institutional analysis of organizations is particularly important when we consider the issues of power and empowerment. Rules, routines, "taken-for-granted scripts," and "shared typifications" can be crucially important in socializing dependent people in their relationships with bureaucracy; they raise critically the problem of acquiescence. At the same time, contradictions in the institutional environment allow for the possibility of change. In subsequent chapters, in discussing empowerment both through cooperation and through conflict, we will see examples of where outside groups have redefined the normative climate of the organizations.

CHARACTERISTICS OF GOVERNMENT AGENCIES

Most of the programs that we will be concerned with are addressed to the states and to lower levels of government—usually county or municipal agencies or special-purpose districts. The significance of the federal role will vary, but complete federal funding *and* administration is relatively

---

[31] Edelman 1988, 112.   [32] Edelman 1988.
[33] McCann 1994.

rare in domestic politics. State and local governments are important actors. Although there is considerable variation among programs, the standard structure is usually the federal grant-in-aid—the federal government sets forth the terms and conditions for cost sharing, which the states are free to accept or reject. The federal terms and conditions will vary in specificity. With rare exceptions, the states usually accept. Other types of federal-state programs provide various forms of cost sharing and state and local government administration under federal guidelines. Finally, of increasing importance are federal (and state) mandates with insufficient funding. This last technique has become a particularly serious issue with the erosion of state and local budgets.[34]

Recently, as part of the Republican's "Contract With America," legislation was enacted that purported to restrict the power of the federal government to impose unfunded mandates. However, the legislation only requires notification of the costs of the mandates and the opportunity for Congress to reconsider. In addition, there are many important exemptions (for example, civil rights). Consequently, it is doubtful whether the practice will change that much.

In looking at specific programs, we tend to concentrate on the particular one we are interested in to see to what extent the specific units of government are it. This kind of analysis usually presents a distorted view of the implementing agency. It gives the impression that the particular program is the exclusive or even an important part of the implementing agency's agenda. In contrast, most of these agencies—the bottom-line agencies that have the responsibility for actually making the field level decisions—are pre-existing, with long histories and traditions. They have other, even more important missions to perform and, as organizations, have extensive vertical and lateral relations with politicians, interest groups, other units of government, clients, and professional organizations. In other words, they are in a complex organizational environment, subject to a variety of incentives, demands, and pressures, all of which are more or less important to the agency's survival, and only one of which is the new federal (or state) mandate.[35]

Take, for example, school districts. From time to time, the federal or state government will address programs or mandates to these districts—regarding, for example, special education or school integration or bilingualism or directives for improved performance. The district will respond in ways that will maximize its own organizational interests, which may or may not coincide with the federal or state directives. School districts are complex organizations embedded in dense networks. At the most basic level, the district is primarily dependent on the local government unit tax base. This means that the district is intimately involved with local politics.

---

[34] Scott and Meyer 1991.   [35] Powell 1991.

Indeed, it is argued that one of the major problems with schools is that political interests, through elected school boards, exercise significant control over the running of schools.[36] Schools are used by politicians, stakeholders, and interest groups for the definition of values as well as patronage. There are extensive interorganizational relationships—with offices of health, mental health, juvenile justice, social services, and legal services—in short, the wide variety of social support systems that affect the families and the students. Many of these organizational relationships are nongovernmental—parent groups, charities, special-interest groups. Schools are also significantly influenced by professional organizations, labor unions, and civil service requirements.

Further complicating the matter is that although a federal education grant-in-aid may ostensibly be in one area (for example, special education or mental health), at the state and local levels, several other programs (public and/or private) may be relevant to the actual delivery of services. Each field has its own traditions, histories, and relationships with the various levels of government and private sectors. It is difficult to overemphasize the importance of the separate bureaucracies within each of the relevant fields. In all of the states, counties, municipalities, and other subdivisions of government, there are schools, police departments, courts, child-protection agencies, social services, welfare departments, hospitals, clinics, and so forth. These agencies have traditions, structures, alliances with special-interest groups, all with their own agendas, which may or may not coincide with the federal or state mandate.

The central mission of the schools, especially those in the politically powerful affluent suburbs, is to prepare mainstream children for college. Success in this area will enhance the survivability of the organization—not educating handicapped children, or coping with at-risk children, or achieving national civil rights goals. The schools may be required to take on these other tasks as a result of federal laws or because of a decision of the state to participate in grant-in-aid programs, but the point to recognize is that these additional tasks then have to compete at the organizational field level for scarce resources in an environment that more often than not is less than enthusiastic about the additional mission. This is not to say that these programs will always fail or that they will be sabotaged at the local level. It is to emphasize that existing bureaucracies are being asked to take on new tasks, and that quite often these new tasks are not within the central mission or goals of the bureaucracy, however broadly they may be defined. The new tasks, while stated in mandatory terms, are often discretionary at the field level, and field level bureaucrats are adept at managing decisions that serve their own interests.[37]

Another familiar example involves work and training programs for

[36] Briffault 1990a; Chubb and Moe 1990.   [37] Lipsky 1980.

welfare recipients. These programs are intended to be run by existing state and local agencies—the state employment service, vocational schools, community colleges, and so forth. How will they respond to the new clients? State employment services compete with private services in presenting themselves as reliable sources of qualified labor to private employers. Sadly, it is not in their interests to devote a great deal of resources to those welfare recipients who could benefit the most from work experience and training. These are the most problematic employees, people who are burdened not only with more serious employment and training deficits, including discrimination, but who will also have family and day-care, and probably health problems as well. The strategy will be to satisfy the minimum funding requirements and somehow deflect the hard cases. Difficult clients (that is, clients with lots of problems) will somehow be excused or dropped from programs instead of receiving extra help and encouragement. Moreover, these decisions are hard to monitor, since they are individualized, discretionary determinations. Similar disjunctures apply to community colleges and adult education; they are not prepared to meet the special needs of welfare clients.

Agencies not only have separate agendas but also are fairly autonomous within the state. By autonomy, I mean latitude in exercising discretion. This is especially true with the major services—education, social welfare, social services, land-use, health, mental health, safety, environmental protection, criminal justice. What this means is that when an upper-level unit of government mandates one of these agencies to do something, the lower-level agency will attempt to respond in terms of their own organizational interests. It will consider what level of compliance will maximize its survival chances.

Further complicating the picture is the existence of the private and not-for-profit sectors. As noted, there has been a significant increase in the public purchase of services, which creates additional autonomous units that have to be bargained with in the implementation process. In the course of time, suppliers become independent forces; they build alliances and become special-interest groups. The characteristics of this relationship will be the topic of chapter 4.

Similar complexities apply between the states and the federal government. Between these two levels of government, there is a complex web of relationships built up over the years across many programs and affecting many units of government. There is no state government and no federal government in the sense of a single entity. There may be a single federal contracting agency—for example, a subdivision of the Department of Health and Human Services—and a single grantee at the state level—the state department of health and social services—but there are many other networks of relationships between the levels of government that have an interest in the particular program. What immediately comes to mind are the interested legislators. The presence in the Congress of an interested delegation from the particular state is of great importance, especially when conflicts arise between the federal executive department and the state or the locality. Within the executive branch, other departments have an immediate interest in the program. On the federal level, one such department would be the Office of Management and Budget; there are equivalent departments at the state level. In addition, agencies that have related programs would also be interested in the particular grant-in-aid. For example, if the particular program had an impact on, say, mental health, then another complex web of agencies, bureaucrats, and special-interest groups enter the picture.

In addition to the agencies and units of government, the private and professional groups and organizations that operate at the state level also are active between the state and federal levels. These include professional organizations and unions, citizen groups, special-interest groups, and charities. Quite often groups and organizations work at multiple levels of government simultaneously.

From the description so far, one might get the impression that the responsible federal granting agency is merely an inert dispenser of funds, caught in a buffeting sea of interests. To some extent, it is valid to emphasize this complex context, if only to correct the traditional simplified version of an active, purposive, effective single centralizing federal government speaking with one voice. The granting agency, the legal and administrative structure of the program, and the funding are of importance; but they are variables rather than fixed determinates.

What usually happens in the grant-in-aid programs is that all federal monies from a large number of programs are received by the state. The state then gathers all of the requests for funds from the other state agencies, local governments, subdivisions, and private agencies and eventually funds the requests from the various pots of federal and state monies. There is usually no segregation of federal funds. There is no separate stream of money coming from the U.S. Department of Health and Human Services for a particular mental health program at a county-level agency that is in fact administering the program. Instead, the state agency receives the request from the county program and allocates money to that program. The state pool of money is made up of state and federal monies from a variety of sources.

Further complicating the matter is the state practice of shifting money. States receive monies from a particular federal grant-in-aid, but often do not allocate the proportionate share of state money. Instead, they may substitute the federal money for the state money, with no net increase in service. This is a common practice, but difficult to pin down because of state accounting practices.

In addition, federal monitoring efforts in general are weak and uncertain. Information systems are inadequate; rules and standards are often vague. It is difficult to find out what is going on below.[38] The politics of enforcement also weakens federal control. State bureaucracies are powerful agencies with friends in Congress who are ready to defend state interests against federal auditors. In most really serious confrontations, the states are able to muster sufficient pressure to force the federal executive agencies to back down.

In an important sense, the role of the federal government is paradoxical; the introduction of the federal government increases state and local discretion. The federal government authorizes and pays for additional or expanded programs, but since the federal government cannot constrain the states significantly, there is an expansion of state and local discretion.

Thus far, I have emphasized decentralizing tendencies. There are centralizing ones as well. Although the regulatory effectiveness of federal law and administration may be problematic, there are other sources of federal influence. In some grant-in-aid programs, the federal share is quite significant, but even in programs where the federal share is only a small proportion, the additional amount can have considerable influence. It can provide the necessary slack to allow an organization to develop or expand a program. Then, over time, the program develops internal and external constituencies and becomes permanent.[39]

Paperwork is also an important influence. The masses of rules, regulations, accounting practices, bulletins, circulars, reporting requirements, and forms affect the delivery of services. In order to lessen these burdens, bureaucrats, teachers, and other line officials will avoid making decisions or changing decisions once made. The state as well as various professions become great rationalizers of practice through the adoption of day-to-day routines. Institutional expectations in dense networks exert great influence on behaviors.[40]

An important centralizing force is the process of social change itself. Again, this presents an apparent paradox. Virtually without exception, all of the major federal social welfare programs start at the state and local levels. There is a long history of testing, experimentation, struggle, and change in the local communities. Local problems start to become unmanageable, they boil up and overflow traditional boundaries of conflict, and various groups and interests seek support at higher levels of government. The classic response of the legislature is reactive and minimal rather than one of seizing the whole issue and absorbing all of the issues and power. Legislatures are normally reactive institutions. Most of their scarce time is taken up with the chief business of government—the budget and con-

---

[38] Stinchcombe 1990.   [39] Farber 1992; Walker 1983.
[40] Powell 1991, 188.

stituency service. All other issues compete for time on a crowded legislative docket. As an institution, the legislature will tend to handle only problems that it has to handle. Most problems that demand scarce legislative time and have budgetary implications are controversial. Problems that disturb existing jurisdictional lines tend to be controversial; there are jealousies between levels of government and concerns about local control. Favoring one group over another will gain both friends and enemies.

The best way in which a legislature can save scarce resources and avoid controversy is avoid dealing with a problem. When it has to deal with a problem, the next best strategy is to handle it minimally and symbolically; and this means delegating the problem back to its source—the local level. If there is conflict at the local level, the preferred technique is to authorize expenditures for a wide range of interests and delegate to the local authority the power to allocate. The granting of discretion satisfies local jurisdictional interests and gets the politically controversial problem out of the legislature's hair. A successful delegation, from the standpoint of the legislature, is one that stays delegated. The problem is "resolved" at the local level and does not rise up and demand more legislative and political capital.

Even though federal intervention is usually reactive, the process can still be centralizing. This is because the groups, organizations, officials, and citizens who have been pushing at the state and local levels are the ones who are interested in federal standards and support, and they keep pushing for more federal authority. These groups draw on a variety of sources of federal support. There is the money, of course, which can fund new positions and mute opposition. Another source of support may be the federal mandates themselves—the statutes, regulations, and court decisions. Law-abidingness and legitimacy will vary from community to community, and by issue, but the law does legitimize the values of the reformers and gives them moral support. While it is hard to pin down the precise effects of legitimacy, social reformers think that it is important to have official, legal confirmation of their position. Social reformers use law in a variety of ways. They appeal to legality and the affirmation of values. They use law for litigation and the mobilization of resources. Law helps mold public opinion; it speaks to the media, elites, and other sources of support.[41]

In sum, when we look at the governmental, administrative system, we do not see a pyramidal structure, with commands and resources emanating from the top down. Instead, we see arenas of competing jurisdictions, both public and private. Programs have long historical traditions at the state and local levels. There are multiple layers of agencies and organiza-

[41] Handler and Zatz 1982; McCann 1994.

tions, with their own perceptions, values, and traditions. There are interest groups, advocates, and professional organizations. Some are vigor-
ously defending state and local interests; others are seeking federal
sources of support and influence. It is a dynamic system of interaction and
reciprocity. The federal-state relationship, especially the grant-in-aid
structure, is best characterized as highly decentralized, with problems of
information, communication, coordination, and control.

The picture, then, of organizations, and especially public organizations, is one of complexity, sometimes resistant and in other situations,
changing. But what accounts for the structure of particular programs?

THE POLITICS OF REGULATORY DESIGN

Federal public organizations are created by the Congress and the presidency. It is here that the politics of regulatory design start. Chubb and
Peterson, in arguing that our institutions of government are no longer
capable of dealing efficiently and equitably with the major issues of the
day, locate at least part of the reason in congressional committees, White
House offices, and bureaucratic agencies. Each institution is substantially
autonomous; each represents different interests, has different conceptions
of effective government, and different concerns about the management of
ongoing problems.[42]

Part of the problem lies in the nature of the U.S. civil service. About
three thousand or more key positions remain subject to the political control of either the Congress, the president, or the political parties. As a
result, the civil service is fragmented; it consists of large numbers of separate departments, bureaus, and agencies, each with its own traditions,
expertise, politics, and constituencies. This suits the constituency-serving
functions of Congress; its specialized subcommittees establish close ties
between the fragmented bureaucrats and local special-interest contribu-
tors who, in turn, make campaign contributions to key committee members, serve on advisory committees, and participate in the exchange of
personnel between government and the private sector.[43]

The White House seeks to assert its interest over the bureaucracy
through its increased staff and the Office of Management and Budget.
Congress fights back with control over statutes, appropriations, influence
in the appointive process, and the capacity to investigate. A growing
problem is that many parts of Congress are involved in a single agency.
With congressional power decentralized, it is difficult to know whether
Congress itself supports the actions of particular leaders.[44]

[42] Chubb and Peterson 1989.   [43] Peterson 1990–91.
[44] Chubb and Peterson 1989.

In any event, Congress, as an institution, is not necessarily interested in effective administration. In response to interest-group demands, Congress will create a bureaucracy, assign the task, but will often fail to provide the authority, autonomy, or resources to act effectively. More often than not, agency structures are a compromise, depending on the interests of Congress, the White House, and the interest groups. They represent more a temporary political resolution than an effective mechanism.[45]

Chubb uses energy policy as an example of the failure of governance.[46] A number of alternatives to the use of imported oil have been considered, and in the process, natural gas pricing, nuclear power, coal plant emission controls, and electricity pricing have all been discussed. But rather than face unpopular choices, politicians delegated responsibility to agencies. Delegation, of course, poses problems as well as advantages for Congress. Once a problem is delegated, there is no guarantee that the bureaucrats will do what the politicians want. Particularly with complex matters, there is an asymmetry of information. Congress tries to control agents through appointing sympathetic personnel, prescribing rules, creating incentives, and monitoring activities. But these techniques are limited. Beginning with the Clean Air Act of 1970, there was a significant shift from broad delegations to trusted administrative experts ("old delegation") to more detailed, circumscribed rules to suspect bureaucrats ("new delegation.")[47] But, as we shall see in the next chapter, the new delegation no more solved governance problems than the old. At the present time, Congress's authority over energy is divided among forty-three subcommittees, accounting for over four hundred in staff. States and federal agencies pursue inconsistent goals. The resulting conflict produces more political intervention, in the form of strict statutes, increased monitoring, political attacks on specific decisions, threats, and delays.

According to Chubb, the new-style delegation works even better for Congress. Politicians look for ways to solve constituents' problems that do not produce obvious problems for other constituents. "If there is a conflict between important groups, the last thing a legislator want to do is to take sides, thereby making political enemies."[48] Energy policies will create losers, at least in the short term. Delegating a problem to an agency creates uncertainty about the allocation of costs and benefits; politicians can limit responsibility by shifting criticism to the agency. At the same time, politicians can claim credit for assisting constituents who have problems with the agency.[49]

[45] Chubb and Peterson 1989.
[46] Chubb 1989.
[47] Chubb 1989, 63.
[48] Farber 1992, 67.
[49] Chubb 1989.

In the meantime, Congress as a governing institution is becoming increasingly impotent. It has become so absorbed in the budgetary process that, as an institution, it has little time for anything else; its work load, as measured by the amount of legislation passed, has declined significantly. Members, with large staffs and resources, devote their energies to serving specific interests.[50]

The effects of politics are that "public bureaucracy is not designed to be effective."[51] This is so, argues Terry Moe, because the political wars over values and interests continue well beyond the legislative phase. The contestants not only battle over the initial administrative design of programs but also throughout a lifetime of implementation.[52] The reason for the continuing, protracted struggles is that the distinguishing characteristic of political institutions is that they are "weapons of coercion and redistribution. They are the structural means by which political winners pursue their own interests, often at the great expense of political losers."[53] This means that "structural choices have important consequences for the content and direction of policy, and political actors know it. When they make choices about structure, they are implicitly making choices about policy."[54] The various actors—the interest groups, presidents, members of Congress, and the bureaucrats themselves—all push for particular structures that will enhance or preserve their particular interests. "The issue of effective organization is right at the heart of the politics of structural choice."[55]

To illustrate his argument, Moe starts with a hypothetical. Assume that a group with a reasonably complex problem—for example, pollution or worker safety—does have dominating political power. Even then, its control will be imperfect. Authority will have to be delegated to an agency. The political group lacks the expertise, situations change, and detailed decision making by political institutions would be too costly and time-consuming. But delegation inevitably raises problems of control; there are conflicts of interests between principals and agents, and asymmetric information. If the group can select its own agents, there is less need for detailed rules. If the agents are selected on the basis of reputation—for example, professionals—this, in turn, also creates control problems. The group might want to grant autonomy as long as they think that they are getting discretion that would be exercised according to their goals.[56]

In most situations, however, one group is rarely that dominant politically. In the face of political uncertainty, it will be forced to compromise,

---

[50] Shepsle 1989.   [51] Moe 1989, 267.
[52] Moe 1990; Farber 1992.   [53] Moe 1990, 213.
[54] Moe 1989, 268.   [55] Moe 1990, 225.
[56] Moe 1989.

and it is here that administrative design becomes compromised. Because a group cannot be sure that its rivals might not come to power and seize the agency, the (temporarily) dominant group tries to insulate the agency from future political capture,[57] using detailed legislation, professionalism, civil service, the location of the agency, judicialization of its procedures, and hindering of political oversight. The important point is that in the effort to insulate the agency from future capture, the proponents will depart from an institutional structure designed in terms of "technical rationality."[58]

Opponents will rarely be completely powerless. Their goal will be to try to neutralize a strong, coherent organizational structure by burdening the agency with structures and requirements designed to insure failure. These include fragmented authority; political access; burdensome data gathering and reporting requirements; monitoring and review; oversight; political control over appointees; access to decision-making processes through judicialized procedures; and requirements of "objective" criteria.[59] Both sides know that "there can be no meaningful separation of structural issues from policy issues" and "that whatever structures are chosen will influence the content, direction, and effectiveness of public policy."[60]

The goals of both the winners and losers do not necessarily conflict with the legislature. While legislators may be responsive to broad public demands, such as consumer or environmental protection,[61] Congress does not have an overarching view as to bureaucratic design. It is not intrinsically interested in efficiency, coordination of management, or even overall control, which can turn out to be politically costly. Legislators would rather be responsive to the interest groups that are often in a better position to monitor the agency and provide legislators with the relevant information. Legislators are satisfied if they can be certified as reliable supporters by the interest groups, while they intervene in specific instances to protect constituency interests.[62] Above all, legislators want to be insulated from future political conflict by shifting responsibility to the bureaucracy.[63]

Presidents, on the other hand, are more responsive to the general welfare and, accordingly, want to assert control over agencies. They want agencies to be efficient, flexible, and capable to taking direction—which happens to be exactly opposite to what the other actors want. The winning group wants the agency insulated from politics. The opposing group favors procedural requirements and protections. The result is that the bureaucratic structure that emerges reflects both the congressional and

[57] Macey 1992.   [58] Moe 1989, 274.   [59] Moe 1989, 275.
[60] Moe 1990, 230; Farber 1992; Fiorina 1986.   [61] Farber 1992.
[62] Farber 1992; Macey 1992; Moe 1989, 275.   [63] Moe 1990, 232.

presidential interests. Moe says that "each agency begins as a unique structural reflection of its own politics."[64]

Agencies, too, have their interests. Their goal is to reduce political uncertainty by courting interest groups and politicians.[65] Bureaucrats favor members of Congress rather than presidents and political appointees, who tend to be more temporary. Bureaucrats gain a measure of autonomy, and this can create fear and uncertainty on the part of interests groups and citizens; after all, the agency does represent the coercive power of the state. This is an additional reason why both winners and losers seek protection through structure.

When consumer groups manage to win, they seek to impose detailed, onerous agency-forcing requirements on the agencies—the new-style regulations mentioned above. Their strategy is to remove crucial decisions from the possibility of capture by regulated interests. As will be seen in chapter 3, in practice, new-style regulation often debilitates the agencies and renders them ineffectual. "In politics, it is rational for social actors to fear one another, to fear the state, and to use structure to protect themselves—even though it may hobble the agencies that are supposed to be serving them."[66]

In sum, throughout the life of the agency, the winning group seeks to defend the agency, the opponents try to cripple it, and the president tries to control it. The players may vary, balances shift, but "structural politics never ends."[67] Moe concludes that as social problems become more complex, politics becomes more competitive, interest groups become more powerful, political uncertainty and compromise increase, and inappropriate structural forms will continue to be created.[68]

IMPLEMENTING PUBLIC PROGRAMS

Given the complexity and diversity of the social system, how then does change come about?

Mayer Zald sets forth four issues that bear on the question of change. The first concerns the relationship of the beliefs and ideologies of the particular program to the broader currents and trends in society. To what extent does the particular program tap into these broader sentiments? Explanations of social problems and solutions will more likely survive if they comport with dominant ideologies. The second issue is how these ideas work themselves out at the state and local levels. States vary in terms of structure, political culture, and the ability to innovate. Some states are "leaders," others "laggards," and still others "nonadopters."

---

[64] Moe 1989, 282.   [65] Moe 1989, 282.   [66] Moe 1990, 234–35.
[67] Moe 1989, 284.   [68] Moe 1989, 329.

Within the states, variation in the subsystems is important. Subsystems include the units of government as well as the interest groups. If certain subunits are particularly autonomous, as for example, school districts, then the likelihood of innovation depends upon the attitude and organization of this particular subsystem.

The third issue concerns the links between the three levels of government. Federal programs can operate as either constraints or opportunities. Zald stresses the personal and professional links between the various subsystems at all three levels—technical and staff contacts, consultative linkages, regional and national contacts—that may contribute to the diffusion of innovation.

The fourth issue concerns the specific intervention of the federal government in the particular program. Prior to the specific federal move, a great deal has already happened. There have been changes in ideologies and beliefs, the formation of groups and interests, and struggles for change at the state and local level. It is into this variable milieu that the federal government intervenes, and it does so with multiple voices: statutes, regulations, court opinions, offers of money, technical assistance, as well as other forms of incentives and disincentives. In some states and communities, behaviors seem to change; in others, they do not. What accounts for the difference?

The traditional method of attempting to answer this question was "impact analysis"—a comparison of changes in "outcomes" with the policymakers' intent. Impact analysis was superseded by "implementation analysis," which pays more attention to the processes of the entire social system. Implementation analysis more critically examines the explicit and implicit theory concerning the relationship between the policy and the expected outcome. Implementation theorists focus on the characteristics and processes of the various agencies and organizations and the relationships between them.

Sabatier and Mazmanian[69] have attempted to identify the relevant variables and hypotheses in implementation analysis. Summarizing their major points, they note, first, that problems differ in terms of their solvability. Some problems are more tractable than others. It is easier to implement an increase in welfare benefits than to provide education and training services. Success will also depend upon the attention that the policymakers pay to the implementation machinery—whether a structure is established and adequate resources are provided.

Major problems in implementation are also attributed to lack of coherence in the causal theory underlying the statute and conflicting or ambiguous policy objectives. Emphasis is also given to the structural arrange-

---

[69] Sabatier and Mazmanian 1981.

ments between the various agencies in the implementation system; there is a greater chance of success when agencies are hierarchically integrated and actions between them are coordinated. Conversely, when agencies are relatively autonomous, they tend to view policy goals in terms of their own organizational incentives. Other important factors internal to the system are, of course, the adequacy of resources and the rules for administrative decisions.

Factors more or less external to the system include the extent to which other actors (target groups, constituency groups, politicians, officials) can and do participate in the process. All major programs require political support; this is especially true if the system is loosely coupled, thus requiring cooperation between various agencies. But public opinion and political support is variable and unstable. Changes in the environment affect perceptions about the nature and seriousness of the problem. Changes in the relative importance of the constituency will affect political support. The media play an important role in maintaining or changing these perceptions.

Sabatier and Mazmanian think that all of these variables affect the success or failure of implementation. Nevertheless, the single most important factors, in their judgment, are the commitment of the agency leadership and their skill in using available resources.

Zald agrees with this analysis but would emphasize three additional factors. The specificity of the mandate is important. Vague standards in effect create discretion and invite conflicting interpretations by lower-level officials. The implementing machinery is important. What precise mechanisms does the supervising agency have for gathering information, monitoring performance, and providing incentives and disincentives? The third factor is variation in what Zald calls the "target objects as social systems." By this he means the difference between implementing systems that have clear coordinating structures and well-established monitoring and compliance procedures as compared to systems that are loosely coupled, do not share the same goals, are not well coordinated, and lack established procedures for the gathering of information and monitoring compliance.

An alternative view of implementation is presented by Elmore.[70] Elmore draws a sharp line between what he calls "forward mapping" and "backward mapping." Conventional implementation analysis is the former. It is the commonsense approach. One starts with an analysis of the policymakers' intent, and then examines the steps taken through the various implementing agencies. The object is to identify and compare the outcomes, the field level behaviors, as measured against the intent.

Backward mapping is the opposite; it is a bottom-up approach. It starts

---

[70] Elmore 1978.

at the field level, with the officials and agencies that have responsibility for the delivery of the services, and looks at the problems of change from their perspective. The choice between forward mapping and backward mapping depends on the assumptions that one is willing to make about the ability of the top to control the implementation process. If one assumes that this ability is fairly decisive, then it is logical to use forward mapping. If, on the other hand, one views the efforts of the top as contingent, as one factor among many in the process of social change, then forward mapping will always show a disjuncture between field level behavior and the policymakers' intent. Backward mapping takes a wider view of the process; it looks at the environment within which the field level agencies are operating. It assumes a loosely coupled, poorly integrated social system of relatively autonomous agencies with different sources of information, perceptions, and goals. It assumes a decentralized system with large amounts of discretion at the field level. For these reasons, according to Elmore, backward mapping more accurately describes the implementation process in most social welfare programs.

Despite the power of Elmore's analysis, it would be a mistake to look at the world only from the bottom up. Local units of government do not operate in a vacuum. Even in a basically decentralized system, there are factors that push toward centralization, that attempt to curb discretion in favor of uniformity. State governments, for example, can create or foreclose options though the use of law and funding. The basic statutory framework, the governmental structures, the funding patterns all set the parameters for the exercise of discretion. I have also mentioned other factors in the environment that push toward centralization—technical assistance, professional and organizational linkages, social reform groups. However, none of the centralizing tendencies lessens the importance of looking at implementation at the field level. The central, overarching fact is decentralization, the presence of widespread discretion at the local level, the decisiveness of the local units in the implementation process. Discretion is bounded by its environment, and that environment includes local, state, federal, and private influences. Nonetheless, the most important sources of influence operate at the local level. Ultimately, it is the community that determines the nature and character of the delivery of services.

CONCLUSION

The picture that emerges from the literature is one of great complexity and diversity. There are many levels of government and many interactions, both public and private. One cannot generalize across programs and issues. Large trends, of course, are unmistakable. There has been a relative decrease in federal spending for certain domestic programs and an expansion of social needs in the urban areas. But, despite common sense or conventional wisdom, changes in federal spending levels do not necessarily translate into changes in federal authority and control. Quite often increases in federal spending increase state and local authority. The complaints that are made today are that with the decrease in federal funding, there has been an increase in federal mandates—from "cooperative federalism" to "coercive federalism."[71]

A few generalizations, however, can be made. In many areas of domestic concern, there always has been and there continues to be substantial amounts of decentralization. Local levels of government exercise considerable amounts of control; this would be especially true where field level decisions are inherently discretionary, such as in the field of services. Moreover, these local units, as organizations, strive to maximize their survival in fields or environments composed of other relevant public and private actors. Organizations try to obtain support and resources from allies and hold off rivals. Thus, there are always an array of public and private relationships that bear on the construction and implementation of programs.

Finally, there is a great deal of rhetoric and many symbols that serve a variety of political purposes. Starting at the very top and extending through every level of government, political leaders use federalism and decentralization as a method of managing conflict. They seek to satisfy demands through the use of symbols, including the enactment of laws, and then delegate the problem to lower units where the struggle continues. From the upper-level standpoint, it is hoped that the problem will stay delegated. However, groups and interests will try to use these same symbols to force change, and problems may not stay delegated. It is in this context that we will consider regulation, deregulation, and privatization—as part of the dynamic political processes of symbolism, delegation, and the management of conflict.

[71] Kincaid 1990.

Chapter 3

THE USES OF DECENTRALIZATION

IN THIS CHAPTER, we consider some major examples of decentralization. The examples show the importance of local administration, despite initiatives from higher levels of government. The first example is welfare. The moral conflicts involved in aiding the poor are most keenly felt at the local level in the communities. For this reason, the most significant actors in welfare policy have always been local officials. During the last thirty years, there have been frequent demands for the federal government to "do something" about the "welfare crisis." Despite frequent federal legislation, in fact the response has been re-delegation to the local level through discretionary programs. More recently, as the "welfare crisis" has escalated, delegation through block grants to the states has become high on the political agenda. Throughout welfare history, the big concern has been setting the poor to work through work programs, but work programs do not create jobs. The clash between the political demands of reducing welfare through work and the realities of local labor markets shows how local discretion is used to de-couple politics from practice.

The second example involves the reactions to command-and-control economic regulation. The initial reactions were informal decentralization; that is, enforcement adjusted to the realities of the local context. Subsequently, there have been a variety of formal initiatives to provide decentralized alternatives—for example, formally structured negotiated rule making, and market-based incentives.

The third example involves the response of Arizona to the Reagan administration devolution. The Reagan devolution is important in its own right—it was the most significant attempt to dismantle or at least change the centralizing course of the contemporary welfare state. This case study shows how a conservative state was forced to increase the welfare state at the local level but it also reveals how the state delegated the tough issues to the local level.

The last two examples are public education and land-use controls, or more specifically, exclusionary zoning. The two are connected, and because they involve both race and redistribution, they are perhaps two of the most salient local policy concerns. Here, efforts at reform at the state level were thwarted at the local level. We return to these issues in chapters 6 and 7, which deal with contemporary education reform.

WELFARE POLICY

Social protection programs are distributed among the various levels of government—federal, state, and local—and, increasingly to the private sector through contracting. Can we explain the distribution?

Social welfare programs, especially when they are public, raise intense moral conflicts. The heart of the issue is the moral construction of the supplicant—is he or she morally deserving? In the United States, the question of deservingness centers on three major ideological fault lines—industrial discipline, or the work ethic, patriarchy, and race. Relief for the able-bodied, it is believed, threatens industrial discipline in that the recipient is less likely to accept a low-wage job, more likely to leave a job, and more likely to engage in collective protest if he or she can fall back on welfare.

Until the last two decades, the proper role of women was considered to be marrying and providing comfort, support, and child rearing for the family. This was the "domestic code." While it was acceptable for a young woman to work prior to marriage, this would only apply to "feminine" work (e.g., teaching, sales). Upon marriage, she was expected to leave the paid labor force. The domestic code never applied to poor women. They had to work to earn money; moreover, their work—in factories, as domestics, taking in boarders[1]—was physically hard and minimally paid. Consequently, these women were viewed with great suspicion. They worked in coarse jobs, exposed to vice. If they were married and had families, they were neglectful of both their husbands and their children. Single mothers were particularly suspect, especially if there were boarders in the home, which, of course, was a very common practice among the working class and the poor. A great many of these poor working women were immigrants and African Americans; thus, they carried the additional burdens of discrimination. They were "degraded to begin with."[2] In sum, poor women and their children had to work, and they were stigmatized for it.

The social welfare codes, as part of the larger normative order, reinforced the ideologies of the work ethic, patriarchy, and race. Those who conformed were symbolically reaffirmed by stigmatizing "the Other." The deliberate humiliation of the poor not only deters the "undeserving," but validates those who play by the rules—the hardworking male head of the household, the proper wife, the racial majority.

Despite the seeming clarity of the dominant welfare ideologies, it turns out that in practice, there is considerable ambiguity and controversy. There is the charitable impulse, especially when the poor are neighbors or

[1] Kessler-Harris 1982.   [2] Gordon 1988.

potentially blameless—such as widows, the disabled, and young children. "Deservingness," in practice, requires judgment as to circumstances and character. Even the unemployed able-bodied command sympathy when they are known in the community to be law-abiding, sober citizens. Consequently, there is always tension and controversy in administering relief. During the nineteenth century, when the state tried to control the spread of pauperism by insisting that all relief recipients go to the poorhouse, there was considerable local resistance. In addition to the increased expense (never a minor consideration in welfare), communities often refused to subject their impoverished, but worthy neighbors to such indignities.[3]

The allocation of jurisdictional authority over the poor depends on the extent and intensity of these moral conflicts. When the particular category of applicant is potentially in the labor force, or otherwise raises issues of gender, child rearing, and race, then giving relief becomes morally problematic, and these controversies are delegated to lower units of government. The relief of the "undeserving" is managed through myth and ceremony—symbolic reassurance to the political victors, token compliance, but delegation to the contending forces at the local level.

During the poorhouse reforms, the myth was that the social evil of spreading pauperism would be checked by abolishing outdoor relief (inevitably indiscriminate in practice) and sending all recipients to the poorhouse. The theory was that the willingness of the poor to put up with the indignities of the poorhouse was an infallible test of necessity. The ceremony was that in certain jurisdictions outdoor relief was abolished; those desperate enough did go to the poorhouse, and no one knows what happened to the rest. But in practice, the issue was locally determined. In most communities, most of the poor continued to receive outdoor relief; the poorhouse was considered too harsh and too expensive.[4]

Practically all of our current major social welfare programs repeat this same pattern—programs that are morally ambiguous are dealt with through myth and ceremony; the controversies are delegated to lower levels of government. We start with our most notorious social welfare program—the one popularly known as "welfare." This is Aid to Families with Dependent Children (AFDC)—the program basically for single mothers of minor children. This program started at the state level during the second decade of this century. Despite its popular name, "Mothers' Pension," the program was born in great controversy. In the late nineteenth century, Progressive Era reformers feared for the traditional American family. Many poor, immigrant, and African American mothers were in the paid labor force; there was spreading social disorder in the festering

[3] Katz 1986. [4] Katz 1986.

urban slums; there were large numbers of single poor mothers; and it was during this period that child abuse and neglect was "discovered." The juvenile courts were established at the turn of the century.

Progressive Era social reformers began to argue that rather than break up a home, a poor, but otherwise proper single mother should be supported so that she could remain at home and raise her children. A "mothers' pension" would reduce child neglect and preserve the domestic code. There was sharp opposition. It was argued by other major social reformers, including most social workers, that such a program would reward vice by encouraging family breakup and male irresponsibility.

Between 1910 and 1920, most states enacted an aid to dependent children program. The proponents prevailed—worthy mothers could now stay at home and raise their children. Or so it seemed; in practice, not much changed. The programs were delegated to the county level, sometimes the juvenile court judge, or, most often, to the county courts. The programs remained extremely controversial. Many counties refused to enact programs at all. In other counties, administration was turned over to the very organizations that opposed the program. Overall, benefits were meager and restricted to white widows. The vast majority of poor single mothers and their children were not touched; they remained in the labor market along with the general mass of the poor. Moreover, by not being on ADC, they bore the additional stigma of being "unworthy mothers." The reformers won a symbolic victory only.

Despite considerable changes, contemporary AFDC retains the same myth and ceremony characteristics. For most of its history, most poor single mothers, especially those of color, were excluded. Starting in the late 1960s, the demographics of the program changed as a result of the migrations of African Americans to the North, and the liberal reforms of the 1960s. The state-run gates were forced open, and large numbers of African American single mothers and their children enrolled. At this point, welfare became a "crisis." Welfare, in the popular mind came to be considered the program for African American unwed mothers, increasingly underclass, living in ghettoes, instead of worthy white widows. As a result, social control features have become more pronounced. The first federal work program for AFDC recipients was enacted in 1967 and continues through the present in the form of the Family Support Act of 1988. Other controls, designed to weed out "waste, fraud, and abuse," have also been introduced. In certain areas, such as financial eligibility and benefit calculations, there has been considerable federal and state centralization to monitor overpayments, but generally, power is at the local level. The states retain authority over the all-important benefit levels; and thus, despite federal eligibility requirements, can exclude large numbers of families. Benefit levels, that is, financial eligibility, have declined, in real terms, during the past twenty years.

The Family Support Act of 1988 is considered to be one of the most significant reforms. The domestic code is gone. The two-earner family is the norm, and the majority of mothers, even of young children, are in the paid labor force. Therefore, it is now morally acceptable for nonpoor mothers to earn incomes. This is the theory of the Family Support Act's JOBS program which is supposed to require welfare mothers to engage in work or training and, as a consequence, to reduce dependency. That is the myth—that work and/or training is now required. However, it is well-known that the most important determinate of exiting from welfare is the availability of jobs, a matter left untouched by the Family Support Act. Employment and training programs, in general, but especially for people with large employment deficits, that is, the long-term welfare recipients, are both expensive and very problematic in terms of effectiveness.

Characteristically, the administration of the Family Support Act is delegated to the states, and then to the counties. State and local programs are underfunded and weakly administered. Under the most favorable circumstances, some recipients will get jobs but the results so far have been very "modest" in terms of both earnings and welfare savings. Most recipients who do find jobs are not much better off financially (they will certainly remain in poverty). This will be the ceremony. But in most jurisdictions, most of the welfare families will be untouched. They will either not be enrolled for a variety of administrative and financial reasons, or the programs will be ineffective, or no jobs will be available in the community. Those who remain on welfare will be further stigmatized because a few will actually have exited welfare through employment and training programs and the myth is that now all welfare recipients are expected to work and that extensive work and training programs are available. Stigmatizing the "failures" will validate the nonpoor working mothers.

The new wave of proposed welfare reforms will not make much difference. The mood of the country is to have time-limited welfare—that is, after two years of work preparation and job search, the recipient must find a job, or be assigned one, but, in any event, welfare is over. It will not be "a way of life." This, too, will be myth and ceremony. Unless there is a significant growth in jobs, financing public jobs will be far too expensive (much more than welfare). In addition to the added cost, reserving public jobs for welfare recipients is controversial at the local level. At the same time, if welfare is cut off, families will show up in shelters and foster care, and these other institutional arrangements are not only controversial but also more expensive than welfare. Moreover, these costs are borne by state and local governments rather than through federal cost-sharing. If history is any guide, time-limited welfare will be enacted; some recipients will find jobs, a few will be cut off, but ways will be found at the local level to defer cutting the vast majority of recipients off welfare. As long as the practice is of low visibility, it is the cheapest and most politically expedient solution. The moral conflicts are delegated to the county level; a successful delegation is one that symbolically satisfies the demand to "do something," but does not disturb other strongly held interests in the community.

In the meantime, the "welfare crisis" continues to boil, with the newly elected Republican Congress rightflanking the Clinton administration. The proposals are more extreme extensions of past policies—tougher work requirements (time limits; pressure to take low-wage work; no funds for education, training, and child care), the ending of welfare as an "entitlement," and further delegation to the states in the form of block grants.[5]

The importance of the moral status of the poor in the allocation of authority is illustrated in other social welfare programs. Two particularly significant examples involve the dependent aged and the unemployed. The Roosevelt administration, as part of the New Deal, put forth two major proposals: old-age insurance pensions and unemployment insurance. The insurance pension program became a national pension scheme, entirely financed and administered by the federal government (Social Security). In contrast to European programs, the unemployment insurance program was largely state financed and administered—individual states set benefit levels and administered the discretionary terms and conditions as to who would qualify. Employers were experience-rated, also unique among industrialized countries. Why the difference?

There were massive numbers of unemployed, both young and old. Clearly, the Depression was a national problem. There were a lot of reasons for the different administrative outcomes, but one important one was that the aged were now considered to be out of the labor market. With Social Security retirement, capitalists wanted and got graduated benefits to preserve work incentives and a uniform national tax to prevent interstate competition.

The unemployed were in a very different position than the aged; they were still part of the labor market and a uniform, generous insurance scheme would lessen both the incentives to take low-wage jobs and the disincentives to strike for better working conditions. It is important for capitalists to keep control over local labor markets to make sure that workers would not be tempted by the cushion of benefits to either quit work or strike. This meant control over state and local administration of the unemployment insurance program.

Race also figured prominently in both programs. The South controlled the Congress, and southern politicians felt that national benefits would disturb existing race relations, especially in the rural areas. Thus, categories of jobs that African Americans filled—primarily agriculture and do-

[5] Handler 1995.

mestic—were excluded from Social Security retirment coverage. At the same time, since state and local agencies had to maintain control, unemployment insurance was restricted to the "deserving" workers either by excluding categories of jobs or by restricting benefits (workers are ineligible if they quit, are fired, or on strike).

The locus of the administration of unemployment insurance was, by far, the single most important political issue concerning this program. The code was that the program had to be sensitive to "local labor markets." Business interests won. Unemployment insurance is administered at the state and local level; despite its name (myth), benefits—as compared to other industrialized countries—are meager and paid to less than a third of the unemployed (ceremony). The conflicts over who "deserves" unemployment and how much are resolved in local, low-visibility decisions.

The Social Security pension program illustrates the reverse side of the thesis: when there is agreement on the moral deservingness of the category of the poor, when the granting of relief is no longer ambivalent, then programs are handled at higher levels of government; they will be more generous and benign. Instead of ceremony, there are real benefits. The aged poor, along with the clear-cut, seriously disabled (e.g., the blind), are the clearest example of the deserving poor. However, this was not always the conception, and the transformation of the dependent aged from a morally ambivalent category to a clear-cut category illustrates the changes in the structural characteristics of the programs.

Prior to the Depression, there was no agreed-upon retirement age. This meant that able-bodied workers in their sixties were still potentially in the labor market. Old-age assistance programs for the poor aged, which began to be enacted in the 1920s, reflected this moral ambivalence. These programs were not widespread; benefits were quite small; and there were many discretionary conditions designed to weed out the morally problematic. There was concern that these programs would undermine the work ethic and family responsibility. So, for example, applicants who had failed to support their families or who had been vagrants would be ineligible. There were restrictions on disposing of property to qualify for relief.

When the Social Security Act pension program was being debated, the paramount goal of the Roosevelt administration was *not* to relieve need among the dependent aged; rather, it was to set up a slowly maturing insurance system that, among other things, would *exclude* the dependent aged. Roosevelt's idea what that the Social Security pension system was for the steady, employed (white, male) worker who would make contributions to an insurance fund. The administration was deeply concerned lest the stigma of the morally problematic poor, which included the dependent poor, taint the Social Security insurance system.

Starting at this time, there was a shift in the moral categorization of the dependent aged. Political movements (e.g., the Townsend movement) urged uniform, flat-grant, relatively condition-free "pensions" for the aged poor. The Roosevelt administration stoutly resisted; it still feared that the pension scheme would become infected by the welfare stigma. This struggle continued until the 1960s. Gradually, the Social Security Administration yielded and benefits were liberalized. Eventually, the dependent aged won the battle for deservingness. The Social Security system, while largely for the nonpoor, does have significant redistributive effects, and poverty among the aged has been significantly reduced. Moreover, for the relatively small number of the aged who are still not covered, the old-age-assistance welfare programs were folded into the Supplemental Security Income (SSI) program (1972). Thus, all of the aged, regardless of work histories and insurance contributions (or other moral behavior), receive most of their public income support from a completely federally financed and federally administered program.

When we look at other social welfare programs, in general, the patterns hold. The clients of workers' compensation and the social security disability program are morally problematic in that generous programs conflict with the work ethic. Workers' compensation, despite the hopes of its proponents, is not an insurance program; benefits are low, and it has always been administered at the state level. The disability programs (whether federal or state) are administered at the state level, although the federal program has tight supervision to control generosity. Both programs are tough.

The toughest social welfare program of all is general relief. This is the bottom-line program for those who fail to qualify for anything else. It is the historic program administered at the lowest level of government (in more than half the states, still at the municipal or county level). It deals with the most morally problematic of the poor—nonaged, childless adults. In the largest cities, the applicants are mostly African American males. While there is great variation, generally it is the most exclusionary, miserly, harshest welfare program of all.

We find the same patterns in in-kind programs as well. Medicare, for the Social Security aged, is federally administered, and is far superior to Medicaid, which is primarily for the welfare poor (plus some other closely similar categories). Medicaid is far less generous than Medicare and is largely state administered. Efforts to expand Medicaid to meet some of the growing health care needs in America are in the direction of sympathetic groups—those not in the labor market, and with an obviously favorable cost-benefit ratio—for example, unborn children.

The food stamps program is seemingly an exception. A broadly based program for many people potentially in the labor market, it is a federal program (U.S. Department of Agriculture) but administered by county departments of welfare. Food stamps has its own particular history and current political support (e.g., farm interests), but even so, is taking on increasing social control characteristics. Qualifying for it requires a work test, and in many jurisdictions violations of other welfare programs (e.g., general relief)—determined at the local level—will also lead to food stamp sanctions. Over the years, food stamps has been losing its nutrition mission and is coming to resemble a welfare program for the undeserving poor.[6]

Recently, the Earned Income Tax Credit (EITC) has been expanded to become a significant form of redistribution. However, the EITC is tied to work—the more one works, the more one gets—and is not considered in the political debates to be part of the social welfare system. Rather, despite its antipoverty effects, it is considered part of employment policy.

We see, then, in the full array of social welfare programs, how decentralization—that is, allocations of jurisdictional authority—is used to manage conflict. When there is agreement on the deservingness of the category, the program is federally administered and fairly routine. On the other hand, when welfare is controversial, and when controversies boil up and demand upper-level attention—such as the "Mothers' Pension" programs, or the unemployed or dependent aged—the preferred response, from the perspective of the legislature, is to try to escape political costs by granting symbolic victories and delegating the controversy back down to the local level. In this way, the legislature can take credit for validating the symbols and the ceremonies and avoid responsibility for the controversial decisions. This arrangement generally suits the lower levels of government as well. It is here that the conflicts are most keenly felt and local interests want to maintain control—whether, as in a prior age, to avoid sending neighbors to the poor house, or to help a worthy widow, or to control local labor markets, or to refuse assistance to the "undeserving."

COMMAND-AND-CONTROL REGULATION AND ITS ALTERNATIVES

There are many changes going on in the management of government. The overarching theme involves rethinking of top-down management in favor of various strategies of decentralization in which lower units, even at the field level, have greater autonomy in making and implementing decisions.[7] The contemporary buzzword is "reinventing government."[8]

---

[6] Lipsky and Thibodeau 1990.
[7] Barzelay 1992.
[8] Osborne and Gaebler 1992.

The sharing of authority can be with lower units of government or with private parties. In this section, we are primarily concerned with the latter.

The widespread move to decentralize economic regulation starts with a description and critique of the command-and-control regime. Previously, the complaint about economic regulation was agency capture by special interests; today the complaint is agency oppression through rigid, bureaucratic command-and-control regulation.[9] In chapter 2, we noted that there was a shift in the approach to regulation. Prior to the 1970s, the usual pattern consisted of broad delegations of authority to administrative agencies that, in general, had wide discretion in terms of substantive standards and enforcement practices. Starting with the Clean Air Amendments in 1970, Congress began to enact much tighter controls over administrative discretion. In response to the growing perception that the Environmental Protection Agency was either not acting when it should, or acting too slowly, there was a flood of highly detailed environmental statutes. Congress prescribed more detailed substantive criteria and imposed action-forcing, mandatory deadlines and schedules on the agency. For example, amendments now require the EPA to list hazardous chemicals or pollution regulations by certain times. This approach was used in several major environmental statutes, including those relating to hazardous waste disposal, underground storage tanks, the transportation of fuel, toxic substances, the discharge of toxic substances, the evaluation of storage facilities, worker safety with hazardous wastes, controlling the contamination of drinking water, storm water discharges, asbestos removal from schools, pesticide ingredients, and lead paint; the list goes on. Further, several amendments provide that if the EPA fails to regulate in the prescribed manner and time, the statutory regulatory result automatically goes into effect. The reasons for the shift to the new style of regulation are said to be lack of confidence in the EPA, the presence of strong environmental groups pressing for action, and public opinion favoring stringent enforcement.[10]

The changes in work-place safety and health reflected similar kinds of distrust of the agency. The perception was that there were serious problems with enforcement under OSHA—leniency, politics, and corruption. The Nixon administration sought to decentralize by encouraging state agencies to take over enforcement. In response, the major industrial unions, the chief constituency of OSHA in Congress, pressed for a strict, legalistic approach. The unions rejected accident rates as a measure of administrative rationality, and instead pressed for enforcement productivity. State agencies would be closely monitored and evaluated according

---

[9] Stewart 1992.   [10] Shapiro and Glicksman 1988, 829–30, 842.

to the number of citations issued, amounts of penalties assessed, and number of cases upheld on appeal. This approach forced state agencies to centralize in order to increase the productivity of their inspectors.[11]

As Bardach and Kagan point out, the changes in regulation were part of broader political and cultural influences. The explosion of protective regulatory law—in the 1960s and early 1970s—coincided with increased knowledge, awareness, and intolerance of being cheated or suffering harm in the environment and the work-place or from products. There were changes in the legal culture; legal rights spread from civil rights and the poor to the economy. Liberal ideology and politics favor command-and-control regulation. It is based on the positive law; it is visible, universal, and equal in treatment. Conciliation, accommodation, bargaining, and flexibility smack of favoritism and corruption. Particular events, such as scandals, scientific discoveries, and catastrophies fuel the demand for more regulation. Protective regulatory law became good politics.[12]

There were other reasons for the spread of regulatory law. Special-interest groups, as discussed in chapter 2, use regulatory law to further or consolidate their position. Bureaucracies expand. Regulations are universalistic; they apply to all businesses of a particular type regardless of variation; and the norms of equal treatment push toward uniform application. Businesses want the security of precision and the certainty that their competitors are not getting an advantage through some secret bargain. Inspectors like the security of quantitative measures of performance. Detailed rules give the appearance of fairness, uniformity, and the absence of corruption; difficult judgment questions can be avoided and higher authority can be invoked in a hostile field environment.[13]

The results of "new-style" regulation were dramatic in agencies such as OSHA. In fact, OSHA began to be cited as one of the prime examples of the "pathologies" of command-and-control regulation. Energy was devoted to close accountability to rules rather than results (i.e, accident rates) in order to avoid the leniency, politics, and corruption of the past. Program integrity would be insured by narrowing administrative discretion, codifying policies, and routinizing decision making. Citations and other enforcement practices went up, but perverse effects also developed—officials rigidly "going by the book," concentrating on trivial offenses that, in turn, created a culture of resistance, an inability to consult and solve problems, and an enormous amount of paperwork. There was great doubt as to whether any of this activity had much effect on improving work safety. In fact, it was argued that the legalistic, command-and-control style probably had perverse effects.[14]

---

[11] Rees 1988.
[13] Bardach and Kagan 1982.

[12] Bardach and Kagan 1982.
[14] Bardach and Kagan 1982; Rees 1988.

Many of the same characteristics applied to other regulatory agencies.[15] Bureaucracies were not considered capable of effective and efficient management. Regulation became rigid, ineffective, and costly. Innovation was stifled. The policy-making process became dominated by faction, and administration was fragmented and irresponsible. Agencies were overwhelmed by exorbitant information and decision-making costs that regulators tried to avoid through simplistic, rigid standardization. Decisions were buried in lengthy adversarial administrative and judicial hearings.[16]

An important criticism of the legalistic approach is what Bardach and Kagan call "regulatory unreasonableness." One meaning of *unreasonableness* refers to the mismatch between regulatory standards and real-world variety. Another meaning, which figures prominently in cooperative-style regulation, refers to the variety of *reasons* or *causes* that produce violations. The authors argue that not all violations occur from deliberate attempts to evade the law. Rather, many come about through incompetence, carelessness, lack of supervision, lack of knowledge, or accidents. But the legalistic, or punitive model of regulation assumes that business firms are amoral calculators, that credible threats to management will induce firms to increase their law-abidingness efforts (e.g., strengthen their safety programs), and that a few bad firms will be able to take an unfair competitive advantage. At the same time, accidents are viewed as industrywide problems caused by insufficient regulation that require industrywide solutions. Problems are exaggerated; solutions are simplistic; and the costs of regulatory solutions are ignored. Either because of lack of understanding of causation or because the problem is not amenable to solution through regulation, proxies are used—for example, staffing ratios, warning signs, records and procedures—that are easily monitored but are only marginally useful.[17]

What punitive, legalistic, command-and-control regulation cannot get at, say Bardach and Kagan, is the *attitudes* of responsible people. This limitation is important, because with the exception of criminal law, regulated activity is favored, indeed essential, activity—manufacturing, construction, consumption, and services.[18] It is not like criminal activity. This means that tough, punitive regulatory enforcement is inherently ambivalent and contested. Business people are not criminals; and there are often trade-offs between regulation, profitability, and employment—or at least employers, employees, and those who rely on the activity think there are. Rules cannot cover everything; compliance needs agreement and cooperation. Yet, it is argued, tough regulation is perverse. Instead of fostering cooperation, it destroys it. By emphasizing violations rather than

[15] Aranson 1990; Rose-Ackerman 1994b.
[16] Stewart 1990; Sunstein 1990, 32.
[17] Bardach and Kagan 1982.   [18] Selznick 1992.

problems and the necessity to cite all violations, regulation creates bitterness and adversariness. Everything must be put on the record. Businesses will not share information; agencies are subject to charges of collusion if they receive information confidentially. A "culture of resistance" sets in. Strict standards and strict enforcement, it is claimed, waste huge amounts of money and resources, discourage innovations, and result in massive counterproductive litigation.[19]

The charge against regulation is, of course, overdrawn. Regulation performs valuable functions, including addressing problems of collective action, coordination, and transaction costs. And despite the failures, there have been significant benefits—for example, air and water pollution has been substantially reduced, with significant health benefits, species have been protected, and significant gains in auto and consumer product safety, and antidiscrimination efforts in the area of disabilities as well as in voting, education, and employment have been achieved.[20]

Still, very serious problems remain. Much of regulation is poorly designed, very costly, and not only produces limited results, but is even counterproductive. There are many examples of "government failure"— in the original statutes, the influence of interest groups, misdiagnosis of problems and inadequate policy analysis, often an undue emphasis on "rights" rather than trade-offs; there is often a failure to anticipate adverse consequences, failures of implementation, perversion of democratic processes through agency procedures, and so forth.[21]

There seems to be a fairly widespread consensus on what is wrong with regulation. As to remedies, there are two basic positions. One, is to return to the market as much as possible. The other is the move toward what is called flexible or cooperative regulatory enforcement.

Market-based incentives are designed to substitute utility maximization for command-and-control regulation.[22] A prominent early proposal was to modify the permit system under the Clean Air Act by auctioning pollution permits and allowing polluters to buy and sell each other's permits.[23] Polluters with high cleanup costs would purchase permits from those with low costs. It is claimed that this scheme would encourage innovation and transfer information tasks from the overburdened agency to the managers and engineers. The agency would no longer be required to determine, through costly adversarial techniques, the best available technology for each major industry and defend these determinations in court. Officials would no longer be required to consider endless adaptations to changing local conditions of every significant source of pollution. Instead, local managers and engineers would be able to determine their own costs,

---

[19] Ackerman and Stewart 1985; Rabin 1986; Rose-Ackerman 1988.
[20] Sunstein 1990, 47–71.   [21] Sunstein 1990.
[22] Rose-Ackerman 1994a, 1206.   [23] Ackerman and Stewart 1985.

and either sell or buy permits as required. The permits would be for a fixed term, after which the polluters would be required to buy new permits in each watershed and air quality control region. Since permits are valuable only if there is strict enforcement, the agency would still have to monitor, but enforcement disputes would concentrate on whether or not the permit was exceeded rather than on complex technology issues.[24]

There is strong support for market-based policies for environmental protection; moreover, this support includes several of the major environmental organizations.[25] The Environmental Protection Agency has already instituted some of these reforms, under its "bubble" and "trade-off" or "banking" or "netting" programs for various air pollutants (e.g., sulfur dioxide, carbon monoxide, lead, hydrocarbons).[26] There is both trading and taxes in the case of chlorofluorocarbons. Other similar programs and proposals, including transferable emission allowances for acid rain, are being considered. There is state experimentation.[27] For example, New Jersey instituted a system of "transferable development rights" to preserve the Pinelands, a forest zone, from excessive development.[28]

At all levels of government, market-based incentives are becoming more widespread. A common example is the deposit-refund systems for waste disposal—one here is the "bottle bills."[29] In the western states, as well as the federal government, there is increasing use of leasing and marketing water resources.[30] Other countries have also adopted market-based incentives. Individual transferable quotas (ITQs) for fishing are apparently successful in New Zealand and Australia. France, the Netherlands, and Germany, as well as other countries, use water pollution charge systems.[31] Proposals continue to be made for much greater use of incentives for environmental protection through the market.[32]

Susan Rose-Ackerman suggests a similar type of approach for OSHA regulation. Assuming that there are trade-offs between health and safety provisions, employment levels, the real value of take-home pay, and product prices, she argues that it is not self-evident that workers are always better off with higher health and safety standards. Instead of the present command-and-control regime, she proposes that information be

[24] Stewart 1992.

[25] Hahn and Stavins 1991. There are, of course, some skeptics (e.g., Blumm 1992, 371; Krier 1992, 325; Menell 1992, 489). Brunet (1992) doubts the efficacy of private enforcement, as a substitute for the public administrative prosecution, to enforce or monitor market rights (311).

[26] Hahn and Hester 1989; Rose-Ackerman 1994a.

[27] Ackerman and Stewart 1985; Hahn and Stavins 1991; Willey 1992.

[28] Stewart 1992.

[29] Hahn and Stavins 1991.

[30] Anderson and Leal 1992; but see Willey 1992.

[31] Anderson and Leal 1992; Hahn and Stavins 1991.

[32] Anderson and Leal 1991; Hahn and Hester 1989.

improved by requiring employers to inform workers and job applicants of risks in clear and nontechnical language and that government sponsor research on risk levels. She then proposes a two-tiered regulatory scheme: The first level would encompass minimal, serious risks, control of which would be enforced by strict requirements that cannot be bargained away. More stringent standards would be covered by the second tier and would be bargained between employers and employees (either individually or through their unions). These standards would only be relaxed in exchange for job-related benefits.[33] Other scholars also propose more flexibility in OSHA.[34]

The proponents of market-based incentives usually argue that regulatory goals will be more likely accomplished if there is a better accommodation, a better balance, between public law and economic efficiency.[35] With the pollution permits, regulation is concerned with the process (the structure of the auction, term limits, etc.) and certain substantive parameters—for example, pollution levels for particular substances within particular areas. But within these ranges, there is autonomy for the regulated industries. Regulatory authority—the ability to choose between various kinds of productive processes—has been delegated to private groups that have the authority to make choices within the parameters. At the same time, the private groups have something of value for the regulators. To the extent that the private groups choose within the regulatory parameters, public goals are accomplished with reduced information and enforcement costs. The regulatory task is made easier. This is an *exchange*.

Vouchers are a variation of market-based incentives. Here, specified consumers are authorized to purchase designated goods and services from eligible vendors. The theory is that holders of vouchers act like ordinary consumers and that vendors, in their efforts to attract buyers, will become subject to market discipline. While the leading example of a voucher program is food stamps, there are significant programs in housing and education (often called "choice").[36]

Voucher proposals are sold on the basis of de-regulation and privatization, that is, the efficiency and quality objectives of external regulation are now to be achieved through the discipline of market incentives. The theory assumes that there is competition among suppliers or vendors and that clients, or voucher holders, are informed, autonomous purchasers. In practice, such conditions rarely exist, and quite often, the items for which the vouchers are issued—housing units, schooling, health care, etc.—become subject to regulation in an attempt to protect the purchaser.[37] In other words, voucher programs become a form of substitution of regula-

---

[33] Rose-Ackerman 1990a.
[35] E.g., Aranson 1990.
[37] Elmore 1991a.

[34] Shapiro and McGarity 1989.
[36] Gormley 1991a.

tory regimes. Others have also noted that privatization is not necessarily deregulation, since privatization is often accompanied by an increase in regulation. Under the Thatcher government, for example, the privatization of telecommunications and nursing home beds resulted in a new regulatory agency for the former, and an increase in the number of nursing home inspectors in the various health districts as well as a more general upgrade of public oversight. Accordingly, if a program for school vouchers for private schools were to be adopted, there would be an increase in regulation to make sure that private schools met minimum certification standards.[38]

Market-based incentives are different from government simply selling a product, for example, an admission ticket to a national park. With market-based incentives, the subjects operate within the regulatory frame. The industrial polluters make choices within the confines of the regulation; moreover, they are subject to regulatory enforcement if there are violations. In contrast, a citizen can, without penalty, decide not to enter the park. The holders of education vouchers are still subject to the compulsory education laws. With other kinds of vouchers, however, the distinction blurs. No one is required to accept food stamps or Section 8 housing certificates. Holders of food stamps and housing vouchers, at least theoretically, can only exercise their choice within the terms of the vouchers, but the vouchers are a very close substitute for cash. In fact, there is a problem of preventing the sale of vouchers.[39] But in any event, the important distinction, for our purposes, is that regulatory goals are accomplished through incentives rather than commands.

Cooperative Regulation

Informal or flexible or cooperative-style regulatory enforcement is usually contrasted with command-and-control regulation. The latter is concerned with the application of punishment for specific violations; the decision-making process is adversarial and relies on legal machinery. The former is concerned with conciliation and accommodation, focusing on prevention rather than punishment. With cooperative regulation, even though regulators respond to a particular problem, the emphasis is on negotiating future conformity. The decision-making process is often private and informal.[40]

Even in a command-and-control regime, flexible regulatory enforcement is ubiquitious.[41] Start with what seems to be a typical example: A regulated firm has been charged with a violation and, after appropriate

[38] Ayres and Braithwaite 1992.   [39] Bendick 1989.
[40] Hawkins 1984.   [41] Hawkins 1984.

process, is ordered to do something—usually make restitution and change future conduct (e.g., stop discharging toxic wastes into a stream). In this situation, which is what we usually think of as command-and-control regulation, authority and power reside in the regulatory agency; the person or entity is commanded to do something on pain of additional state punishment.

However, even where there is detection, conflict, and an ordered change in behavior, regulated persons are not completely passive. It is rare that there isn't some sort of bargaining, some sort of interaction between the enforcement personnel and the regulated persons, that influences decisions. This is a familiar story with the police—attitudes and responses of suspects influence police decisions. Thus, even within these constraints, there is some exercise of power on the part of the citizen. In most situations, regulated citizens exercise varying and important degrees of power in their relations with regulatory personnel.[42] When we move from criminal law enforcement to regulation, then, despite the public insistence on command-and-control regulation, with its formal characteristics of prosecution and deterrence, bargaining, or the cooperative style of regulation, is much more the norm.[43] Because regulation concerns activities that are valued by the community, there is an inherent slant toward cooperation.[44]

The cooperative model uses persuasion, consultation, and accommodation. Regulated businesses are legitimate enterprises producing valued goods and services. The purpose of regulation, therefore, is to protect these core activities, but control for harmful externalities. Many violations are often morally ambiguous (i.e., accidents). In addition, firms are not monolithic. They have a variety of motives. Generally, firms are law-abiding; managers adhere to basic societal norms, they are responsive to peer pressure, and the opinions of customers, employees, and the public at large.[45] Many regulations don't quite fit; they are either overinclusive or underinclusive, and regulators have to be responsive to the needs and intentions of firms.[46]

Even in its most legalistic period, OSHA enforcement proved to be "flexible" in the field. In a recent study of OSHA agencies in thirty New York counties over a ten-year period (1975–85), it was found that local political officials and their coalitions exercised considerable influence on enforcement. The study looked at rates of inspections, penalties assessed, and amount of penalties in both manufacturing and construction sites.[47]

It is at the field offices where the actual work takes place—inspecting

---

[42] Sarat 1990; Ewick and Silbey 1992; White 1990.
[43] Hawkins 1984.   [44] Selznick 1992.
[45] Ayres and Braithwaite n.d.; Gray, Wayne, and Scholz 1993; Rees 1988.
[46] Bardach and Kagan 1982; Rees 1988.   [47] Scholz, Twombly, and Headrick 1991.

places of employment, issuing citations for violations, and prosecuting appeals. Enforcement involves the process of interpreting national regulations under diverse, changing local conditions. There is broad discretion in determining how closely to inspect, whether a condition constitutes a violation, and whether a violation should be considered "intentional" or "accidental." The former will be cited; the latter dealt with informally. Discretion leads to considerable variation between actions of officers and between offices.

The central office attempts to control field level discretion by three principal methods. First, enforcement activities are governed by detailed regulations requiring officers to spend considerable time and effort documenting and justifying their activities according to the rules. In addition, enforcement decisions can be appealed to a special, independent review commission that was set up in part to restrict enforcement activities. Appeals require additional time and effort on the part of the field staff. Second, a great deal more monitoring information is now available as a result of computer technology. Every inspector is recorded in the central information system; all of their official acts are recorded. Third, OSHA attempts to recruit field staff that are professionally trained safety engineers and industry hygienists, and provides in-service training to develop common beliefs about appropriate enforcement policies.

Nevertheless, there are limits on OSHA's control. One source of limitation is directly traceable to the political conflicts surrounding OSHA at the national level. Political polarization starts with business, labor, and other interest groups and is reflected in the extremely partisan congressional committees and a hostile White House. Labor scored initial victories when they got OSHA into the Department of Labor and won the right of workers to file complaints, but business got an independent review commission that can reduce the level of enforcement. In addition to budget cuts and morale problems, there has been a steady stream of formal, but nevertheless ambiguous rules, guidelines, and symbols emanating from the top. Despite the presence of a powerful integrating technology, the political conflicts work against the development of standardized beliefs and values at the field level. Conflicts among central political authorities lead not only to more delegation to the bureaucracy, but also to more delegation within the bureaucracy to the field office.[48]

But the principal reason for variation at the field level is that it is easier for the central office to control inspections than penalties. The central office can estimate the number of inspections (number, dispersion, and complexity of work sites) and can command more inspections without increasing resources by decreasing the time allotted for each inspection. Although penalties are more important than inspections in decreasing

---

[48] Scholz, Twombly, and Headrick 1991.

work-place injury rates, it is more difficult to control penalties. Despite detailed guidelines, inspectors differ in how they apply criteria to penalties. The frequency and amount of penalties depends on the relative level of compliance, which is more difficult for the central office to evaluate. In addition, it is harder to command an increase in penalties because more penalties require more documentation and appeal time.[49]

The authors found that local politics influenced field level enforcement by affecting the local climate. Local political leaders can encourage negotiation by meeting with local businesses to iron out problems, or to help coordinate efforts of unions, local health officials, or trade associations, or to crack down on particularly troublesome employers. A supportive, conciliatory atmosphere can translate into easier access to firm sites, and better information about safety and health conditions, and make it easier to document violations. Conversely, local leaders can encourage confrontational, legalistic tactics on the part of business—for example, requiring warrants for all inspections and appealing all citations. Confrontational inspections can produce considerable psychological pressure in the day-to-day work affecting agency morale.[50]

This is not to argue that OSHA enforcement has been completely discretionary at the local level. The Reagan administration, as well as Congress, has influenced enforcement activities. But especially in the discretionary areas—penalties as compared to inspections—local political influence has been important. It is not direct partisan intervention; rather it is more subtle, more in the nature of providing or withholding bargaining and cooperative resources and lending legitimacy to the agency. The study found more vigorous enforcement when there is local support, and less enforcement in a hostile environment.[51]

Now, it is argued that cooperative flexible enforcement is more efficient—with OSHA, for example, there is more safety and fewer accidents at less cost.[52] This is so for two reasons. First, because the behavior that is to be regulated is favored economic activity and most of the regulated people are considered to be responsible citizens, the attitudes of the regulated firm as well as the strong policy goals of not unduly discouraging economic activity are important considerations. Second, the legalistic approach works best where the the conduct is discrete and there is no basis for a continuing relationship. But where the conduct is continuous and more in the nature of a state of affairs than a number of discrete acts, there is a "problem" and problems are amenable to correction over time.[53]

Keith Hawkins's study of water pollution control in two large districts in England is an important example of cooperative regulation in a com-

[49] Scholz, Twombly, and Headrick 1991.
[50] Scholz, Twombly, and Headrick 1991.
[51] Scholz, Twombly, and Headrick 1991.   [52] Rees 1988.   [53] Hawkins 1984.

mand-and-control context.[54] Water pollution control enforcement agents initially rely on negotiation. Prosecution is rarely used, although it is always in the background. In fact, prosecution is regarded by the agency as a sign of failure. Water pollution control is something most people are ambivalent about, because it competes with the demands of economic activity and although sometimes conduct is clearly blameworthy, more often pollution is the result of accidents. Judgments of blameworthiness mediate the use of law. Sanctions are imposed when violations are deliberate, or, if negligent, are accompanied by uncooperativeness, that is, if the firm challenges the authority and legitimacy of the agency. In other words, enforcement is less a reflection of the law than of the agency's concept of self-preservation.

Field level agents concentrate on major problems, figuring that small problems will be taken care of. They give warnings, advice, information, and consultation. The emphasis is on surveillance and prevention. Because they need easy access to property and information and the ability to raise sensitive issues, they seek to preserve or build good relations. It is not unusual for dischargers to self-report, which means, in effect, that the act will normally not be penalized. Further, if the polluter has the right attitude, compliance may proceed by increments. In addition, if the infraction has been corrected, the agency considers prosecution to be wasteful and vindictive.

The agency does prosecute from time to time, but it does so for symbolic reasons—to demonstrate that it is enforcing the law and to maintain its credibility. The agency carefully selects a small number of important but winnable cases. But the main goal of regulation is to secure change, not to mete out punishment, and to this end, negotiation is the preferred strategy.

Hawkins emphasizes that the cooperative style of regulation is rooted in *reciprocity*—the agency bargains on the less serious offenses, treats the regulated with respect, exchanges information, is responsive to the problems of compliance, and is considerate of good faith. Forbearance is exchanged for access, information, and compliance. The agency achieves regulatory goals at less cost. It is important to emphasize that there is an exchange—each gives the other something of value—and both are better off as a result. This is especially true with continuing relationships.[55]

Ayres and Braithwaite, in their research, also found a great deal of economic cooperative regulation. Corporate executives have a variety of motives in addition to utility maximization; as individuals as well as executives, they are concerned about good reputations. They care about adverse publicity; "they viewed both their personal reputation in the com-

---

[54] Hawkins 1984.   [55] Axelrod 1984.

munity and their corporate reputation as priceless assets."[56] In practice, regulation often responds to both the desire to make money and a sense of social responsibility. A punitive strategy would undermine the cooperative impulse and create a subculture of resistance.

In many areas of business there is a long history of formally delegated self-regulation including the authority to promulgate enforceable standards. Perhaps the most prominent example is professional licensing and self-regulation. Under broad statutory authory, many important professions—law, medicine, accounting, and engineering, among others—have been given wide latitude in setting standards for qualifications, practice, and discipline. The professions are not completely autonomous. There are statutory standards; state and federal constitutions and laws of general applicability apply; and there is state oversight. Nevertheless, a substantial amount of public authority—the monopoly and regulation of the professions—is in private hands.

In civil aviation safety, in every country, a public regulatory agency approves route patterns, safety procedures and equipment, and other operating procedures that are written by the individual companies, tailored to their needs. Violations of the rules can result in fines or license revocations.[57]

Another prominent example involves United States coal mine safety and health. Mine operators can petition to modify the application of mandatory safety standards if the alternative method will achieve the same measure of protection. Several hundred petitions have been granted, and there have been cases where companies have been fined for violating their own regulatory standards. In addition, mine operators can submit plans for ventilation, dust control, and roof support, all subject to agency approval.[58]

Another example involves the Good Laboratory Practices (GLP) rules imposed on pharmaceutical companies by the FDA. These rules require each drug-testing laboratory to have a Quality Assurance Unit (QAU) that acts as an internal compliance office. QAU status reports must be routinely sent to study directors and management, thus eliminating the defense of not knowing. In fact, not knowing about a discovered violation is itself a violation. In all of these situations, enforced self-regulation is a form of "subcontracting regulatory functions to private actors."[59]

Scholars, and now the government, argue that the cooperative style of regulation should be extended farther back in the administrative process—to the policy and rule-making stages.[60] Vice President Gore's *Improving Regulatory Systems* recommends increased use of both regula-

---

[56] Ayres and Braithwaite n.d., 22.   [57] Ayres and Braithwaite n.d., 116.
[58] Ayres and Braithwaite n.d., 117.   [59] Ayres and Braithwaite n.d, 103, 120.
[60] Shapiro 1983.

tory negotiation and incentives.[61] Traditional adversarial adjudication and rule making would be replaced by negotiation, bargaining, mediation, arbitration, or market-based incentives. An example would be a situation in which the Evironmental Protection Agency, the regulated firms, and other interested parties negotiate a standard for emissions. The advantages, claim the proponents, would be flexibility; a mix of incentives; the encouragement of innovation; and the reduction of uncertainty, delay, and the costs of compliance. These would eliminate the special burdens on new products, and reduce the effects of a cumbersome and inefficient decision process.[62] The proponents of negotiated regulations have been somewhat successful. The Negotiated Rulemaking Act of 1990 encourages formal participation of "affected interests," with help of a "facilitator," in the drafting of proposed rules.[63]

Of course, there are a number of concerns with cooperative regulation. Who is included in the negotiations? Will the agency be co-opted? What about regulatory "entitlements" such as worker safety? In much of the literature on the compliance style, there is little discussion of victims—workers, consumers, those who are exposed to environmental hazards.[64] Some think that the bargaining style will preserve the status quo, and discourage reconsideration of current paradigms. Part of the unease about the cooperative style is rooted in the tensions between the symbols of command-and-control regulation and the inevitable need for discretion. No enforcement agency can enforce all of the law all of the time—indeed, such a result would be unacceptable in most cases—but we worry about corruption and capture and about the bargaining away of regulatory goals.

Agency capture by regulated industries is a familiar story. While examples of enforced self-regulation are not so rare, there are weaknesses.[65] Undoubtedly, there is firm pressure to slant the rules. Private rules would not have the legitimacy of universal, public rules. Internally, compliance may be more effective when compliance officers can say that government, rather than company policies, insists on particular practices.[66] But government regulatory vigilance cannot be assumed.

Maintaining the independence of internal compliance units is always problematic. But, Ayres and Braithwaite argue, empirically—in pharmaceuticals, coal mining, and nursing homes—tough compliance units have maintained their independence. Furthermore, corporations are not monolithic organizations. Subunits within organizations, including compliance units, can generate their own political power, their own constituencies.[67]

Again, as with cooperative regulation, the relationships will vary de-

---

[61] Rose-Ackerman 1994a.   [62] Stewart 1992.   [63] Rose-Ackerman 1994b.
[64] Rose-Ackerman 1994b.   [65] Ayres and Braithwaite n.d., 120.
[66] Ayres and Braithwaite n.d., 125.   [67] Ayres and Braithwaite n.d., 127.

pending on the characteristics of the private group and their environments. Strong business firms will either exert dominating pressure, as when agencies are captured, or hold their own in a bargaining context. Depending on the context, one could find adversarial confrontation under the guise of participation, cooperation, co-optation, or corporatism. All of these arrangements involve a *process*. They are not stable. Although the stakeholders have common goals, they come from different positions, have different languages, and different world views. The environments are constantly changing. There are changes in personnel and resources; sometimes crises occur that threaten the basis for trust and cooperation. In short, procedural forms can never be taken for granted.

THE RESPONSE OF ARIZONA TO THE REAGAN DEVOLUTION

A critical dimension of decentralization is federalism—the allocation of authority between various levels of government. Governance in the United States has always involved the distribution of authority between federal, state, and local governments. From the time of the colonies through the Great Society and the Reagan administration, there have been shifting allocations between the three levels of government. Most domestic programs involve complicated intergovernmental relations. They may have varying amounts of federal dollars and, sometimes, significant amounts of federal regulation, but they are actually run by other units of government or private enterprises. This is true for welfare, health, education, housing, social services, workers' compensation, unemployment insurance, and on and on. Various combinations of ways of financing and providing the goods and services are used: (1) federal financing and provision of goods and services; (2) federal financing and state (local) provision; (3) cost-sharing (federal, state, and local) and state (local) provision; (4) state financing and provision; (5) state cost-sharing and local provision; and (6) local financing and provision. Social Security, an enormous program that is completely financed and administered by the federal government, is the exception.

The Reagan administration, called the "decade of devolution," represented a reversal of more than fifty years of increasing centralization and federal activism.[68] The 1970s set the stage. That period was judged by many as one in which an overloaded federal system proved incapable of responding to the economic or social needs of the cities. The federal grant system became unmanageable; local spending incentives were distorted; and regulations created inflexible, onerous obligations on states and localities.[69] "Stagflation" added to the perception of a weakened federal

[68] Liner 1989.   [69] Thomas 1990.

government incapable of managing the economy. It was a government failure—the relative paralysis of the Carter administration—that increased public concern.[70]

California's Proposition 13, enacted in 1978, signaled the start of a taxpayer revolt that is still very much alive. The resistance to taxes, the decline in revenues, and the increase in the federal debt deprived liberal reformers of their principal tool—revenue—which undermined the argument that the federal government could more easily raise tax revenues than could the state and local governments. This led to the collapse of liberal "cooperative federalism."[71] Over time, the share of the federal government money in state and local budgets changed significantly. Between 1958 and 1978, federal aid had increased from 11 percent to about 26 percent of state and local budgets. In 1978, federal aid peaked at $85.5 billion, and has been declining ever since. In 1988, federal aid was about 17 percent of state budgets, and is expected to fall to about 13 percent in 1998.[72]

Reagan's view of federalism was that domestic responsibilities should be handled by the states, and that localities were creatures of the states without direct links to the national government. This meant reducing the domestic role of the federal government, increasing the role of the states and local governments, increasing the role of the private sector, reducing the size of the welfare state, and increasing the role of profit and not-for-profit services. The framework for the reversal was built into the Omnibus Budget Reconciliation Act (OBRA) 1981; a comprehensive set of swaps and turn-backs proposed in 1982 (e.g., Medicaid to the federal government and AFDC to the states); and the megablock grant proposals of 1983 (more than forty education, transportation, community development, and social service programs were to be consolidated into four major block grants); tax reform legislation; and the termination of General Revenue Sharing and Urban Redevelopment Grants.[73]

There was another devolution trend that has also continued. In the 1960s, Congress adopted a new type of federal preemption. Congress or a federal agency promulgates rules and regulations that establish minimum national standards. If a state desires to have regulatory responsibility, then it submits a plan containing standards at least as stringent as the federal standards. If the plan is approved, the federal agency delegates enforcement responsibility to the state. The delegation can be revoked if the state fails to enforce the statute. Contingent or partial preemption offers a number of political advantages that have already been discussed. Congress or the president can claim credit for the legislation, yet cloud

---

[70] Elazar 1990.   [71] Kincaid 1990.
[72] Liner 1989.   [73] Thomas 1990.

implementation in a set of involved, uncertain, and often ambiguous intergovernmental arrangements. The national leaders can defend against the criticism of an overbearing national government while, at the same time, permitting members of Congress or high executive officials the option of intervening to serve constituents. If gross implementation failures occur, the politicians can blame the bureaucrats. Finally, the politicians can practice fiscal austerity by placing the costs on the states. Since 1965, an increasing number of such statutes have been passed, particularly in the environmental and health areas.[74] In the 1970s, of the twenty-five environmental statutes enacted, eighteen contained a contingent preemption.[75]

The results of the Reagan devolution were mixed. There was no doubt that cuts made in the grants-in-aid during Reagan's first year were historic.[76] On the other hand, there was disagreement as to what should be turned over to the states as well as reluctance on the part of the states to assume new fiscal burdens.[77] Congress rejected the more revolutionary proposals. For example, the swap of Medicaid for AFDC and the mega-block grant proposal were never seriously considered. Cities and advocacy groups wanted to maintain federal ties. On the other hand, there was a significant reduction in federal regulations across a wide range of programs. The administration was generally responsive to local concerns about regulatory burdensomeness.[78] In the end, though, most targeted programs survived through a combination of congressional compromise and bureaucratic staying power.

The Reagan administration was much more successful in cutting budgets. In many instances, however, the administration's unwillingness to spend money did not diminish the desire of the federal government to continue to pass legislation directed at states and localities. Congress resorted to unfunded mandates.[79] Some mandates were direct orders with civil or criminal sanctions; others were crosscutting requirements attached to federal programs; and others imposed conditions on whole systems as a condition for federal grants.[80] "Cooperative federalism" was replaced by "coercive federalism" in the form of federal preemptive statutes, a tightening of eligibility criteria, and, when feasible, a devolution of federal functions to states and localities.[81] Nevertheless, while a substantial shift occurred, there still remains an extensive federal presence. The money may be less, but there are still over six hundred federal grant programs for state and local governments.[82]

In general, the states welcomed the reduction in federal requirements

[74] Zimmerman 1990.   [75] Wright 1990.   [76] Nathan and Lago 1990.
[77] Elazar 1990.   [78] Farber 1989.   [79] Liner 1989.
[80] Rivlin 1992, 107–8.   [81] Kincaid 1990; Liner 1989.
[82] Rivlin 1992, 109.

and were eager to assume more control. However, the shift in authority did have a substantial impact on state budgets. The re-routing of block grant monies through state government rather than directly to the cities, as well as more federal mandates for state and local provision of services, forced greater fiscal burdens on state and local governments. During the 1980s, the search was on for new ways to raise revenues to cope with escalating expenditures—for example, management improvements, privatization, and functional transfers to other units of government.[83] The unfunded federal mandates caused an increase in state and local taxation.[84] At first state and local spending grew slowly, reflecting the tax-revolt movement of the late 1970s and the 1980 and 1981–82 recessions, but since 1983, spending by both state and local governments has increased sharply. Much to the surprise of the Reagan administration, state government expanded.[85] State reform—of the executive, the legislature, and the revenue systems—had been taking place since the mid-1960s. States were far more ready to respond to the Reagan challenge.[86] The Reagan cuts, in effect, energized the states.

One of the most important impacts of the Reagan devolution was that the bias toward centralization definitely shifted. States, rather than cities, were now the preferred vehicle for delivering federal aid.[87] There was no doubt about the antigovernment, antibureaucratic ideology that developed. By shifting priorities, reorganizing existing grant programs, and reducing federal domestic expenditures as a proportion of the total federal budget, the Reagan administration did succeed in introducing new attitudes among state and local officials and their constituents—in a word, state and local officials henceforth would have to rely more on their own initiatives than seek help from federal government. Both the substantive and symbolic consequences of the Reagan Era altered local officials' approaches to their problems. They engaged in new discussions about their responsibilities. There was more emphasis on management skills rather than on grantsmanship, more initiative in seeking alternatives, and more incentives to develop stronger ties to their states.[88] This shift in orientation away from Washington was accompanied by a reduction in federal regulation of state and local activities and oversight of intergovernmental programs.[89]

The Reagan administration also produced significant changes in state-city relations. During the 1960s and 1970s, the premise was that urban problems were nationally defined and ought to be solved by direct federal aid to cities and to individuals. The federal government responded to a

[83] MacManus 1990.   [84] Liner 1989.   [85] Nathan and Lago 1990.
[86] Rivlin 1992, 102–7.   [87] Thomas 1990.   [88] Thomas 1990.
[89] Elazar 1990.

wide variety of needs—for sewage treatment facilities, airports, roads, hospitals, as well as for assistance with social welfare functions. As the federal government channeled money to the cities, the cities became more autonomous. This pattern began to change somewhat during the Nixon and Carter administrations; there was some attempt at decentralization and devolution, but there were contradictions as well. Regulation began to increase during these periods. The federal government decided not only who should benefit from programs, but how states and cities must run them.[90]

Under the Reagan administration, the cities, which have always carried major service burdens, were especially hard hit. They lost federal aid, both directly or through the states, and were forced to both raise revenues through property taxes and user fees and cut costs by reducing or eliminating services, restricting eligibility, and contracting out.[91] Just as federal requirements can dramatically change state budgets and social welfare programs—for example, Medicaid requirements have had a significant impact on state budgets and significantly influenced the ability of states to finance other social welfare programs—so too, states can alter local budgets. The reduced federal aid placed significant burdens on states to develop new state-local fiscal cost-sharing arrangements. As we shall see in the Arizona case study, states adopted the same pattern—lawmakers require another level of government to provide the services, but they do not provide the funds for them to do so. This has squeezed local governments.[92]

Thus, there were contradictory directions. Decentralization occurred from the federal government to the states, but within the states, there was centralization vis-à-vis the cities.[93] The result has been a relative increase in state revenues as compared to the localities (previously, cities raised more money than state government) but a relative increase in local spending as compared to state spending. Local governments not only spend more than state governments, but also employ more people; they are now the primary public service provider.[94]

In sum, while the results in many specific programs were ambiguous (e.g., environmental protection), the actual overall pattern of federal-state-local relations was changed significantly during the Reagan administration. In many areas of the social welfare state, energy and initiative is more now at the state and local level, and, although state governments have grown in importance, cities and localities are even more significant than ever in the actual delivery of services.

[90] Thomas 1990.   [91] Liner 1989.   [92] Brizius 1989.
[93] Liner 1989.   [94] Brizius 1989.

Bipartisanship

It should be noted, however, that although the start of decentralization is identified with the Reagan administration, there is another side that is politically important. Decentralization, historically and today, is not exclusively championed by the conservatives. In fact, some date the start of the current deregulation movement to Senator Ted Kennedy's hearings on the Civil Aeronautics Board, as well as other consumer movements in the mid-1970s. By 1980, everyone was in favor of deregulation—consumers, liberals, conservatives; it had become a buzzword, a symbol turned into a fashion.[95]

While liberals understandably reacted with suspicion to the Reagan initiative and the legacy of states' rights with its history of racism and parochialism, there is also ambivalence. Even during the heyday of centralization—the days of the Great Society—there was also a communitarian, community control tradition. The War on Poverty, in a very significant sense, was a strategy of citizen-based empowerment. Community Action was local control. While that program ceased to exist in its original form, many of its legacies survive.[96] There are strong elements of local, parental participation in its most successful surviving program—Head Start.

Today, many people, not just conservatives, are worried about the competency of government and the pathologies of large-scale public bureaucracies. There is increasing attention paid to local governments and local communities in terms of responsiveness and flexibility. Alice Rivlin, a long-time scholar at the Brookings Institution, the first director of the Congressional Budget Office, and now head of the Office of Management and Budget, published a book calling for the restructuring of the American federal system.[97] She argues for a much clearer distinction between the functions of the federal government and the states. Under her plan, the federal government would be responsible for tasks that are inherently central responsibilities, such as national defense or foreign policy, or that require a national system (e.g., Social Security, health care) or that have significant spillover effects (e.g., air traffic control, pollution, scientific research). The federal government would also have responsibility for moving the budget from deficit to surplus. The states would take over primary responsibility for what Rivlin calls the "productivity agenda"—education, work-force preparation, and improving the public infrastructure. The federal government would eliminate most of its programs in education, housing, highways, and so forth. She proposes a new system of common shared taxes (e.g., value-added) for state financing. The primary rea-

---

[95] Derthick and Quirk 1985, 40–53.
[96] Boyte 1980.   [97] Rivlin 1992.

sons for the state taking over these responsibilities is Rivlin's conviction that certain policies, if they are to be successful, require "bottom-up community effort." She says, for example, that "education in America will not improve significantly until states and communities decide they want better schools. Making education more effective will take parents who care, committed teachers, community support, and accountable school officials," rather than an " 'education president.' "[98]

Two Examples

We have noted that states and localities have responded in fairly significant ways to deregulation and decentralization. What matters, though, are the details. States and localities are complex organizations, and they vary considerably. Federal mandates, grants-in-aid, or responses to local demands will vary by community. For purposes of this study, I have selected two case examples. Arizona is an example of a conservative state responding to the increased pressure of domestic needs. In that state, we will see political and administrative techniques similar to those that scholars have described at the federal level. I follow this with a case study of local control over two central issues—education and exclusionary zoning. These two issues are selected because of their crucial policy implications. Education reform and residential segregation are critical policy issues. In short, these two areas involve two of the most intensely felt domestic concerns—race and redistribution.

ARIZONA

The discussion of Arizona is based on a case study by John Hall.[99] Hall was interested in state-local relations. As in all states, all local governments in Arizona are creatures of the state. State government controls many of the functions of local governments. Nevertheless, argues Hall, one should not conclude that local governments are even relatively powerless. The important starting point is state government itself—it is not a single entity; rather, it is many structural units, often working at cross-purposes. As in many states, throughout government, power is fractionalized. There are many executive officers, often with short terms, as well as a wide array of boards, commissions, and agencies with both legislative and executive powers. There is direct popular legislation through referendum and initiative, as well as recall of elected officials. The bicameral legislature is becoming increasingly professionalized. The governor has important powers of appointment and an item veto, but is constrained by the fourth branch of government—over one hundred fifty boards, com-

---

[98] Rivlin 1992, 11.   [99] Hall 1989.

missions, and other offices that are more responsive to the legislature. In practice, the power of the governor derives from personality and style—his or her ability to work with the legislature, key state agencies, the media, and other units of government, both nationally and locally. But whatever the role of the governor, "most of the state-local interaction is between 577 units of local government and approximately 35 state agencies."[100]

Starting in the early 1970s, public programs in Arizona have grown substantially in terms of costs, coverage, and responsibilities. Hall asks how this could have come about "in a state known for its conservative philosophy—and during a time of widespread allegiance . . . to tax and spending limits, Reagan domestic budget cuts, and state tax reductions?" The reason was the increased demand for services fueled by the tremendous growth in population (doubled between 1970 and 1987) and urbanization. Twin pressures—from outside and inside the state—were felt at the state legislative level. In addition, court decisions, the threat of litigation, and the financial plight of local governments all had their impact.[101]

The structure of the state's revenue system helped the local governments—major portions are automatically allocated to local units on the basis of population. This system provides for a certain amount of local financial stability, allows for the growth of revenue to meet needs, and lessens reliance on the local property tax. But there are constraints, especially the self-imposed revenue and spending limits that were imposed with increasing frequency from the late 1970s. In addition, some significant state programs (public education, health care, and prison construction) are open-ended, formula-driven programs.

By 1988, Arizona faced a significant deficit. Local governments were hard hit as a result of the decline in federal spending at both the state and local levels. While needs increased, there were reductions in housing, employment and training, social services, and community development. There were some small increases in nonprofit services and user fees.[102]

During this period, there were two major shifts in state policy. Arizona finally bought into the Medicaid program (1982) which greatly reduced county responsibility for indigent health care while at the same time greatly increasing the state's responsibility. In public education, the state also assumed a major financial and policy role—state funds now account for 60 percent of total school spending. Despite the complaints from local school districts about unwarranted state intrusion (e.g., guidelines on curriculum), the 200-plus school districts have managed to retain substantial autonomy.[103]

[100] Hall 1989, 134–35, 137.   [101] Hall 1989, 138–39.
[102] Hall 1989, 143–45.   [103] Hall 1989, 147.

As noted, under the Reagan administration devolution, block grants were shifted from local governments to the states. In Arizona, the response of the various state agencies varied, but generally, the state agencies have been cautious about exercising control. For the most part, the agencies have taken the politically safe route—following the legislative pattern of revenue sharing, funds are allocated according to population-based formulas and local units are given wide latitude in developing and administering programs within broad guidelines. Despite complaints about lack of state leadership, it turns out that "local officials really would not have it any other way, as their state counterparts know, which is why it works that way." At the same time, "the system also operates under an iron law of inter-governmental relations that requires each layer of government to be critical of governments above them for telling them what to do and to chastise those below them for not doing what they are told."[104]

In general, the Arizona system of government, both state and local, was doing far more and costing far more in 1989 than it did in 1980. Both state and federal revenues had increased; new programs were developed and old programs expanded. To some considerable extent, the power of state government had expanded, but state officials "consider themselves as winners only of headaches previously shared by national and local actors."[105] Despite the Reagan devolution, the overall change in intergovernmental relations in Arizona has been modest and incremental, reactive, and needs-driven, primarily due to population growth, and other economic, social, and political trends. In Arizona,

> there is a natural negative reaction . . . to state-imposed solutions of local problems. . . . Local governments are interested in continued revenue sharing with the state; they would like the state to continue to manage and deliver some of the tougher human and social services, but they are adamant about the need to retain local control. . . . Local governments stress self-determination, self-help, and local option, not assistance."[106]

At the same time needs and the demand for services grow in this very politically conservative state. Politicians respond in the classic tradition—they use the intergovernmental system. By this, Hall means that

> It is in the best political interest of all units in our complicated federal system to work together to maximize response and credit and to minimize responsibility for finance and failure. It is also in the best interest of the partners to keep the system complicated. That is because, when seen clearly and in total, both costs and responses are far greater than many people would imagine and are easy pickings for new politicians at all levels. . . . [I]ntergovernmen-

[104] Hall 1989, 152–53.   [105] Hall 1989, 155.   [106] Hall 1989, 155–56.

tal arrangements often succeed because they are not tested by full democratic review. So it is as sometimes silent partners that Arizona governments have grown, prospered, and provided public services in a climate of limited government. . . . All partners will, of course, continue to negotiate profits and losses (credit and blame, responsibilities, and revenues). . . .[107]

In sum, as at the federal level, state officers would just as soon delegate the hot issues to the local level, to which we now turn.

"Our Localism"—Education and Exclusionary Zoning

Public education is deeply rooted in local government. The part of the story that concerns us involves the reform efforts to mitigate some of the major disparities that followed from local control—principally racial segregation and inequalities in resources, which, of course, are linked.

Richard Briffault, in an extensive study of the structure of local government law,[108] illustrated the central role of local government in its control over school finance and exclusionary zoning, which are intimately connected in preserving class and racial segregation.[109] The setting for local control is the broad delegation of power and responsibility from the states to the localities, with very little oversight by the states. The localities provide the basic public or social services; they are authorized to raise the necessary revenues through taxes on real property within their boundaries. They have similar broad authority, again delegated by the states, to regulate the use of land, including the right to zone it. As we know, localities differ greatly—enormously—in the amount of wealth that lies within their borders. The differences in locally based wealth depend on where industry and commerce is located and where the rich and poor live. Locally based wealth is not related to need, which also differs greatly.[110]

Rich localities provide far more resources for education at lower taxes than poor districts. These differences are reinforced by exclusionary zoning. Local governments, through the power to zone, seek to exclude residents who will lower the local wealth average; and quality education attracts high-income families. Low-income families are not only excluded from nice neighborhoods and good schools, but usually from better jobs as well.[111]

In the late 1960s, both school financing and exclusionary zoning began to be attacked in the name of equality. It was argued that if the state assumed greater responsibility for financing local schools, this would re-

[107] Hall 1989, 157–58.
[108] The phrase "our localism" in the subhead above is from Briffault 1990a.
[109] Briffault 1990a.   [110] Briffault 1990a.   [111] Briffault 1990a, 20–22.

duce the local tax burden and the incentives to exclude lower-income families. In general, both the courts and the state legislatures turned these claims aside in the name of local autonomy. In the two-dozen school finance cases, most courts rejected both equal-protection claims as well as arguments that existing disparities violated the state constitution requirement that a free public education must be provided. While some courts upheld either or both of these arguments, they declined to order equalization remedies on the grounds that these remedies would violate local autonomy. For example, the New York Court of Appeals held that it was only through local control of the school budgets that local residents could exercise administrative control over the education in their districts, a crucial matter of local autonomy.

The basic issue was that, given the huge disparities in wealth, guaranteeing equal resources would mean either significant state taxation or limits on spending by the wealthy districts. Both alternatives—each requiring either significant state financing or control—were fiercely opposed by the wealthy districts, and many courts agreed, either because they held they would be violations of local autonomy or out of deference to legislative policy to fund education through local tax revenues.[112]

Briffault uses New Jersey as a major example of the importance of local control in school financing. The New Jersey Supreme Court, one of the most active in the country, held that the unequal, locally based school financing system violated the constitutional requirement that the state must provide a "thorough and efficient" education. The court said that while the state could delegate that responsibility to local government, the state had to ensure that the districts were providing a constitutionally adequate system. The court, however, did not require equalization, only that more resources had to be given to the poorer districts. In response to that decision, the state enacted the Public School Education Act of 1975 which increased the state's role in defining standards, mandated state oversight of local schools, and increased provision of state financial assistance.

However, local education was still to be financed primarily by local taxes. In fact, under the new statute, much of the state aid was based on levels of local spending rather than need and thus went to the rich districts as well as poor. In other words, disparities were not reduced. The myth was state standards and supervision; the ceremony was increased state aid to poorer districts; but the reality was that strongly held local interests were not disturbed. There was no redistribution. Nevertheless, the act was held constitutional.[113] Recently, the New Jersey Supreme Court held that the latest attempt by the legislature to equalize funding between dis-

---

[112] Briffault 1990a, 27–33.   [113] Briffault 1990a.

tricts was unconstitutional because achieving parity remained discretionary with state officials. However, the court did not grant immediate relief; rather, it gave the state an additional three years to amend the statute.[114]

There have been other courts that have invalidated education financing. Some have held that as long as some increased financing is made available to the poorer districts, equalization will not be required. With others, it is uncertain what will emerge, except for a prolonged conflict over the elusive goal of equality. Throughout, local autonomy remains the predominant justification. "The basic structure of school finance—the state delegation of authority—is predicated on the desirability of local power."[115]

Exclusionary zoning is a similar situation. Again, New Jersey provides an instructive example. Over fifteen years ago that state's supreme court held, in the *Mount Laurel* case, that communities are constitutionally required to assume a fair obligation to provide housing for low- and moderate-income families. For eight years, local governments were able to resist the court's mandate and very little low- or moderate-income housing was built in the suburbs. Finally, the court decided it could no longer wait for local governments or the state to come up with regional plans and it issued tough orders to local governments.[116]

New cases were brought to enforce the new obligations, which produced an intense political controversy, including an attack by the governor on the court for intruding into local affairs. Finally, the state enacted the Fair Housing Act of 1985, which created the State Council on Affordable Housing. The administrative agency was to develop local housing plans that would respect "the established pattern of development in the community." Localities were not to be required to finance low- and moderate-income housing. Rather, the state would undertake that obligation, but only in low- and moderate-income neighborhoods, and not in the more affluent suburbs. Moreover, localities subject to the court's obligation would be permitted to transfer half of their "fair share" of their housing obligation through payments to other localities. The act further provided for a moratorium on litigation (principally brought by builders seeking to overturn restrictive zoning); instead, the cases were to be transferred to the new administrative agency.

The council went into business. It halved the court's projections of low- and moderate-income housing needs. It provided that more than half of these needs could be satisfied by units in central cities rather than through the construction of new units in the suburbs. In the meantime, partly as a result of eliminating the spur of litigation, localities have been

[114] *Abbott v. Burke*, 1994.   [115] Briffault 1990, 33–39.

[116] For example, localities had to remove excessive restrictions and provide appropriate incentives for the construction of low- and moderate-income housing (Briffault 1990, 53).

very slow in submitting plans and not much low- or moderate-income housing has been built.[117]

The New Jersey experience with low- and moderate-income housing is only unique in that an activist court took seriously the impact of exclusionary zoning on race and class. Other courts refuse to interfere, bowing to the stubborn intense resolve of local exclusionary interests to protect their tax base and preserve class and racial homogeneity.[118]

School financing and exclusionary zoning involve two of the most sharply contested issues in the United States—race and redistribution. In both of these examples, despite strong challenges on the basis of equality, state governments continue to defer to local autonomy.[119] These decisions are framed in terms of the traditional symbols of local autonomy. To resolve the conflicts, the myth of solutions is offered, for example, "fair housing," "school reform," and some aid is dispensed to poor districts, some low- and moderate-income housing is provided for. However, the status quo is maintained. Patterns of racial and class segregation continue. Most state school aid is not based on need; in fact, the richer, higher-spending districts may receive more aid than the poorer districts. Very few states, reports Briffault, have provided additional funds to implement state-imposed requirements to improve schools.[120] Deflect and re-delegate is the preferred tactic of the more powerful economic and political interests. State governments are very reluctant to use their powers in areas that are of fundamental concern to localities. What is notable, says Briffault, is the relative absence of conflict overall between state governments and localities, indicating the strength of local power. Instead, state governments are increasingly delegating, without significant interference, to local governments the authority to raise and spend revenue and to regulate.[121]

In the end, "local governments often get what they want."[122] Cities are not necessarily better off under these arrangements because their resources are poor compared to their needs; rather, the affluent suburbs are the big gainers—they have the most resources and the fewest needs.[123]

Special districts, or limited-purpose governments, are other systems set up to manage state and local conflict. These devices provide an infrastructure for the provision of services without disturbing local power arrangements.[124] They often span local boundaries, but they have no general public authority over citizens or territory within their jurisdictions. They do not disturb race or class homogeneity. They provide technical solutions to problems rather than engage in social or economic policymaking.

[117] Briffault 1990, 39–55.
[118] Briffault 1990, 49, 57.
[119] Briffault 1990, 60.
[120] Briffault 1990, 63.
[121] Briffault 1990, 354.
[122] Briffault 1990, 112.
[123] Briffault 1990, 355.
[124] Briffault 1990, 375.

They are usually financed through user fees and thus minimize distributive effects.[125] Local government contracting produces similar effects. It allows smaller localities to purchase services from larger units; the smaller suburbs can thus benefit from economies of scale without disturbing race or class interests.[126]

There have been some efforts in some states to assert more control over local authority, but the overall pattern remains the same. Nor, thinks Briffault, is this likely to change in the future. This is because the largest and most influential bloc of state legislators come from the suburbs and it is in their interest to retain local control to preserve race and class homogeneity rather than to help the communities with the greatest needs.[127] States have the power to override localities, but the ideology of localism and its rhetoric—*efficiency, participation, community,* and *local self-determination*—are used to mask powerful economic and social interests.[128]

Conclusion

Once again, the picture that emerges from both a theoretical and empirical analysis is one of great complexity and diversity. There are many levels of government and many interactions, both public and private. One cannot generalize across programs and issues. Large trends, of course, are unmistakable. There has been a relative decrease in federal spending for certain domestic programs and an expansion of social needs in the urban areas. But, despite common sense or conventional wisdom, changes in federal spending levels do not necessarily translate into changes in federal authority and control. We have seen that quite often increases in federal spending increase state and local authority; and the complaints are made today that with the decrease in federal funding, there has been an increase in federal mandates—from "cooperative federalism" to "coercive federalism."[129]

A few generalizations, however, can be made. In many areas of domestic concern, there always has been and there continues to be substantial decentralization. Local levels of government exercise considerable control; this is especially true where field level decisions are inherently discretionary, such as in the case of services. Moreover, these local units, as organizations, strive to maximize their survival in fields or environments composed of other relevant public and private actors. Organizations try to obtain support and resources from allies and hold off rivals. Thus,

[125] Briffault 1990, 376.   [126] Briffault 1990, 378.
[127] Briffault 1990, 450.   [128] Briffault 1990, 452.
[129] Kincaid 1990.

there is always an array of public and private relationships that influences the construction and implementation of programs.

Finally, there is a great deal of rhetoric and symbolism that serves a variety of political purposes. Starting at the very top and extending through every level of government, political leaders use federalism and decentralization as methods of managing conflict. They seek to satisfy demands through the use of symbols, including the enactment of laws, and then delegate the problems to lower units where the struggles continue. From the upper-level standpoint, the hope is that the problem will stay delegated. However, groups and interests will try to use these same symbols to force change, and problems may not stay delegated. It is in this context that we will consider regulation, deregulation, and privatization—as parts of the dynamic political processes of symbolism, implementation, and delegation.

Chapter 4

PRIVATIZATION

As NOTED IN chapter 1, privatization means different things and takes different forms. If viewed as the sharing or delegating of authority to nongovernmental agents, then privatization, both formally and informally, is a common practice in both civil and criminal regulatory regimes. Many social and regulatory programs start with public subsidization of private organizations.[1] At the other end of the spectrum, privatization means the public sale of assets—government withdrawing, or "load shedding." Although a favorite of the conservatives, this form of privatization has never really amounted to much in the United States.[2]

Privatization here will refer primarily to contracting, a system in which government continues to provide the funding for services but contracts the implementation or delivery to the private sector, either nonprofit or for-profit firms. This is the dominant form of privatization, by far.[3] At the conclusion of this chapter, we will take a short look at vouchers. The remaining large area of privatization, in which various nongovernmental agents share in the exercise of authority, will be the topic of chapter 6. These include worker safety committees, tenant management organizations, and nursing home resident councils; it also encompasses industry self-regulation, and cooperative-style regulation.

The principal justification for contracting is efficiency: the theory is that the same or similar services or goods can be provided by the private sector at less cost than government can furnish them. Contracting can also be looked at in terms of effectiveness, equity, accountability, and legitimacy, as well as other criteria.[4] Privatization is a form of decentralization, and thus also a method of managing conflict.

The ideological justifications for privatization emphasize client autonomy. Large bureaucracies, it is claimed, are unresponsive to clients, consumers, and workers. The private sector, in contrast, has to compete for consumers. Efficiency depends upon satisfied clients. Therefore, privatization, by breaking the public monopoly and increasing private sector competition, enhances consumer autonomy.

Similarly, the theoretical justifications of the voluntary sector are based on satisfying client needs. Under the *public goods theory*, nonprofits serve as a private producer of public goods to satisfy the residual demand

[1] Feeley 1991.   [2] Donahue 1989.   [3] Kramer 1994.
[4] Gormley 1991a.

that the public does not meet. The argument under the *contract failure theory* is that because there is an asymmetry of information, the consumer is not able to assess the service and therefore will be more likely to trust the nonprofit because of the nondistributional constraint.[5] Thus, under either theory, contracting with nonprofits makes provision of services more effective. Other justifications of privatization, such as accountability, emphasize the consumer.

Nonetheless, I shall argue that both theoretically and empirically, consumers and clients will be better served under privatization only under rare circumstances. They may not be worse off than under public provision, but the claims of enhanced consumer autonomy or empowerment under privatization are simply not plausible. Under privatization, client empowerment is subordinate to the overriding demands of managing political and organizational conflict. Sometimes privatization will be responsive to empowerment concerns—for example, agencies will listen to clients when they are seeking new business—but for the most part, client interests will not be paramount.

In this chapter, I will first discuss the idea of privatization, why it has become so popular as a policy initiative, and present a more precise definition. These points will be brief, as the story has been well told elsewhere. The bulk of the chapter will deal with government contracting, since this is the most important form of privatization in the United States. I will discuss the theory of contracting, the concerns raised about contracting, and the experience thus far. I then draw conclusions as to the impact of privatization on clients.

THE IDEA OF PRIVATIZATION

Traditional laissez-faire libertarians have always challenged the welfare state, but without success. Today, political leaders, academics, public and private commissions, and research institutes are all recommending increased participation of the private sector in areas traditionally within the domain of government. What explains this ideological sea change? The privatization proponents have succeeded because they have been able to convince the public that reducing and changing the size of government will not compromise the benefits of the welfare state.[6] They have argued that government, as a public monopoly, is, in practice, inefficient, unresponsive, and, as such, anticonsumer; that there is a difference between government responsibility and government provision and that the latter could be accomplished more responsively and efficiently through private firms in a competitive environment.[7]

---

[5] Hansmann 1987.   [6] Donahue 1989.   [7] Henig 1989–90.

The privatization argument fell on fertile soil. By the 1960s and 1970s, confidence in government was shaken by the urban riots, Vietnam, the persistence of poverty, and the urban fiscal crisis. The reputation of the welfare state was tarnished by charges of corruption and inefficiency. At the same time, a formal theory and proposed mechanism for providing public services without renouncing government responsibility was put forth.

The privatization theorists argued that a great deal of contracting was already going on at the local level. In the 1970s, local governments, under increasing financial constraints, began using a variety of market strategies, including contracting. Studies of municipal contracting claimed to show that services could be delivered more efficiently in a competitive environment. At the national level, airlines, trucking, securities, and banking were deregulated.[8]

The blossoming of privatization occurred during the Reagan administration. There were aggressive proposals for the sale of government assets, contracting, subsidies, tax incentives, deregulation, vouchers, franchises, and divestiture. Privatization was a political strategy designed to reduce the welfare state by reshaping the interest group environment through competition.[9]

The Reagan administration started with the wrong target—the sale of public lands—which aroused the strong opposition of the environmentalists, and this controversy plagued further efforts to sell government assets. Privatization still runs into strong opposition when it is highly visible and arouses strong interests—for example, proposals to privatize schools.[10] In contrast, privatization has spread more easily when justified on the basis of pragmatic efficiency.[11]

THE THEORY OF CONTRACTING

Contracting focuses not necessarily on the size of government but rather on its performance.[12] "The question is not *whether* governments *provide* a given service, but rather *how* they *deliver* it."[13] Government contracting is sold on the idea that it is a management strategy. The most common practice is to publicly finance goods and services but to have them privately produced or delivered. In fact, nearly half of all government spending for goods and services is handled in this manner.[14] Another form of privatization involves the use of vouchers; eligible consumers are authorized to purchase specified goods or services in the private market from government-specified providers. Food stamps is an example of a voucher program. There have been several voucher programs associated with

[8] Henig 1989–90.   [9] Henig 1989–90.   [10] Henig 1989–90.
[11] Kramer 1994.   [12] This section relies extensively on Donahue 1989.
[13] Van Horn 1991, 262.   [14] Bendick 1989.

housing, and today, vouchers are part of the discussions about educational reform.

Trash collection, laundry service, building, highway and fleet maintenance, parking lots and garages, utilities, data processing—these and similar services have been contracted by local governments for a long time and the practice is now very extensive.[15] These services are referred to as "physical and commercial services" or "intermediate goods and services." The private providers are customarily for profit. The current battleground has been the expansion of contracting into "protective and human services" or the "production of final goods and services." These include health, education, and social and welfare services. The extension of privatization here is considered to be far more problematic.[16] In this area, the nonprofits predominate, although there has been an increase in the use of for-profit firms.

As stated, the justification for contracting is efficiency. Efficiency not only saves public money, but is based on consumer sovereignty. Competitive markets are driven by consumer choice. In order to survive, for-profit firms have to be *accountable* to their customers. Accountability is used to contrast competitive firms with large, bureaucratic, unresponsive government agencies.

Under what conditions, then, are providers of goods and services accountable? This is the question that John Donahue asks in analyzing the case for contracting. The fundamental issue is *"relationships among individuals."* Different tasks call for different kinds of relationships. The task is to structure efficient arrangements that enforce accountability on those who act on behalf of others. Accountability is especially important in matters of public authority because citizens are particularly vulnerable to officials who fail to take account of their interests. For Donahue, accountability is a question of institutional design—how well does organizational design deter opportunism and irresponsibility and promote "faithful stewardship"?[17]

Defining and achieving accountability is a complex matter. We favor individual choice but at the same time distributions must be efficient and fair. We deter free riders through compulsion but then lose information (i.e., real preferences). Elections are often only blunt signals of preferences since voters often can't register intensity on specific issues. Information has other problems: it is often too costly to collect. Some questions are unanswerable, and a large fraction of the citizenry are uninformed. Moreover, there is a systematic bias in the lack of information.[18]

Donahue analyzes accountability as a question of agency. The "agency

---

[15] In his recent book, John Donahue (1989) lists over a hundred different governmental functions now performed by private agencies.

[16] Gormley 1991a; Kramer 1994.   [17] Donahue 1989, 11.

[18] Donahue 1989, 25–37.

problem" is the difficulty of ensuring that the principal is faithfully served
and the agent is fairly compensated. The agent is commissioned to act on
the principal's behalf, but their interests do not always coincide. If the
principal does not have complete control over the agent, how does one
avoid exploitation by the agent? With the profit seeker, the customer is
the principal and the entrepreneur is the agent. The agent carries out the
commission for a price, and is motivated to do so efficiently in order to
make a profit. The obligation of the agent is to deliver the goods as promised. Whereas civil servants agree to accept instructions in exchange for a
wage, profit seekers agree to deliver a product in exchange for a price.
This is the *output-based* contract. Accountability is enforced by the customer, who can opt out of the contract. Thus, principals select agents
on the basis of price and quality, and agents who can perform well will
prosper.

Donahue says that in practice, output-based agency arrangements are
not that common. Instead, many agency relationships are based on inputs. There are two reasons for this. One, it is often difficult to measure
outputs, especially when more than one agent may be involved. And two,
it is often too risky to compensate on the basis of output when other contingencies are involved. A common example is health care. Who bears the
risk of outside contingencies? However, once the relationship between
the payment and the ultimate result is severed, then the principal becomes
vulnerable to agency manipulations (e.g., unnecessary health care). On
the other hand, with inputs, there are problems of measurement, risk, and
opportunism. Principals try to protect against this by using proxies for
outputs, but then, says Donahue, agents are motivated to deliver the
proxies instead of the outputs.

A variety of devices are used to ensure accountability and efficiency in
the face of measurement problems, risk, and opportunism. With employment contracts, the agent agrees to follow instructions. The agent-
employee has less need than an independent agent to demonstrate the
value of the output and thus less incentive to manipulate or ability to
exploit. The principal has more control over how the product is delivered.
On the other hand, once the employment contract is signed, the discipline
of competition may be lessened and the principal bears the risk and loses
the benefit of the agent's expertise.[19]

According to Donahue, it would be more advantageous to employ
agents when the task is uncertain, revisions more likely, when measuring
the value of the output is ambiguous, changing agents would be disruptive, and the principal is confident about the method or technology by

---

[19] Some of these defects can be remedied if output measures are built in, or, where the
expertise of the agent exceeds that of the principal (e.g., the agent is a professional), independent contractors are used (Donahue 1989).

which the task is to be performed. Contracting is preferable if the performance requirements can be specified with a high degree of precision in advance, if results are more important than means, if monitoring is difficult, and if agents can be replaced easily. These distinctions will be important in considering contracting for human services rather than for intermediate goods and services.

Donahue identifies three major problems in public sector accountability—efficiency; excessive compensation for agents; and distorted spending decisions. Inefficiency—a major problem with public bureaucracies—comes about through the loss of discipline, the lack of contractual ties between principal and agent, opportunistic or rent-seeking behavior by agents, and managers who become less able to resist drift, deter waste, and focus resources on the organizational mission. Because ownership interest—that is to say, the interest of the citizens—is minute in the public sector, there is less pressure to make government more efficient.

With private firms, competition and the profit motive force owners to resist the self-interest of agents. Donahue thinks that rents—unfair or inefficient, or both—are a real problem in the public sector. When public functions are transferred to private contractors, wages are usually lower, which may mean the elimination or reduction of rents.[20] In addition to rents or random inefficiency ("slack"), collective spending decisions can become distorted when self-seeking agents form alliances with producers or key constituencies, all at the expense of the dispersed citizenry.

Donahue uses garbage collection as an example to explain his theory of efficiency as accountability. There are three basic types of garbage collection arrangements: (1) public; (2) contracting—private firms submit bids to the city; and (3) competition—individual households contract with private companies. Evidence from a wide variety of sources indicates fairly conclusively that competition is the most efficient (cheapest) method of collection, followed by public agencies, followed by contracting. The conclusion that competition would be more efficient than either the public provision of services or contracting is not self-evident. There should be higher transaction costs (e.g., billing) with competition, as well as collusion and problems of "economies of contiguity" (pickups next to each other). On the other hand, private firms tend to use bigger trucks and smaller crews and have more flexible schedules and more complete packages of incentives and penalties. There are low entry barriers, economies of scale, flexibility in switching contractors, and ease of monitoring (the industry is the most visible of the public services).

Donahue concludes that the crucial determinate is the presence of *com-*

[20] This does not necessarily resolve other issues. Donahue (1989) asks, "Is it bad to transfer wealth—good pay, benefits, job security, working conditions—to individuals, as compared to corporations?"

petition rather than *organizational form*. According to a variety of studies, competition improves the performance of both public and private agencies. In fact, when the public agencies are forced to bid against private contractors, they begin to resemble each other in cost structure and organizational style. And without competition, both public and private agencies are plagued by inefficiency.

Reviewing the evidence on efficiency from a variety of sources—military support services; office cleaning firms; fire-fighting organizations; the transportation industry; water and power utilities—Donahue concludes that profit-seeking firms are potentially more efficient. Part of the efficiency comes at the expense of workers. But the determining factor is the presence of competition. Without a credible prospect of replacement, it is difficult to control private firms. Moreover, it is hard to maintain competition. Private firms with contracts may have inside information, expertise, and special relationships with government officials. And, the profit drive, without meaningful specifications or competition, may be the worst situation of all.[21]

Under what circumstances, then, should the public opt for private contracting rather than civil servants? Donahue says that when the task can be more precisely specified in advance and its performance evaluated after the fact, then it is more likely that contractors can be made to compete and can be replaced or disciplined. And when the government is more concerned with ends rather than means, then the conditions are better for real competition. Bidding only becomes meaningful if performance can be evaluated and contractual terms enforced; otherwise, the bid process will be inflated. As long as the government does not care about means, contractors can be more flexible and innovative.

Conversely, the more uncertain the task and the harder to measure the results, then, according to Donahue, the less likely it is that there will be open competition, and the less there is to gain from profit seekers. In addition, problems arise when the task is redefined, which is quite common with government. Civil servants can change. But with profit-seeking firms, contracts have to be renegotiated; there may not be any competition, and market discipline disappears. Finally, if means matter as much as ends, than the profit seeker's advantage in innovation lessens. With public agencies, while there is a loss of the market discipline and the benefits of innovation, there are the gains of control over methods and the ability to change mandates.

But in any event, according to Donahue, "the fundamental distinction is between competitive out-based relationships and noncompetitive input-based relationships rather than between profit seekers and civil servants per se."[22] There is an inherent tension between paying for activity

---

[21] Donahue 1989, 78.   [22] Donahue 1989, 82.

and paying for results. And, to the extent that civil servants adhere to output-based contracts, they will tend to resemble profit seekers. Conversely, to the extent that profit seekers contract to accept instructions, they will tend to resemble civil servants. In sum, the choice between profit seekers and civil servants depends on whether the product is definable, performance can be evaluated, competition is feasible, contractors can be replaced, and whether means are important.

The issues raised by Donahue give rise to a number of concerns about contracting. The benefits of contracting only accrue to the extent that there is competition and a credible threat of replacement. We will see that it is not so easy to locate and maintain competitive markets, and if there is a lack of effective competition, then a symbiotic relationship will develop between government agencies and favorite suppliers. This would be especially so if government officials are more interested in diffusing conflict than in efficient performance.[23]

In the case of human services, both availability and continuity of contractors will be problematic. Particularly as programs get under way, there will be considerable pressure to contract with those organizations that best meet the needs of the government agency, and this is not necessarily efficiency. In many instances, government will have to, in effect, create suppliers. In other instances, there will be an irresistible need to favor those suppliers who can best meet the demand for an acceptable level of continuous service, thus avoiding repeated bidding as well as the bureaucratic, red tape that accompanies the dispersal of public funds. This means, of course, favoring the large, entrepreneurial firm, whether for-profit or nonprofit. The effects on both for-profits and nonprofits, it is claimed, is that they will come to resemble government itself—large, bureaucratic, concerned with organizational maintenance, with process and paperwork, stability of funding, and not necessarily with service. Nonprofits will lose their differential advantages over both government and for profits. The result will be goal displacement, a focus on funding strategies that will be decoupled from service.[24]

Contracting may very well serve to *increase* rather than decrease the welfare state. One of the claimed benefits of contracting is the creation or empowerment of "mediating institutions," that is, voluntary organizations that will then press for increases in services.[25] But contracting can just as easily produce corporate-style for-profit enterprises, which is what happened with the Medicaid funding of nursing homes.[26] It is for these reasons, that "true" conservatives, those interested in reducing the size of government, have always been suspicious of contracting. The principal danger they see is the increase in government spending as the result of the

---

[23] Brodkin and Young 1989.   [24] Kramer 1994.
[25] Bendick 1989.   [26] Starr 1991.

creation of powerful private interests now dependent on public funds. The analogy would be the defense industry. Efficiency, Brodkin and Young remind us, is more than a technical calculation of costs and benefits; it involves the distribution of political power and material benefits.[27]

These are some of the concerns about contracting. What has been the experience?

THE EXPERIENCE OF CONTRACTING

Local Services Contracting

The sources of private sector cost advantages are claimed to be in management practices, technology, and labor costs. With workers, there is "more flexibility"—translated, this means less unionization, younger workers, lower wages, fewer benefits, less job security, less due process, stronger incentive systems, and more employee control over maintenance. Much of the saving from privatization comes at the expense of employees.[28] In addition, contractors can spread their costs among several cities, are more flexible, and have more incentives to innovate with capital equipment.

On balance, Donahue thinks that in theory a substantial portion of state and local services meet the privatization criteria—that is, outputs can be specified in advance, there is competition and the ability to monitor. Privatization provides superior productivity and the potential gains are quite large; but, the loss to labor is considerable. However, Donahue emphasizes, there has to be competition. Efficiency comes from competition, not from privatization per se. In practice, the record is mixed, both at the national level and locally.[29] In the case of contracting, privatization is generally more efficient with relatively straightforward services (garbage collection, data processing, streetlight maintenance) than with complex services.[30]

In New Jersey, both state and local government contracting was studied by Carl Van Horn.[31] As elsewhere, local and county contracting is an old, established practice. At the local level, contracted services included refuse collection, road construction and maintenance, solid waste disposal, towing, parking enforcement, water treatment, as well as specialized services, such as engineering, legal services, and planning. At the county level, there were also contracts for health and social services. State

---

[27] Brodkin and Young 1989.

[28] On the other hand, according to Donahue, city workers are usually better paid than a great many taxpayers (Donahue, 1989).

[29] Kramer 1994.   [30] Bendick 1989.   [31] Van Horn 1991.

contracting is relatively recent. Contracts have been entered into for the design and construction of roads, for cleaning up toxic waste sites, and for the delivery of health and child care to poor populations. Some state departments contract for routine services; others, for specialized skills not readily available in government, such as programmers, evaluators, public relations people, and test development specialists. There is great variation among state departments. Generally governments contract with for-profits for public works and public safety services, and with nonprofits for social and health services. However, in both situations, governments rely entirely on the private sector rather than split the responsibility between public and private.[32]

Van Horn found that in practice there is very little competition between the bidding firms. In effect, contracting results in the creation of private monopolies for the delivery of services. Most New Jersey officials were satisfied with the contracting process. However, while they gave "efficiency" as an important reason for contracting, it was not the principal reason. When pressed, officials could not give evidence of cost savings, and "if cost comparisons were ever made they were forgotten."[33] *In fact, most officials were worried about cost increases under the contracting system.* A substantial number were worried about quality, accountability, and reliability. Other important reasons for contracting were in-house limitations, quality, and convenience. "Effectiveness," that is, improved management or services, was not mentioned much as a reason for contracting.[34]

Once established, there was very little change in the mix of service delivery contracting. For governments to try to change course—for example, to regain refuse collection or road maintenance—would require not only a large increase in financial investments, but also a potential battle with the current suppliers.[35] In effect, governments became captives of the private providers without whom they cannot run their programs.[36] The experience of contracting—at least in New Jersey—was no secret. In those areas where government did not contract, officials resisted contracting on the grounds that they would lose in-house capacities and loss of control over prices.[37]

It is estimated that one half of New Jersey's $12 billion state budget is contracted out to private firms. Thus, it is no surprise that privatization is highly politicized and that contracting practices are strongly influenced by political contributions. The links between government officials, private contractors, and political contributions are cemented through the

---

[32] Van Horn 1991.   [33] Van Horn 1991, 271.   [34] Van Horn 1991.
[35] Kramer 1994.   [36] Bernstein 1991.   [37] Van Horn 1991.

bidding process. Many contracts are let through no-bid practices, but even the laws requiring bidding are full of loopholes, especially in contracts for services. Then, there is the revolving door—many public officials join the private firms doing business with the government as soon as they leave government service. Finally, serious accountability problems are raised by the lack of systematic evaluation procedures. For these reasons, says Van Horn, many state departments are reluctant to embark on new privatization initiatives. The New Jersey experience, he concludes, casts doubt on the claims of significant improvements in government performance, that services are now being performed more effectively and more efficiently. Rather, there are significant political, economic, and administrative constraints on changing persisting practices.[38]

Human Services

By the mid-1980s, the Massachusetts Department of Mental Health had over two thousand separate contracts with over five hundred vendors.[39] Contracting was supposed to (1) give the state more flexibility by avoiding bureaucratic rigidity; (2) lower costs, primarily by avoiding civil service and union requirements; and (3) provide greater responsiveness to local needs by decentralization. Most of these hopes were apparently not realized. Monitoring, oversight, and accountability concerns led to a detailed, lengthy, and complex contract review process and to the use of line-item budgets, which not only add to administrative costs, but also inhibit innovation and flexibility (it is difficult for vendors to shift funds). Wage costs have been reduced significantly, but turnover has increased, compromising quality of care.[40] However, contractors have asked for increased wage rates, employees are unionizing, and a state ethics commission has classified the employees as "state employees." Thus, wage costs are expected to increase.[41] The private provider industry has boomed, creating a major special-interest group.[42] On the other hand, contracting has promoted both an expansion and a decentralization of services. There is considerable geographic variation, with mixed results.[43]

Significantly, the system has evolved from one that was "explicitly designed to promote competition among private contractors to one that substantially inhibits competition."[44] Even though between one-third and one-half of all contracts should be subject to competitive bidding

---

[38] Van Horn 1991.   [39] Schlesinger, Dorwart and Pulice 1986; Pack 1991.

[40] Continuity of care is considered to be particularly important in mental health services. Low salaries have contributed to high turnover rates. For some services, such as residential care, turnover has approached 80 percent annually (Schlesinger et al. 1986, 250).

[41] Pack 1991.   [42] Schlesinger, Dorwart, and Pulice 1986.

[43] Schlesinger, Dorwart, and Pulice 1986.

[44] Pack 1991, 302.

each year, in fact, only 20 percent are competitively bid. Moreover, within the bidding process, the extent of competition is quite limited—averaging less than two responses per solicitation. "Several evolutionary factors have limited and will limit further competition. The 'goal of maintaining continuity of care,' economies of scale, and the difficulties associated with evaluating providers without a 'track record' have led to an increasing concentration of contracts with large organizations."[45]

Similar conclusions were reached in another study of contracting with nonprofit agencies in Massachusetts. In 1986, the Massachusetts Department of Social Services had 1,700 contracts with nonprofits, constituting 70 percent of its budget. Steven Rathgeb Smith found that government departments became increasingly dependent on the private agencies to deliver basic services and that newly established nonprofits had no existence apart from government programs. The government's dependence on these nonprofits meant that the government had to continually prop up inefficient and mismanaged organizations in order to maintain continuity and long-term relationships. In addition, in view of the sensitivity of the services—child care, care of the elderly and the infirm—as well as the large sums of money being spent, there had to be extensive government regulation, again reducing flexibility and increasing administrative costs.[46] Janet Pack says that in time, "the performance of the private nonprofit organizations may be expected to differ little from that of the public agencies."[47]

In sum, in order for contracting to achieve its goals, the government contracting agency has to be able to evaluate performance in a relatively short period of time, be willing and able to shift contracts to other vendors, and to base its decision on efficiency and effectiveness performance.[48] Apparently, not much of this happened in Massachusetts with human services contracting. Similar findings have been reported in other states.[49]

In general, studies of the effects of contracting on clients are sketchy and ambiguous. Shalom Malka described Pennsylvania's subsidized daycare program as a "centralized closed contract system."[50] In most of the state, a monopoly was established with a small group of large providers, depriving parents of choice. Contracts were almost always renewed, and turned out to be more expensive than either private day care or a mix of public and private. Despite the higher costs, there are no detectable differences in quality. The study concluded that the Pennsylvania state system,

[45] Schlesinger, Dorwart, and Pulice 1986, 252; Pack 1991, 302.
[46] Smith 1987.
[47] Pack 1991, 302–03.
[48] Schlesinger, Dorwart, and Pulice 1986, 248.
[49] Schlesinger, Dorwart, and Pulice 1986, 255; Donahue 1989.
[50] Malka 1990.

by sole source contracting, actually restricted the availability of day care by excluding potential vendors from the subsidized program and, at the same time, affected quality of care by undercutting consumer feedback. Since the study, the state has abandoned the close contract system in favor of a locally managed parent-choice-driven system.[51]

Donna Hardina, in a survey of social welfare agencies in Chicago, found that external funding led agencies to be much more bureaucratic and less client-oriented in terms of access.[52] It is commonly asserted that contracting adversely affects the poor.[53] Kamerman and Kahn analyzed the effects of Reagan policies on child care.[54] Instead of directly providing child care or financing providers, the Reagan administration chose to increase demand primarily through the Dependent Care Tax Credit. However, because the subsidy came through tax credits, it primarily increased the relative demand of those in higher income brackets, those for whom the tax credit was worth more. There seemed to be an increase in the supply of day care for the better-off and a reduction in options for low-income families. There also was some evidence of a lowering of quality for low-income families. For example, given a choice, for-profit chains would not locate in states with high minimum standards.[55]

Schlesinger and Dorwart found that ownership did make a difference in mental health services. Specifically, private agencies—both for-profit and nonprofit—were "less likely to admit patients who cannot fully pay for care than are government-owned institutions."[56] On the other hand, contrary to earlier predictions, in a recent study of home health organizations, Clarke and Estes found that there was no significant difference between for-profits and nonprofits in terms of client income.[57]

CONCLUSIONS FROM EXPERIENCE

Contracting has exploded, but research and evaluation studies are still quite scarce.[58] While some generalizations can be made, conclusions must remain tentative.

The Contracting Process

The contracting process involves five stages: (1) requesting bids; (2) comparing and selecting firms; (3) drafting, negotiating, and processing the contracts; (4) monitoring and evaluating performance; and (5) renewing or terminating the contract. In practice, the contracting process is depen-

---

[51] Malka 1990.   [52] Hardina 1990.   [53] Bernstein 1991.
[54] Kamerman and Kahn 1989a.   [55] Kamerman and Kahn 1989b.
[56] Schlesinger and Dorwart 1984, 959.
[57] Bergthold, Estes, and Villanueva 1990; Clarke and Estes 1992.
[58] Kramer 1994.

dent on the organizational environment of the government agency. As discussed in chapter 2, bureaucrats are subject to many pressures and have various interests and goals, including dependence on the supply of potential providers, the history of government-provider relations in that particular community, political relationships, and the avoidance of adverse publicity or political controversy.[59] Any or all of these may be more important to the bureaucrat than efficiency.

The social service market, like other markets, is influenced by a variety of factors, in addition to supply and demand. The request for proposals (RFP) typically prescribes the type and quantity of service needed, the populations to be served, costs, procedures, and often personnel standards, facilities, affirmative action, citizen participation requirements, and so forth. In practice, the RFP processes are burdensome and inefficient, especially for the smaller agencies.[60] The basic assumption that there are multiple, qualified agencies available is faulty; more often than not, there are few appropriate sellers. When confronted with a scarcity of sellers, government agencies will try to establish some—that is, they will help groups organize facilities and programs through loans, technical assistance, and consultation, even though this activity is a departure from competitive bidding. At the other extreme, government agencies will define services so narrowly as to steer the contract to an agency already providing the service; this practice is justified in terms of continuity. This tactic furthers the government's organizational interests and is responsive to political pressures. The government, like any major purchaser, seeks to stabilize its environment and one of the ways to do so is to maintain the support of needed suppliers. In any event, the RFP process imposes high, indirect costs on agencies; this favors the larger, established agencies.[61]

Despite the fact that many public agencies use complex rating systems purporting to be based on explicit criteria, the decision-making process is still fundamentally political. Final judgments almost always involve matters of judgment and considerations of power. There are numerous opportunities for political and personal influence, and there is a tendency to select the larger, more bureaucratic organizations, especially if past performance was relevant.[62]

The Bargaining Process

Government contracting requirements are highly technical and although some elements are nonnegotiable, drafting usually involves a lot of bargaining. Voluntary agencies try to resist requirements that reduce their flexibility—for example, those involving accounting procedures, staff cre-

[59] Kramer and Grossman 1987.   [60] Bernstein 1991.
[61] Kramer and Grossman 1987; Smith and Lipsky 1992.
[62] Kramer and Grossman 1987.

dentials, restrictions on client selection, or specified treatment goals. The outcome of these negotiations depends on the importance of the issue and the relative power of the parties. Generally, the larger, well-established agencies are usually able to obtain more flexible contracts. After agreement is reached, there may be months of processing before the required number of approvals are obtained, and then additional months before the first payments are made. All of this can create serious cash shortages for agencies. The negotiation and processing of contracts represent important nonreimbursable indirect costs, which, again, hurt the smaller, newer agencies.[63]

The Monitoring Process

Most government agencies have systematic monitoring procedures—for example, the filing of monthly or quarterly reports, which have to include client profiles, access, referrals, staff assessments, summaries of training and technical assistance, and so forth. Guidelines can be quite specific. Monitors customarily pay more attention to fiscal matters rather than to service-related items. When services are monitored, the emphasis is usually on inputs rather than results. In fact, effectiveness evaluation is rare. There are costs in monitoring as well as in staff resentment. And in the final analysis, the government agency is dependent on the provider for the delivery of the service or is subject to the political influence of the contracting agency.[64] Susan Bernstein, in her study of agencies in New York City, lists the multiple ways in which managers are able to manipulate the contract requirements, sometimes with the tacit cooperation of the monitors. "The conflict between contractual requirements and reality is frequently so blatant that collaboration appears to be necessary if the service is to be provided."[65] In short, in an environment of mutual dependency, close monitoring doesn't pay.[66]

Renewal, Termination

Not surprisingly, unless funds are no longer available, contracts are rarely terminated.

In the final analysis, because of reciprocal dependency, the government is seriously limited in its efforts to secure greater accountability.[67] Con-

---

[63] Kramer and Grossman 1987; Smith and Lipsky 1992.

[64] Kramer and Grossman 1987.   [65] Bernstein 1991, 125–43.

[66] Kramer and Grossman 1987.

[67] Kramer and Grossman 1987; Salamon 1987. Smith and Lipsky (1992) acknowledge the reciprocal dependency, but argue that it is unbalanced, with the government holding the upper hand. Bernstein (1991) gives a much more ambiguous assessment as to who is the more powerful. A not untypical quote from an agency manager: " 'My sense is that most

tracting is rarely competitive; in fact, the competition requirement seems to be satisfied as long as markets are potentially "contestable."[68] Bureaucrats, in order to manage their own environment, become dependent on large suppliers, that is, the established agencies. The established agencies, both for-profit and nonprofit, are increasingly the service providers. As critics have feared, contracting seems to have resulted in an increase in government spending.

THE IMPACT ON THE NONPROFIT SECTOR

While there is no doubt about the tremendous growth of the nonprofit sector as a result of contracting, there is considerable dispute as to what these changes mean in terms of the structure of nonprofits, their role, and their relationship to their clients.[69] Some argue that for a variety of reasons—principally government dependence on nonprofits and its lack of monitoring ability—that nonprofits have taken the money but have essentially retained their autonomy.[70] Smith and Lipsky argue that while there is mutual dependence, it is unequal, with government holding the upper hand, and that the mission of the nonprofits is in jeopardy.[71] There is concern that in response to changes in the funding sources, the big nonprofits have also changed; they have become more bureaucratic, more professionalized, and that fund raising, the principal activity, has been decoupled from services. Clients only become important when organizations need to recruit.

Changes in Size

The most significant growth in the nonprofit sector occurred between 1972 and 1982. Employment increased 43 percent; the payroll more than tripled. Social services grew the most, with its labor force doubling during this period. All the social services experienced significant increases: individual family services, job training and related services, child day care, residential care, as well as others. Within the social services, the nonprofit organizations accounted for 82 percent of employment. The for-profits had a significant amount of employment in only two areas—residential care and day care. A unique feature of the philanthropic sector was the volunteer labor force. In 1980, about 80 million volunteers did at least some work, while there were only 6.7 million paid staff members. Never-

---

government contracts don't really care how you do it as long as you can justify it to them because then they can justify it to somebody'" (149).

[68] Starr 1991.   [69] Kramer 1994.

[70] Kramer 1994.

[71] Smith and Lipsky 1992.

theless, despite the large number of volunteers, their total labor time was less than the paid nonprofit labor force.[72]

Most voluntary agencies are considered small in terms of budgets, staff, and clients. In a 1982 survey, three quarters had annual budgets of under $500,000; 40 percent had less than $100,000. Three-quarters of all expenditures were made by 15 percent of the large agencies—those with budgets of $1 million or more. These larger agencies were also older and more established, and relied heavily on the increased availability of federal funds.[73]

At the smaller end of the scale are the neighborhood-based organizations. The traditional examples are in ethnic communities, and are the focus of local social life and the source of a variety of mutual-aid and community-betterment services. Often these are church-connected, especially in Catholic and black communities, but organizations are also affiliated with unions, civic associations, and political wards. While neighborhood-based organizations were created to address particular social problems, especially those related to poverty, several of these organizations eventually developed into large-scale social service agencies with broad service responsibilities and a large clientele. Today, there are a wide variety of organizations claiming to serve local needs and aid community participation, even though many may be large and bureaucratic.[74]

The historical pattern in the United States is that when a need arises, the initial response of government is to contract with a nonprofit to implement a response.[75] Thus, from the earliest days of social welfare programs, government has contracted with voluntary agencies for the care of indigents, the deaf, handicapped children, and orphans.[76] The earliest correctional programs were contracted out.[77] Eventually, state institutions took over, but various forms of subsidization of voluntary agencies continued to grow. The reasons for the preference for the voluntary sector, according to Ralph Kramer, were: the idea that individualistic, moralistic, and religious caring were unsuited for government, the distrust of government in view of the spoils system and the generally low level of administration, the assumed superiority of voluntary agencies, and political pressure.[78]

As stated, beginning in the 1960s, government financing of voluntary agencies increased dramatically and it is now the dominant source of funding for the voluntary sector. As a result, the voluntary sector was transformed. It became competitive and new agencies developed—crisis centers, free clinics, hot lines, community mental health centers, mutual aid organizations, consumer-oriented associations, and peer self-help

[72] Rudney 1987.   [73] Kramer 1987.   [74] Milofsky 1987.
[75] Smith and Lipsky 1992.   [76] Kramer 1987.   [77] Feeley 1991.
[78] Kramer 1987.

groups. During the civil rights campaigns and the War on Poverty, alternative organizations were added. The pace continued in the 1970s. By this time, the trend was aided by the loss of confidence in public agencies, the preference for voluntary agencies, and the political pressure of an expanding social-service interest network.[79] At the same time, despite an increase in actual charity dollars raised, there was a relative decline due to inflation and increased costs, and the proportion of charity dollars devoted to social services dropped from 15 percent to 6 percent. With the exception of churches, the government is a more important source of revenue to nonprofit service providers than all private giving combined, exceeding private giving by a factor of 2 to 1.[80]

At the present time, the federal government provides about 35 percent of the total expenditures of nonprofit organizations (excluding religious). There is variation; 55 percent of social service and over 40 percent of community development expenditures come from the federal government. Government provides more than half the funding for mental health; housing/community development; legal services/advocacy; social services; employment/income assistance; institutional/residential services; and multiservice organizations. The second largest source of income for the voluntary sector—28 percent of total—comes from service fees and charges. Fees and service charges dominate in health providers (exclusive of hospitals) and education and research institutions. Private giving from all sources—individual, corporate, and foundation—provides 20 percent. Private giving predominates in arts, culture, and recreation.[81]

The rapid expansion of federal funding from the 1960s to 1980 comprises one side of the story; the effects of the Reagan administration another. By cutting spending and reallocating responsibilities to the states, many nonprofits became more dependent on the fiscal health of the states. During the recent economic hard times, nonprofits were increasingly squeezed, leading to further consolidations, and increased efforts to stabilize funding sources.[82]

As more public funds became available, for-profits have entered into social services delivery. In some fields, for-profits are now the predomi-

---

[79] Kramer and Grossman 1987; Kramer 1987.   [80] Salamon 1987.

[81] Salamon 1987, 103. Federal funding of nonprofits takes a variety of forms: direct grants or contracts; grants to states and local governments, which can then decide whether to deliver the services themselves or contract with nonprofits or other public or private providers; and payments to individuals or to financial agents on their behalf (e.g., Medicare; college students). Generally, the federal influence is greatest when there is a direct relationship—the grant or the contract—and weakest where assistance goes to the private citizen who is then free to purchase from the market. But the direct route is used the least—only 20 percent of federal social service dollars, as compared to 53 percent that goes to individuals, and 27 percent that goes to state and local governments (Salamon 1987, 105).

[82] Smith and Lipsky 1992.

nate contractors and are becoming increasingly important in community-based alternative care.[83] By 1984, for-profits were firmly established in several areas, including: homemaker/chore; employment/training; special transportation; and meals-on-wheels. They are dominant in nursing home care, day care, residential child welfare (residential, institutional care, group home) and substance abuse.[84] In effect, what we now see is an increasingly mixed social service delivery system—public, voluntary, and for-profit.

Methods of Fund Raising

The goals of nonprofits are to stabilize their funding sources but maintain their autonomy. Nonprofits sell social services to the government for an agreed-upon price. If the price does not provide for full reimbursement, the nonprofits must make up the difference. If the price represents the full cost, then competing for-profits will enter the market. This has happened with day care, home health care, vocational rehabilitation, counseling, and residential care. Generally, the price is set below the full cost and the nonprofits must seek additional funds.[85]

In one sense, government grants are a source of stability. Most grants are, in fact, renewed. Yet, it is argued that the granting process causes great instability and seems to have produced dramatic changes in the internal organizations of the nonprofits. Delays in the contracting process cause cash-flow problems for agencies and result in start-up costs, and unplanned expenses in securing and implementing new or renewed contracts. Then, the twelve-month cycle of most grants and contracts ("annualization") requires extensive resources to prepare for next year's proposals. These efforts result in the diversion of energy and resources, considerable stress, and the displacement of goals. The process is particularly burdensome for the small agency, those that specialize in community-based services, rely on local initiative, and have single programs, and favors the larger, bureaucratized agencies with specialized staff. Larger agencies with "track records" tend to be favored. The small agencies that are successful grow large and become bureaucratized. Agencies become "miniconglomerates" whose scope and content tend to reflect changing government priorities. Each program within the umbrella agency becomes responsible for its own funding, constituency, mission, and accountability requirements; the staff become identified with a particular program rather than the agency. The agency becomes loosely coupled. Accounting becomes an ongoing problem.[86]

[83] Kramer 1987.   [84] Gilbert n.d.   [85] Kramer 1987.
[86] Kramer and Grossman 1987.

Problems of underfunding are serious and recurrent—reimbursement rate cuts; cuts in grants because of budget restrictions, cutbacks, and cancellations; preparation errors; unforeseen but nonreimbursable contingencies; and cash-flow delays. One study found that a 15 to 20 percent average loss to nonprofits on most government contracts and grants.[87] Agencies try to press for longer contract terms, for higher and more stable reimbursement rates, for reimbursement of indirect costs, and for additional funds for more costly clients. They seek supplemental funds from donors and fees from clients who can pay, and set up various types of enterprise (e.g., thrift shops, direct sales). Noncash, in-kind contributions (e.g., volunteers, space in public buildings) also help. Some agencies engage in collaborative ventures—for example, sharing a fiscal service division—that occasionally lead to formal mergers. Agencies will "cream" to demonstrate positive outcomes. Agencies depend heavily on the political and entrepreneurial skills of their executives. In addition, boards change to include the corporate world; savings are made in staffing through the use of unpaid or low-paid personnel There are costs to these personnel policies—high turnover and training, coordination, and morale difficulties.[88]

On the other hand, Bernstein quotes many agency managers who are adept at working out arrangements with government contractors, know how to distinguish between formal compliance and informal practice, and maintain considerable leverage for their agency.[89] She points out that the growth and development of nonprofits demonstrate that the risks of fund raising are not that great. However, while many organizations survive, they pay the price in the amount of resources that are devoted to fund raising. Over the last fifty years, fund raising has become highly standardized, bureaucratic, and professionalized. The requirements of fund raising now are so pervasive that most volunteers engage in this activity rather than in service. Fund raising takes on a life of its own, in that agencies become invested in programs that generate income.[90]

Kirsten Gronbjerg looked at the funding strategies of six human service organizations, all medium-sized.[91] Her basic finding is that funding strategies become institutionalized over time. Successful organizations showed great continuity in relying on particular funding streams. They developed particular skills, contacts, and vested interests. Fees and other sources of earned income are valuable, but are also uncertain in that the nonprofit usually cannot control either the supply or competition. In order to secure this source of income, the nonprofit has to develop long-term client relationships, repeat clients, fiscally sound clients, and clients

[87] Kramer and Grossman 1987.
[88] Kramer and Grossman 1987.
[89] Bernstein 1991, 86–95, 112–14.
[90] Kramer 1987.
[91] Gronbjerg 1992.

that are organizations rather than individuals. With donors, nonprofits have to also engage in marketing activities, usually by board members. Only institutionalized relationships (e.g., with United Way or various religious federations) provide a reliable, stable source of income. Gronbjerg thinks that nonprofits have even less control over donors than over clients, and thus, donations drive the organization even less than fees or government grants and contracts. Gronbjerg argues that the ongoing nature of public funding (at least in the human services area) makes these relationships predictable, and the organizations institutionalize particular management practices. Despite the difficulties in dealing with government, Gronbjerg says that nonprofits view government grants and contracts favorably because they provide stable, predictable sources of funds. It is the combination of the attractiveness and the requisite complexity of securing and managing the contracts that now dominates nonprofit activities.

The basic finding is that securing and managing public funding becomes the driving force in these organizations, absorbing and dominating management activities. Success in obtaining public funds confers legitimacy on management. Intense and prolonged relations give agencies the opportunities to learn how to negotiate the system and circumvent or adjust to funder demands. Those agencies that can make these adjustments are the most successful. The costs, however, are the decoupling of funding management from the actual delivery of services. In addition, because few funders (public or private) are able or inclined to evaluate agency performance, patterns of accommodation and informal understandings develop between funders and providers.[92]

As a result of these trends, fund raising has become highly standardized, bureaucratic and professionalized.[93] Organizations in specific fields tend to become similar over time, without necessarily becoming more efficient. Sometimes, organizational conformity is caused by substantive requirements. For example, Medicaid has become an increasingly important source of funds, but to qualify, an organization must be certified as a health care clinic.[94] But even absent formal legal requirements, as the new institutionalist theory predicts, organizations develop "institutional mind sets" that consist of widely shared assumptions about what an organization should look like and how its work should be performed. Otherwise, an organization may lose legitimacy and risk sanctions by regulatory agencies and funding sources. Organizations tend to conform to fieldwide norms. A common example is acquiring certified professionals

---

[92] Gronjberg 1992. Many of Bernstein's (1991) managers would dispute this conclusion. They argue that they are able to maintain their agency mission, even when the funding is basically public (178–81).

[93] Smith and Lipsky 1992.   [94] Smith and Lipsky 1992.

and standardized accounting practices. As Powell and Friedkin point out, nonprofits may be particularly susceptible to institutional mimicry because their technologies are ambiguous and not susceptible to careful evaluation, their environments are both highly organized and uncertain, their relational networks are important, and there is a growing professionalization of the field. They have to show that they can provide the same services as their competitors.[95]

There are other forces, in addition to public funding, that tend toward bureaucratization. After all, similar changes have been noted in the absence of extensive contracting.[96] There are invariably trade-offs with outside sources of support. Powell and Friedkin think that the forces of change work quietly, and often it is too late for the organization to realize that its purposes have been neglected and even that its legitimacy may have been eroded. The example they give is one in which donors give money with no particular programmatic purpose in mind but prefer a centralized executive leadership, accountants, financial managers, and so forth. These changes, in turn, may lead to elite domination and the disenfranchisement of broad-based participants. Other forces produce organizational change. The goals of strong constituents are more likely to prevail over those of weak ones; middle-income services are more likely to replace those that are provided to the poor and the powerless; mainstream and more acceptable programs will tend to replace confrontational or controversial programs, especially when finances run short. To the extent that programs and activities are complex, experts will tend to dominate in groups with broad-based participation and pluralist governance. While these tendencies are not inevitable, they do point to the vulnerabilities of nonprofits.[97]

In addition to funds and staff, agencies need a steady, predictable, sufficient source of appropriate clients. Problems vary. Because governments are under different constraints, sometimes, as a condition of public funds, agencies have to accept larger numbers of clients, or clients with more difficult problems, or they have to provide a minimum basic service (which is all government will pay for) or a different service (e.g., a twenty-four-hour hot line). A not uncommon problem is forcing agencies to take clients with more serious problems (e.g., substance abuse) because government has no other alternative.[98] Other agencies face opposite problems; they may have difficulty in recruiting enough clients despite apparent need. There may be faulty information. Sometimes agencies are reluctant to refer to new programs or programs with short-term funding. Conversely, agencies may be swamped with clients and unless the agency can

---

[95] Powell and Friedkin 1987.   [96] Kramer 1994.
[97] Powell and Friedkin 1987; Kramer 1987.   [98] Smith and Lipsky 1992.

quickly develop ways to delay or deflect the flow, the grant may be exhausted prematurely. Dumping creates considerable tensions between government and private providers. But usually, developing a clientele takes time and energy and agencies have to engage in a variety of marketing strategies.[99]

Governance

Nonprofits are governed by boards and executive officers. Boards are part of both the organization and its environment. Members serve as resources; they connect the organization to the environment to ensure a flow of resources. They help the organization meet demands and seek to reduce constraints.[100] At the same time, one may question the democratic character of voluntary agencies in view of the composition of their boards and executives.[101] Members are drawn from a relatively narrow range of society—predominately white, male, Protestant, in their fifties and sixties, wealthy, in business or law. Consumers, women, and minorities are seen as not having access to needed economic, social, and political resources. Not surprisingly, women constitute less than 20 percent of the members.[102]

The structure of nonprofit boards calls into question the assumption that nonprofits are more able to innovate and experiment than the public and private sectors. The boards are embedded in the organization's environment, which is congruent with the status quo. While lower-status community members who serve (less frequently) on lower-status nonprofits may be more likely to try to redistribute resources, their lack of access to resources make such efforts problematic.[103]

In theory, boards are responsible for making final policy decisions including the selection, tenure, and supervision of the executive. In fact, the executive is usually the functional authority. Above all else, the executive (CEO) must be an entrepreneur. It is the executive's job to overcome constraints, bring in and distribute the resources, and provide for internal incentives for participation. The other key role is personnel management, since performance depends on the quality and motivation of the work force.[104]

[99] Kramer and Grossman 1987.   [100] Middleton 1987.

[101] Kramer 1994. Charles Perrow questions this objection. He argues that internal democracy is less important than the advocacy role in representing special or diverse interests and groups in the community; that is, the democratic contribution of voluntary agencies should be judged by their contribution of pluralism as expressed through their advocacy and service to their clients. Kramer is skeptical of this argument; he thinks that the costs of minority rule may cancel the contributions to pluralism, responsiveness, and flexibility (Kramer 1987).

[102] Middleton 1987.   [103] Middleton 1987.   [104] Young 1987, 167–69.

The executive must deal with the professionals, especially in organizations with complex technologies. The influence of the professionals derives from their external power base, their professional ideology, and their control of information and technical knowledge. Nonprofits seem to be particularly dependent on professionals, and agendas are shaped to attract professionals of high quality and prestige. On the other hand, professionals may prefer nonprofits because they tend to value professional values, autonomy, and opinion of peers, and to resist managerial systems of performance measurement. They prefer a collegial environment, which can lead to the practice of protecting each other from scrutiny by nonmembers. At the same time, professional standards can be inflexible and constrain responsiveness to changing circumstances. If they are powerful enough, professionals often maintain a monopoly on the delivery of particular services.[105] For these reasons, professionals can create problems for managers.[106]

A unique feature of nonprofits is their extensive use of volunteers. In the 1970s there was a resurgence of volunteerism not only in the number and range of the volunteers, but also in the diversity of organizations involved.[107] Nevertheless, the most frequent reported use of volunteers is in fund raising, rather than in direct services. Volunteers, too, can create problems with the executive and the paid staff. They can have their own agendas and political connections with the board. Volunteer trustees or board members may expect altruistic motivations from the paid staff.[108] The exploitation of volunteers is a major concern among feminists. The charge is made that most women volunteers in the social services function as substitutes for paid staff, thus contributing to the low status of women in society. Volunteers can also be viewed as threatening the social workers' tenuous hold on professionalism. Volunteers, in short, are not cost-free.[109]

Measuring Performance

Henry Hansmann claims that it is almost certain that in the absence of a subsidy or a substantial degree of market failure, nonprofits will produce a given product at a higher cost than a for-profit. Otherwise, he says, we would expect nonprofits to be operating successfully in a broader range of industries than is now the case. Nonprofits seem to have survivorship

---

[105] Kantor and Summers 1987.   [106] Kantor and Summers 1987.

[107] A widely publicized "guesstimate" is that one in four people over age thirteen does some form of volunteer work weekly, of which at least 10 percent is in social welfare. United States Department of Labor studies estimate growth in volunteers from 22 million to 37 million between 1965 and 1974, including 4.5 million sixty-five and over (Kramer 1994).

[108] Young 1987.   [109] Steinberg 1987.

properties superior to for-profits only where particular forms of market failure give them an efficiency advantage. Nonprofits, he says, are not found where contract failure is not a significant problem.

Furthermore, nonprofits tend to respond more slowly to increases in demand than do for-profits; for example, where demand is expanding rapidly (e.g., health, education) the ratio of nonprofits to for-profits is lower than when demand is stable or declining. One reason could be that nonprofits are constrained in the access to capital. There could also be differences in entreneurship. Because of the nondistribution constraint, nonprofit entrepreneurs are unable to capture the full return from innovation.[110]

Nevertheless, the nonprofit sector was the fastest growing sector in recent years. Obviously these constraints are not that significant.[111] Comparing three for-profits and three nonprofits, Dennis Young found no clear-cut differences in economic behavior. The for-profits faced financial risk, which did not necessarily fall on the entrepreneurs; and there was risk to professional standing and reputation to the nonprofit leadership. Other kinds of constraints—for example, access to capital, government regulations, employment, bureaucracy—operate differentially. Entrepreneurs in the different sectors have to work with different constituencies and sources of support and abide by different rules.[112]

Evaluating performance is difficult. In contrast to other organizations, the "raw materials" are people; goals are ambiguous and problematic; the technology is indeterminate; the staff usually controls the most relevant information; and valid measures of effectiveness are usually lacking.[113] But ambiguity in the evaluative criteria is probably not the prime constraint on the ability to evaluate performance. The accountability process is more political than technical. Organizations have a lot at stake in performance measurement. Competing interests, both inside and outside of the organization, have differing views on what the organization should produce and seek to use the organization for their purposes. Performance standards favor some groups over others.[114]

Organization performance measures serve a number of different functions. There are institutional functions—evidence that the organization is meeting standards necessary for legitimacy, which, in turn, leads important donors to reaffirm their support. These performance measures are addressed to boards, volunteers, and other constituencies. Performance measures may serve managerial functions, such as providing information about progress, or problems, or about how resources are being allocated. Then, performance measures serve technical functions, that is, they pro-

[110] Hansmann 1987.   [111] Young 1987.   [112] Young 1987.
[113] Hasenfeld 1992a; Kramer 1987.   [114] Kantor and Summers 1987.

vide information on the efficiency and quality of the services. The constituency here is the customer. Often, there are contradictions or gaps between the various measures and the constituencies. Nonprofits (as other organizations) live with the contradictions because they are loosely coupled between the sources of legitimacy and the standards of management and between those providing resources and those receiving them, that is, between donors and clients. In between are the managers and professionals who have their own agendas. The result is that the focus of the nonprofit is likely to shift from outcomes to inputs. Rather than focusing on results, evaluation is more likely to concentrate on the development and expenditure of resources. Planning becomes more concerned with fund raising than with service. Because objectives are vague and planning concentrates on development, managers gain considerable freedom of action in their activities, which can lead to even more goal displacement, internal politics, and favoring key donors over clients.[115]

Is there a difference, then, between nonprofits and for-profits in terms of performance? The evidence is mixed. Marc Bendick argues that for socially complex programs, nonprofits have a distinctly better record than for-profits.[116] In health care, ownership does seem to make a difference. With nursing homes, controlling for the characteristics of patients, services, and other attributes of the facility, for-profits' costs average 5 to 15 percent lower than nonprofits. In contrast, cost averages are inconsistent with hospitals; here, professional standards and incentives may mitigate some of the incentives for cost reduction that otherwise might be associated with for-profits. With nursing homes, there seems to be a lower quality of care in for-profits; although evidence as to *average* quality of care is inconsistent and controversial, there does seem to be a disproportionate number of for-profits in those institutions offering the lowest quality of care. For-profits screen location, kinds of service offered, and individual patients more than nonprofits do.[117] On the other hand, in a recent study of home health agencies based on extensive surveys, Clarke and Estes found very little difference between nonprofits and for-profits. There were no systematic differences between types of services provided, waiting lists, proportions of low-income and minority clients served, staffing credentials, and sources of income (e.g., Medicare, insurance, co-payments). Nonprofits serve more clients per month than for-profits, but this is because nonprofits are more likely to be older and more established. Significantly, the authors state: "We . . . find no support for the charge that for-profits serve better-paying, less troublesome clients while nonprofits are beneficent providers."[118]

---

[115] Kantor and Summers 1987.
[116] Bendick 1989.
[117] Marmor, Schlesinger and Smithey 1987.
[118] Clarke and Estes 1992, 963.

An Extension of Government?

Contracting favors the large, established agencies over smaller, more innovative ones. Contracting has resulted in major internal changes within nonprofit organizations, among them entrepreneurial executive officers, a dominating focus of securing government funding, the imposition of accounting and other standardized financial procedures, professionalization and other credentialing services, public requirements on the recruitment of clients and the services that are provided. From the government side, this means, paradoxically, that contracting has not lessened the role of government. Instead, the role of government has been extended through its mutual dependence on the private sector.[119]

What are the consequences of these differences? Many argue that the nonprofit sector has been seriously compromised by the interpenetration of government and that it is rapidly losing its distinctive qualities; that the differences between nonprofits and government are diminishing; in many cases, the organizations are indistinguishable. The prior formulations of "pioneer," "gap-filling," and "partnership" are inadequate. Now, there are two coexisting organizational systems, occasionally collaborating and exchanging resources, infrequently competing or in conflict. Sometimes the nonprofit is the only or primary provider (e.g., hospices); or complements government with a service that is qualitatively different in kind (e.g., sheltered workshop); or supplements or extends the government system with a similar type of service; or is a substitute for government provisions (e.g., homemakers).[120]

Again, the evidence is mixed. Some of the most important claimed advantages of the voluntary sector center on what might be called its progressive character, that nonprofits play a vanguard or pioneering role; they are advocacy- and consumer-oriented. The theory is that nonprofits are inherently particularistic in that they specialize in particular problems, or groups, or methods of intervention. They can more easily be selective and exclusive than public agencies. Whereas a public agency has to have the *appearance* of equity and accountability, these norms do not apply to the voluntary agency.[121] Thus, there can be a positive value in being *particularistic*. It allows for the concern for specialized interests, or groups that do not have widespread support and are often overlooked by the public—for example, pregnant adolescents, battered women, immigrants, runaways, teenage prostitutes, and so forth. On the other hand, particularism can also result in undue specialization and parochialism.[122]

However, Ralph Kramer says that the most important innovations in

---

[119] Kramer 1994; Smith and Lipsky 1992.
[120] Kramer 1994; Smith and Lipsky 1992.
[121] Douglas 1987.   [122] Kramer 1994.

the social services in the recent decades—for example, in juvenile delin-
quency, community action, community care of the mentally ill, model cities, and so forth—were primarily the result of governmental activity.[123]
The older, established agencies rarely develop new methods or new programs. That they have changed in recent decades is due primarily to government funding.[124] Furthermore, much of what is called pioneering or
innovative is really the "discovery" of small groups of overlooked or underserved populations. "Almost without exception, the vanguard programs are small-scale, noncontroversial, and incremental—extensions or
improvements of conventional personal services to a clientele previously
underserved."[125] The "cult of innovation" is basically entrepreneurial,
the search for new funds. Few of the new programs developed by voluntary agencies are, in fact, adopted by government. Nevertheless, despite
the evidence, the myth persists. Exaggerated innovation becomes part of
the game of grantsmanship. While there has been some important innovative work with specialized groups (e.g., drug addicts, the frail elderly), for
the most part, present-day pioneering is more likely the development
of a small number of low-risk extensions or improvements of existing
programs, which are then continued with government funds. Finally, voluntary agencies retain their innovative characteristics for only a short
period of time; if they are successful, they become bureaucratic and
professionalized.[126]

It is also said that voluntary agencies mediate between the citizen and
the government and engage in social action on behalf of their clients.[127]
In addition, clients themselves organize self-help groups and associations. This function has increased with the diffusion of the ideology of
citizen participation and the rights of disadvantaged populations. Today,
many, if not most, voluntary organizations give a high priority to consumer involvement.[128]

A major issue is whether the reliance on government funds has compromised this advocacy role. Ralph Kramer argues that nonprofits, despite their rhetoric, have considerable discretion in the allocation of their
resources. They can select a mission. There seems to be no relation between advocacy and degrees of government support; in fact, the most active advocacy agencies are among those receiving the highest percentage
of government funds. Kramer thinks that the most important reason why
autonomy is not compromised is the low level of accountability demanded by government and that this level is low because government
lacks both the incentives and the capacity to do more. Agencies complain
about the extensive record keeping and burdensome reporting require-

[123] Kramer 1994.   [124] Smith and Lipsky 1992.   [125] Kramer 1987, 177.
[126] Kramer 1987.   [127] Kramer 1987.
[128] Hasenfeld and Gidron 1993; Kramer 1987.

ments; but these are not perceived as restricting agency freedom. Kramer argues that in several respects, United Way requirements are regarded as even more unacceptable. Even government requirements concerning eligibility, staffing, board representation, and so forth, are not regarded as serious threats to independence; they are either considered legitimate or a small price to pay or the result of insufficient monitoring. In general, agencies do what they want to do, but now have the funds.[129]

The degree of government constraint varies with the method or form of financing—differences between a loan or a grant or a subsidy and whether for construction, research, demonstration, or reimbursement for entitlements. While purchase-of-service requires a nonprofit to channel its services into what the government defines as reimbursable, generally there is room for negotiation. And because the nonprofit is usually in a monopoly position, it can assert its interests. An additional factor is the type of service that is purchased. If performance standards can be specified and monitored, then government can avoid specifying internal operations. But where outcomes are difficult to define and measure, then inputs have to be measured—for example, number of interviews, meals served, hospital days—rather than results.[130]

In any event, what evidence there is does not seem to show that agency independence has been compromised, that they have become dependent, have been co-opted, or have lost their advocacy zeal and autonomy.[131] In fact, Susan Ostrander reports that as a result of government cuts, the agencies that she studied assumed a more active advocacy role to improve benefits for the poor.[132] Nonprofits have been able to maintain their missions, and they express little concern about the assumed distortion caused by the rise in government funding.[133] But this may be because organizational goals have shifted toward the rewards of stabilized fund-raising via government contracts. If the analysis of Grongberj and others is correct, then it would be hardly likely that the entrepreneurs who are now running the successful nonprofits, and reaping the rewards of contracting, would be seriously complaining about the loss of their mission.

Advocacy is also believed to be constrained by bureaucratization, professionalization, a federated structure, or service delivery. Ralph Kramer finds no evidence on these dimensions either. He argues that the existence of an active advocacy role depends less on the organizational structure than on the environment, the fiscal resource systems, and leadership. In the agencies that he studied, the most active were also the largest, the most bureaucratized and professionalized, and the recipients of the largest amounts of public funds. Those that had the lowest amounts of service

[129] Kramer 1987.   [130] Kramer 1987.   [131] Bernstein 1991.
[132] Ostrander 1989.   [133] Salamon 1987.

activities, bureaucratization, and professionalism also engaged in the least amount of advocacy. The ideological commitments of the executive leadership were the most significant for the improver role.[134]

In Sosin's research on voluntary agencies giving material assistance, he found that a majority of agencies did not view advocacy as part of their mission. Perhaps this resulted from pressure from funding sources or from a definition of their mission and the need to maintain internal integrity. On the other hand, agencies that deal with the developmentally disabled and the handicapped were more likely to advocate.[135] Could the difference in advocacy be related to the political acceptability of the clientele—the difference between the disabled (deserving) and the morally questionable poor?

Relation to Clients

Human services are, or ought to be, about clients. Are they better or worse off under a regime of contracting? This issue has been raised extensively on the theoretical level. As noted, a principal justification for privatization is to enhance client autonomy—firms bid for client votes—in contrast to the unresponsive, bureaucratic, public monopoly. At the same time, critics of privatization raise concerns about the citizen (client) and the state. The argument is that dispensers of services—the new "street-level bureaucrat"—is under the control and direction of private masters, that the citizen no longer deals directly with her government, and that state responsibility is diffused. Privatization is an erosion of entitlement.[136]

We know from extensive empirical work that citizen-state relations in human service agencies are quite often characterized by anything but entitlement, fairness, equity, uniformity, or legality. Public agency goals are more often than not de-coupled from service. Clients are recruited, selected, and processed to fulfill agency goals rather than client needs.[137] But in any event, there is very little research on client-agency interactions comparing public and private or for-profit with nonprofit. Very little is known about what difference organizational form has in terms of either access or quality.[138] Bernstein reports that real problems of client confidentiality arise under government contracts. Government agencies view the clients as "theirs," since they are paying the bill; these agencies want client files in order to track them through various systems. The nonprofits, says Bernstein, are strongly resistant; they view the clients as theirs and entitled to confidentiality.[139]

[134] Kramer 1987.
[135] Sosin 1986.
[136] Smith and Lipsky 1992; Starr 1988.
[137] Hasenfeld 1992a; Lipsky 1980.
[138] Kramer 1994.
[139] Bernstein 1991, 182–86.

The Clarke-Estes study, comparing private home health agencies, noted only that there was no difference in the kind of services offered and the proportions of low-income and minority clients. While these are important findings, they do not address the question of the quality of service or agency-client relations. In the child-care area, Mary Touminen argues that quality does vary between for-profit and nonprofit. The National Child Care Staffing Study says that staff wages are the most important predictor of child-care quality and that wages and other working conditions are much worse for for-profits than for nonprofits. Annual turnover was 74 percent for for-profit chains as compared to 30 percent for non-profits.[140] Sosin, in his study of homelessness, claims that contracting results in less flexibility and responsiveness because the government and the providers become vested in the status quo.[141] Others make the same argument.[142]

On the basis of the research dealing with the organization of contracting, one would doubt that clients would have much importance. Nonprofits are focused on maintaining the public funding stream. Clients would only be important when new ones are needed.[143] But the experience with various forms of neighborhood organizations suggest that even they can become as institutionalized, rigid, inaccessible, unresponsive, and undemocratic as professionalized bureaucracies.[144]

VOUCHERS

Vouchers represent a different approach to privatization. Here, specified consumers are authorized to purchase designated goods and services from eligible vendors. The leading example is Food Stamps; in addition, there are programs in housing and education.[145] De-regulation is the theory behind vouchers ("choice" in education); the idea being that, the efficiency and quality objectives of external regulation will now be achieved through the discipline of market incentives. However, it is argued that vouchers are really more in the nature of a substitution of regulatory regimes.[146]

Housing Vouchers

The beneficiaries of housing vouchers, like all renters, select apartments in the private market. Their share of the rent is based on a formula, and the rest is subsidized by the government. However, voucher beneficiaries

[140] Touminen 1991.
[142] DeHoog 1990; Gronbjerg 1992.
[144] Kramer 1994.
[146] Elmore 1991a.

[141] Sosin 1990.
[143] Kantor and Summers 1987.
[145] Gormley 1991a.

are not in exactly the same position as beneficiaries of income transfers, in that the former are restricted to housing that has passed certain minimum quality inspections. Housing vouchers are a form of privatization that replaces the government production of housing with a process that uses the private market.[147]

In the 1960s, the Department of Housing and Urban Development (HUD) sponsored the Experimental Housing Assistance Program (EHAP) which provided housing allowances to thirty thousand households in twelve experimental sites. This was the largest social experiment ever conducted. The principal findings were as follows: Program participation rates were lower than anticipated. Only about 42 percent of all eligibles eventually participated. Finding acceptable housing was apparently a problem. The allowances were modest. Of those renters who did qualify, 51 percent had substandard units, another 38 percent persuaded landlords to make repairs; and 11 percent moved.

Housing quality did improve, but the effects were modest. For those living in standard units, cost of housing was reduced from 47 percent of income to 25 percent. When repairs were necessary, only modest ones were done. The experiment had very little effect on household mobility. Very few moved to qualify for better housing. Thus, at least on the basis of this experiment, vouchers are not likely to disrupt neighborhoods or disturb existing patterns of segregation. Nor did the experiment cause rent inflation in the sites. Too small a percentage participated, and the subsidy funds went to increasing nonhousing consumption. On the other hand, the per unit costs were significantly below those of the production program. There were much simpler administrative requirements (and costs) than in production programs. Thus, experimental allowance programs were able to keep low-income families in decent housing at reasonable rents at a very low public cost. However, while the allowance program was efficient, it was far from dramatic. It did not stimulate new construction or even much substantial rehabilitation.[148]

Section 8 "certificates"[149] operate like housing vouchers, with two exceptions: (1) With vouchers, the beneficiaries receive payments equal to the difference between the fair market rate (FMR) and the fraction of their income that it is considered that they can afford for rent. Thus, there is a shopping incentive. If the voucher holders find a unit that is less than the FMR, they still get the same subsidy and pocket the difference. With Section 8, the payment is the difference between the actual rent and the affordable fraction, so the incentive does not exist. (2) Voucher recipients

[147] Kingsley 1991.
[148] Kingsley 1991.
[149] Lower Income Rental Assistance Program, Housing and Community Development Act of 1974.

could occupy units with rents higher than the FMR, but assistance would not increase. Thus, the range of choice is lessened under Section 8. Section 8 continues to be popular and to grow. In 1987, 4.3 million households received HUD rental assistance; it is estimated that this is about 34 percent of the eligibles.[150]

Both vouchers and Section 8 perform pretty much as expected. While there are no major supply impacts, there is considerable budgetary relief for the individual households, and the programs are a lot cheaper than production. Nationally, there is a strong consensus building for support of the voucher concept. While there continues to be concern about the supply of housing, there seems to be agreement on a consumer-oriented program. However, while vouchers are a good form of privatization, they are not a solution to America's housing problem. Affordability continues to get more serious, and major efforts have to be done about the supply, particular in areas with severe shortages.[151]

Education

Education will be the subject of chapters 7 and 8, so here, I will mention only briefly some of the major findings on vouchers, or educational choice. Richard Elmore,[152] in his review of three choice programs, the Minnesota Postsecondary Enrollment Options Program, the Community District 4 Alternative School Choice Program (East Harlem), and the Washington State Education Clinics Program, concluded that educational choice policy, although touted as "de-regulating" education—that is, substituting the discipline of market incentives for external regulation—actually is a substitution of one regulatory regime for another. In these three projects, the overall, existing school systems accommodated the projects, and did not change very much.[153]

CONCLUSIONS

While contracting out to the private sector presents a complicated, mixed picture, with only scattered research findings, it nevertheless seems safe to conclude that turning to the private sector—by itself—does not necessarily increase client autonomy. Economic theory may predict that consumer autonomy will be enhanced through market incentives, but that prediction will only come true to the extent that market incentives are present. Instead, what we seem to find are patterns of organizational behavior that

---

[150] Kingsley 1991.   [151] Kingsley 1991.
[152] Elmore 1991a.   [153] Elmore 1991a.

closely resemble the public sector. This is Donahue's principal conclusion: It is not the *form of ownership* that matters; rather it is the institutional arrangements. In most organizational arrangements, whether public or private, client empowerment is not important to organizational survival. Clients are simply not important stakeholders. We now turn to Part II to examine situations in which client empowerment does become important to organizations.

PART II

The View from Below:
Empowerment by Invitation,
Empowerment through Conflict

Chapter 5

POWER AND EMPOWERMENT

EMPOWERMENT is the ability to control one's environment. Here, the environment is the citizen-bureaucratic or -regulatory relationship. In practice, relationships between agencies and people are matters of degree; they can range from completely coercive—for example, police subduing a suspect—to citizens dominating the agency—for example, regulatory agencies being captured by special interests. There is a full range of bargaining, which may be more or less voluntary. In most human service relationships—welfare, health, mental health, education, and so forth—the agency is in the dominant position. It may not be completely dominant, but it clearly has the upper hand.

Part II examines efforts to empower dependent people—workers, parents, clients, tenants, citizens—in a variety of contexts. It is concerned with the attempt to redress the balance so that dependent clients can meaningfully participate in decisions that affect their lives. This is what is meant by empowerment—not necessarily clients controlling the agency—but clients or citizens having a genuine voice.

Before we can consider empowerment, we first have to understand the nature of power in bureaucratic or regulatory settings. As will be discussed in the next section, power is not always direct and observable; it is often subtle and manipulative. Similarly, empowerment involves not only direct, observable forms of behavior, but also the subtle, psychological reactions of clients. Empowerment involves not only challenge and confrontation but also consciousness raising. We are especially concerned with the problem of acquiescence. What does the absence of challenge mean? What does consent in a hierarchical relationship mean? If participants are relatively equal and the relationship is voluntary, then agreement is usually not an issue. Agreement or acquiescence, on the other hand, is an issue when power relationships are unequal. It then becomes important to determine why clients acquiesce.

We consider first the nature of bureaucratic power. As we shall see, there are a variety of views or approaches to power. We then look at power from the perspective of the client; and, not surprisingly, empowerment, too, has multiple meanings. Empowerment is usually discussed in a zero-sum framework—what the client gains, the agency or the worker loses. But this is not always the case; in fact, I argue that the most interesting situations are where both gain as a result of sharing power. We conclude the theoretical discussion of power with an analysis of power in human service agencies from a political economy perspective.

Empowerment is part of the current decentralization debate in regulation. In fact, it has become a buzzword in the more generalized critique of government. The reaction to command-and-control regulatory regimes includes a variety of reforms that have implications for client empowerment. Accordingly, in the next chapter, I briefly review the case against command-and-control regulation. The principal examples are Occupational Safety and Health (OSHA) and environmental protection. Although many other examples could be used, reforms in these two areas are illustrative of empowerment strategies such as cooperative regulation, privatization, and legally structured participation. The chapter then considers major examples of empowerment by relatively powerless people—parents of students, the frail elderly poor, construction workers, public housing tenants, and neighborhood organizations. The chapter concludes with some generalizations about the conditions for empowerment in a decentralized welfare state.

THE MANIFESTATIONS OF POWER

The standard explanation of *power* is, A has power over B to the extent that he can get B to do something that B would not otherwise do.[1] At first blush, the definition seems unproblematic, especially in the context of the dependent bureaucratic client. The client, as the price of receiving something that is needed, has to do something that the official insists upon—participate in a work program, reveal a private matter, or engage in other kinds of behaviors. The model assumes an objective conflict of interests; there is a direct exercise of power and a knowing, albeit unwilling, submission.

[1] While this may be a common, and for our purposes useful explanation of power, there is, in fact, no agreement on the various meanings of power. According to Talcott Parsons,

> Power is one of the key concepts in the great Western tradition about political phenomena. It is at the same time a concept on which, in spite of its long history, there is, on analytical levels, a notable lack of agreement both about its specific definition, and about many features of the conceptual context in which it should be placed. There is, however, a core complex of its meaning having to do with the capacity of persons or collectivities "to get things done" effectively, in particular when their goals are obstructed by some kind of human resistance or opposition. (quoted in Lukes 1986, 94)

The Lukes volume contains a series of essays on various approaches to power. At the end of the introduction, Lukes says: "[I]n our ordinary unreflective judgments and comparisons of power, we normally know what we mean and have little difficulty in understanding one another, yet every attempt at a single general answer to the question has failed and seems likely to fail" (Lukes 1986, 17). For further discussion of power, see, e.g., Clegg 1989; Honneth 1991.

Suppose, however, that the client willingly submits? Has there been an exercise of power if B *appears* to do what A wants? Now the situation becomes more problematic. What does consent mean in a hierarchical relationship? Can we take the client's position at face value? What other choice do we have? Steven Lukes, in an essay, *Power: A Radical View*,[2] addressed the problem of power and quiescence. Lukes argued that there are three dimensions of power. The one-dimensional approach is the example given above in which A gets B to do something he otherwise would not have done. This dimension focuses on observable behavior— "who participates, who gains and loses, and who prevails in decision-making."[3] As such, it assumes that grievances and conflicts are recognized and acted upon, that participation occurs within decision-making arenas that are assumed to be more or less open, at least to organized groups, and that leaders, or decision makers, can be studied as representatives of these groups. Nonparticipation, or inaction, then, is not a political problem; "the empirical relationship of low socio-economic status to low participation gets explained away as the apathy, political inefficacy, cynicism or alienation of the impoverished."[4] As Gamson puts it, inactivity can be seen as confidence (consent), alienation, or irrelevance.[5] Quiescence lies in the characteristics of the victims; it is not constrained by power.

The two-dimensional view of power seeks to meet this last point. Bachrach and Baratz argued that power has a "second face" that not only influences the participants within the decision-making arenas but also operates to exclude participants and issues altogether; that is, power not only involves who gets what, when, and how, but also who gets left out and how.[6] Some issues never get on the political agenda—for example, the issue of pollution in a company-dominated town, or the failure of southern African Americans to register and vote prior to the 1965 Voting Rights Act. Apparent inaction is not related to the lack of grievances. Bachrach and Baratz argue that the study of power has to also include the barriers to even expressing grievances.

Lukes argues that the two-dimensional view, while a considerable advance, does not go far enough; it fails to account for how power may effect even the *conception* of grievances. The absence of grievances may be due to a manipulated consensus. Furthermore, the dominant group may be so secure that they are oblivious to anyone challenging their position—"the most effective and insidious use of power is to prevent ... conflict from arising in the first place."[7] This is the third dimension of

---

[2] Lukes 1974.
[3] Gamson 1968, 3; Polsby 1963, 55.
[4] Gaventa 1980, 7.
[5] Gamson 1968, 46.
[6] Bachrach and Baratz 1962; 1970; Bachrach and Botwinick 1992.
[7] Lukes 1974, 23.

power. A exercises power over B not only by getting him to do what he does not want to do, but "he also exercises power over him by influencing, shaping or determining his very wants."[8] Lukes argues this may happen in the absence of observable conflict even though there is a latent conflict between the interests of A and the "real interests" of excluded B.

An important characteristic of the third-dimensional view is that it is not confined to looking at the exercise of power in an individualistic, behavioral framework; rather, it focuses on the various ways, whether individual or institutional, by which potential conflicts are excluded. It is much more sociological than either the one- or perhaps the two-dimensional views. Under the third dimension, two theoretical approaches are combined—the hegemonic social and historical patterns identified by Gramsci[9] and the subjective effects of power identified by Edelman.[10]

The two- and three-dimensional approaches promise to be particularly relevant when one is considering dependent or relatively powerless people: "In the two-dimensional approach is the suggestion of barriers that prevent issues from emerging into political arenas—i.e., that constrain conflict. In the three-dimensional approach is the suggestion of the use of power to pre-empt manifest conflict at all, through the shaping of patterns or conceptions of non-conflict."[11]

What are the mechanisms of power in the three dimensions? In the first dimension are the conventional political resources used by political actors—votes, influence, jobs. The second dimension adds what Bachrach and Baratz call the "mobilization of bias." These are the rules of the game—values, beliefs, rituals, as well as institutional procedures—that systematically benefit certain groups at the expense of others. The mobilization of bias operates not only in the decision-making arenas but also, in fact primarily, through "non-decisions" in which demands are "suffocated before they are voiced, or kept covert; or killed before they gain access to the relevant decision-making arena; or failing all of these things, maimed or destroyed in the decision-implementing stage of the policy process."[12] Quiescence can be the product of force or its threat, co-optation, symbolic manipulation, or the silent effects of incremental decisions or institutional inaction.[13]

The mechanisms of power in the third dimension are the least understood. Here is where,

[8] Lukes 1974, 23.   [9] Gramsci 1971.

[10] "Political actions chiefly arouse or satisfy people not by granting or withholding their stable, substantive demands but rather by changing their demands and expectations" (Edelman 1971, 8). Also see Gaventa 1980, 13.

[11] Gaventa 1980, 13.   [12] Bachrach and Baratz 1970, 43.

[13] Gaventa 1980, 15.

power influences, shapes or determines conceptions of the necessities, possibilities, and strategies of challenge in situations of latent conflict. This may include the study of social myths, language, and symbols, and how they are shaped or manipulated in power processes. It may involve the study of communication of information—both of what is communicated and how it is done. It may involve a focus upon the means by which social legitimations are developed around the dominant, and instilled as beliefs or roles in the dominated. It may involve, in short, locating the power processes behind the social construction of meanings and patterns that serve to get B to act and believe in a manner in which B otherwise might not, to A's benefit and B's detriment."[14]

Third-dimensional mechanisms of power not only include the control of information and socialization processes, but also fatalism, self-deprecation, apathy, and the internalization of dominant values and beliefs—the psychological adaptations of the oppressed to escape the subjective sense of powerlessness. Voices become echoes rather than grievances and demands. Behaviors and beliefs intertwine. Political consciousness and participation are reciprocal and reinforcing; those who are denied participation will not develop political consciousness. As Paulo Freire puts it, because dependent societies are prevented from either participation or reflection, they are denied the very experience necessary for the development of a critical consciousness; instead, they develop a "culture of silence." Moreover, it is the culture of silence that may lend legitimation to the dominant order. Finally, if their voices do emerge, they are especially vulnerable to manipulation by the powerful.[15]

Gaventa argues that the various mechanisms of power as well as the attributes of powerlessness, in all three dimensions, are interrelated and cumulative; they serve to reinforce each other. Repeated defeats lead to quiescence, which give the dominant group more opportunity to create barriers of exclusion. The maintenance of power becomes "self-propelled"; thus, "power relationships can be understood only with reference to their prior development and their impact comprehended only in light of their own momentum."[16]

While Lukes's three faces of power has been very influential, it has been criticized as presenting a view of power that is overly monolithic, sovereign, top-down—in short, hegemonic. It emphasizes negative, prohibitory power, the denial of sovereignty to sovereign individuals. Stewart Clegg, taking a poststructuralist approach, argues that power is never that complete, that there is always a dialectic between agents.[17] Rather than a "sin-

---

[14] Gaventa 1980, 15–16.   [15] Freire 1985; Gaventa 1980, 15–16.
[16] Gaventa 1980, 23.   [17] Clegg 1989.

gle all-encompassing strategy," power is a "shifting, inherently unstable expression in networks and alliances."[18] Rather than a sovereign view, power is a " 'capillary form' which 'reaches into the very grain of individuals.' "[19] Power, according to Foucault, is exercised through disciplinary practices or discourses, the construction of routines.[20]

Power, according to the post-structuralist view, is

> neither in specific individuals (Lukes) nor in concrete practices (Foucault) but in the way in which agents and practices are articulated in a particular fixed ensemble of representations. There is only representation; there is no fixed, real, hidden or excluded term or dimension. To the extent that meanings become fixed or reified in certain forms, which then articulate particular practices, agents and relations, this fixity is power. . . . Power is textual, semiotic, and inherent in the very possibility of textuality, meaning and signification in the social world.[21]

Power, then, is not a "thing," rather it is "property of relations."[22] Networks of interest are constituted and reproduced through both conscious strategies and unwitting practices. The study of power is how agents constitute interests, how they attempt to enroll others to their strategies. Power is relational. When these relational interests are reproduced, when they become fixed or reified, then power tends to be regarded as thinglike, material, concrete. This means that despite theoretical instability, in practice, power can be "as 'objective' as the policeman's power to arrest" because of the "fixity of stabilized disciplinary powers and discursive practices."[23] However, according to Clegg, power rarely achieves this form; rather, there is always some resistance.

Agents—which can be either individuals or collectivities—exercise power. According to Clegg, existing social relations constitute the identities of agents. Agents posses varying control of resources and varying means of producing outcomes. Power will automatically reproduce the existing configurations of rules and domination; transformation comes about only when existing practices are challenged. Domination, however, is not challenged that often because agents are embedded within organizations controlled by others and thus lack the collective organization to resist. They may not know about the existence of other resources—they may not know the rules of the game or even recognize the game. Often they are unaware of potential allies; in which case, resistance is isolated, and easily defeated. Or, there may be conflicts within potential allies. Or, they may be aware, but the cost of resistance is too high. Clegg also says that conditions of the agents may be such as to render whatever

18 Clegg 1989, 154.   19 Clegg 1989, 155.   20 Honneth 1991, 155–56.
21 Honneth 1991, 184.   22 Honneth 1991, 189.   23 Clegg 1989, 177.

knowledge they have useless. He uses as an example labor's need to earn a living and the deadening effect of ceaseless, routine activity as a form of discipline. Routine, he says, "takes on the form of ritual; myth and ceremony serve to reinforce and make meaningful the routines of everyday subordination."[24]

Rules of meaning and membership in organizations are fixed by institutional isomorphism. Certain meanings are privileged and certain membership categories are aligned with these meanings. Organizational fields develop when other organizations and agencies are enrolled, producing a stabilizing network of alliances and coalitions. Agencies in the field are reflexively aware of their constitution as a field. Clegg adopts the views of Meyer, Rowan, DiMaggio, and Powell (discussed in chap. 2) about the sources of organizational stability and change. Transformation is most likely to occur when there is a lack of fit between the core institutional order and the material substructure, where there is a "strain" arising from the functional incompatibility between the institutional order and the material base.[25] The tendencies toward contradiction are contingent upon relations of meanings and membership. With higher degrees of isomorphism, there is more of an equilibrium of power ("thought-control" and "hegemony").[26] The dialectic of power and structure is "our irremediable entrapment within webs of meaning together with our organizational capacity to transform these."[27]

In sum, there appears to be a high degree of convergence as to the characteristics or manifestations of power.[28] Whatever the various definitions, "power" (A getting B to do what B would not ordinarily desire) at times can be objectively observed, from the subtle manipulations of the agenda to the construction of ideologies and meaning that leave B unaware of alternatives. Structuralists emphasize the multiple ways in which the powerful dominate. Poststructuralists argue that power is not always total, that there are contradictions and forces of change in society, and that there is often resistance on the part of seemingly powerless people.

[24] Clegg 1989, 222.   [25] Clegg 1989, 233.   [26] Clegg 1989, 237.

[27] Clegg 1989, 239–40. Honneth (1991): "Physical violence and ideological influence, Foucault believes, show a common characteristic as means of procuring power: They work by way of directly or indirectly forcing opponents to abandon their own objectives" (164).

[28] In describing the evolution of Foucault's theory of power, Honneth (1991, 173) writes:

> Accordingly, he no longer regards individual actors or social groups as the subjects of this developed form of the exercise of power, but instead social institutions such as the school, the prison, or the factory—institutions that he himself must comprehend as highly complex structures of solidified positions of social power. The frame of reference for the concept of power has, therefore, secretly been shifted from a theory of action to an analysis of institutions.

Not surprisingly, concepts of empowerment mirror the multiple meanings of power. Power or empowerment is "the ability to act effectively."[29]
Empowerment is both psychological and behavioral. It involves a sense of
perceived control, of competence, a critical awareness of one's environment, and involvement in activities that, in fact, exert control.[30] Empowerment is more than an absence of alienation or sense of helplessness. It
involves a sense of connectedness.[31]

Charles Keiffer, in his study of participants in grass-roots organizations, argues that empowerment is a long-term process of learning and
development.[32] He emphasizes the importance of the connections between the experiences of daily life and perceptions of personal efficacy.
The contrast is powerlessness. Building on the ideas of Freier—in which
the individual becomes powerless when he or she assumes the role of object rather than subject—powerlessness is a sense of loss of control over
social relations, "a construction of continuous interaction between the
person and his/her environment. It combines an attitude of self-blame, a
sense of generalized distrust, a feeling of alienation from resources for
social influence, an experience of disenfranchisement and economic vul-
nerability, and a sense of hopelessness in socio-political struggle."[33] Keiffer quotes one of his respondents: "It would never have occurred to me to
have expressed an opinion on anything. . . . It was *inconceivable* that my
opinion had any value. . . ."[34]

How then do individuals move "beyond . . . situations of powerlessness and oppression?" Keiffer argues that the process must be specific;
generalized feelings of injustice or consciousness raising are not sufficient.
According to his participants, tangible and direct threats to individual or
familial self-interests were necessary to provoke responses that would
eventually lead to empowerment. There must be a "personally experienced sense of outrage or confrontation."[35] Examples include a woman
being assaulted, or the betrayal of a tenant farmer's trust by a landlord.
The next phase is what Keiffer calls the emergence of "participatory competence." By this he means getting over being scared, demystifying the
symbols of power and authority, that is, coming to realize that officials do
not know everything, and that ordinary people can change things. The
process continues with the help of more experienced allies (role models,
mentors, instructors, friends), supportive peer relationships, and the development of a more critical understanding of social and political relations. Action must be reflective. Direct experience is used not only to gain
skills, but also to increase understanding and confidence, which, in turn,

---

[29] Bachrach and Botwinick 1992, 57.   [30] Zimmerman 1993.
[31] Zimmerman and Rappaport 1988.   [32] Keiffer 1984.
[33] Keiffer 1984, 16.   [34] Keiffer 1984, 16.
[35] Keiffer 1984, 19.

increases motivation. Eventually, the participants achieve an "increasingly self-conscious awareness of self as a visible and effective actor in the community. . . ." and they use their skills to integrate their "new personal knowledge . . . into the reality and structure of their everyday life-worlds."[36]

In discussing the relationship between thought and action, Keiffer is careful to point out that his respondents are not talking about theoretical conceptualization. Rather, thought is used to inform action, to make future activity more effective. There has to be both thought and experience, extending over a period of time. "Empowerment is not a commodity to be acquired, but a transforming process constructed through action."[37] Empowerment is a "long-term and continuing *process* of adult development."[38] Empowerment as "participatory competence," involves the development of a sense of self-competence, a more critical or analytical understanding of one's social and political environment, and individual and collective resources for social and political activity.[39] Keiffer argues that this definition of empowerment "places the notion of competence and coping within an explicitly political context."[40]

Subsequent research confirms Keiffer's conception. Thus, Zimmerman and Rappaport report that studies of participants in a wide variety of settings and organizations suggest that empowerment is a combination of personal beliefs about control and involvement in activities to exert control, as well as a critical awareness of one's environment. They, too, emphasize *experience*—behaviors designed to exercise control—as well as consciousness raising.[41]

The three faces of power and empowerment as mirror image involving both psychological and behavioral processes will be used in the various examples presented in this and the next two chapters. The conceptualizations of power and empowerment become particularly important in analyzing the most radical school restructuring, now taking place in Chicago. Before proceeding, however, I illustrate the three faces of power in human service agencies.

POWER IN HUMAN SERVICES AGENCIES

Human service organizations perform major caring, nurturing, and individual improvement functions in society—health, education, social welfare, employment and training, occupational safety.[42] At the same time,

---

[36] Keiffer 1984, 23–24.   [37] Keiffer 1984, 27.
[38] Keiffer 1984, 31.   [39] Keiffer 1984, 31.
[40] Keiffer 1984, 32.   [41] Zimmerman, 1993; Zimmerman and Rappaport 1988.
[42] This section relies extensively on Hasenfeld (1992a, 1992b).

they are social control agencies. They regulate, exclude, and punish devi-
ant behavior. They are supposed to be responsive and professional, but
they are often huge bureaucracies with rigid, incomprehensible rules,
staffed by distant, overworked, seemingly uncaring workers.

Hasenfeld describes the enigmas or dilemmas of human service organizations as follows. The first distinguishing characteristic is that the core
activity of these organizations involves human beings. The purpose of
these organizations is to process or change people. People, as clients, react
to the processing, and thereby can affect the work. They can also participate in the organizational work.

A second distinguishing characteristic is that the work of human services organizations is *moral work*. The very nature of selecting, processing, and changing people conveys a judgement as to the moral worth of
that client—a judgment that the student is worth educating, that the patient is worth treating, that the poor person is worth helping. However
technical or rule-bound the decision, somewhere along the line a value
judgment has been made about the client. Rationing is a moral decision;
some clients will receive scarce resources before others. The manner in
which the client is treated also conveys moral decisions. Should the client
be consulted or is the client a passive recipient only? That is to say, is the
client a subject or an object? A statement of moral superiority is made
when official decisions are expected to be unchallenged.[43]

Because human service organizations are engaged in moral work, they
have to constantly seek moral legitimacy. They adopt the moral systems
of dominant political leaders, interest groups, and organizations in their
environment. "[S]urvival depends less on the technical proficiency of
their work and more on their conformity with dominant cultural symbols
and belief systems."[44] However, human service agencies are not merely
passive responders. They are also "'moral entrepreneurs'"; they seek to
influence the moral conceptions of their organization, their environment,
and their clients.

Cultural beliefs determine what values are legitimate and appropriate
in working with clients. Service technologies become reified into "*practice
ideologies*"—beliefs as to what is good for clients, and these beliefs provide both the rationale and the justification for the practices. However,
because the technology of human services organizations is indeterminate
and clients vary in terms of needs and problems, clients may not conform
to the agency's conception of client values and may not respond to the
agency's technology. The agency will attempt to select those clients who
fit organizational needs and compartmentalize client needs into "'normal'" service categories. Other client problems will be considered ir-

---

[43] Hasenfeld 1992b.   [44] Hasenfeld 1992b, 10.

relevant. The selection and diagnosis is designed to establish a "set of behavioral expectations for both the clients and the workers."[45] Tracking clients ensures compliance in two senses. It allows the workers to proceed according to their rules. At the same time, the organization exercises broader social control functions by "reinforcing socially sanctioned client roles." Finally, "by assuming such a social control function, the organization pays homage to the moral systems it adopts to garner and maintain its legitimacy."[46]

In responding, adopting, and adapting the broader cultural influences and values—processes described by the new institutionalists (see chap. 2)—human service organizations establish their worth with those organizations, politicians, interest groups, and other elites that are essential to their survival. Schools reward conforming students and track others. Employment and training programs select and train the most promising students and somehow defer or deflect those who may need the services the most. Welfare agencies from time to time punish the undeserving poor.

In the selecting, sorting, and processing of clients, the individual field-level decisions are relatively immune from upper-level supervision. Individual field-level decisions are shrouded in factual assessments. It is difficult for supervisors to uncover the relevant information, assuming there was the will to do so.[47]

In confronting and resolving these dilemmas, how is power exercised? Social work practice theory recognizes that there are natural unequal power relationships between the worker and the client but that in most relationships, the power advantages will be neutralized through the voluntary mutuality of interests. This is because according to the traditional view of social work practice theory, the client-caseworker relationship is voluntary, mutual, reciprocal, and trusting.

Hasenfeld challenges this view; he describes the exercise of power from a political economy perspective.[48] The principal source of social worker power derives from the resources and services controlled by the agency. Workers are members of organizations, and it is the organizations that determine how their resources are to be allocated. If the clients want these resources, then they must yield at least some control over their fate. In addition to control over resources, workers have other sources of power: expertise, persuasion, and legitimacy. They have specialized knowledge and interpersonal skills. All of these sources of power are used in various combinations to exercise control over clients.

A great deal of an organization's power is exercised through its standard operative procedures; these control the type of information that is

---

[45] Hasenfeld 1992b, 15.   [46] Hasenfeld 1992b, 17.
[47] Hasenfeld 1992b.   [48] Hasenfeld 1992a.

processed, the range of available alternatives, and the decision rules. The agency is concerned with maintaining and strengthening its core activity—the delivery of services. The environment matters; goals represent the interests of those who control the key resources of the agency, and those goals may or may not incorporate professional norms and/or the interests of the client. In public agencies, which chronically lack the resources to meet demand, social workers are relatively powerless to change the situation; thus, they develop various personal coping mechanisms, such as withdrawal and client victimization.

Hasenfeld rejects the concept of mutuality of interests—that agencies and clients share the common goal of helping the client—in favor of a transactional approach. The interests of the client and the agency are determined by their respective systems. Each wants to maximize its own resources while minimizing costs. A person becomes a client to obtain needed resources but tries to do so with a minimum of costs; the social worker needs the resources controlled by the client, while minimizing his or her and the agency's costs. The relationship is governed, then, by the power that each person has over his or her own interests. Thus, the amount of power that A has over B is a direct function of the resources that A controls and B needs and the inverse function of the ability of B to obtain those resources elsewhere. Agencies that have a monopoly of services exercise considerable power over clients. On the other hand, clients can exercise considerable power if they possess desirable characteristics. Thus, the exchange relationship between the client and the agency can be voluntary or involuntary depending on the degree of choice that each possesses.

However, even in situations where social workers possess considerable power, that power may not necessarily be used. There are rules and regulations, and workers, in varying degrees, are influenced by professional norms and values. But in any event, the traditional social work practice theory assumption of client self-determination is largely untrue for vulnerable groups. For these groups, relationships tend to be involuntary. The agency is not dependent on the client for its resources. Demand exceeds resources, and most agencies are in monopoly positions. The agencies have the resources that the clients need. The clients usually have no alternatives.

The asymmetrical power relationship between the agency and the client, and hence between the worker and the client, is maintained throughout the structure of social services. Social workers increase the power advantage through their monopoly of expertise, limiting client access to other workers, making the offer of services conditional on compliance, and limiting options for alternatives.

Agency processes reflect the evaluative criteria of the external funding and legitimating sources. The more powerful the agency, the more it will use its advantages to maintain its position; it will maintain a superior practice and select the more desirable clients. Within the agency, the more powerful workers are better able to control the conditions of their work. In this way, the dynamics of power perpetuate the unequal distribution of quality practice. Poor clients tend to receive poor services. This results not only in an inequality of practice, but, Hasenfeld argues, the practice of inequality.

The exercise of power becomes more subtle when one considers agency technology. As stated, human service agencies are designed to change people; thus, the agency practice or technology is a *moral* system. Clients are invested with moral and cultural values that define their status. The processes of the organization—intake, intervention, and termination—are crucially shaped by the workers' moral evaluation of the client. Moreover, as clients progress within the system, moral and social attributes change. The technology is based on a conception of human nature, and this conception is reinforced through the selection, processing, and evaluation of the clients—what Hasenfeld calls, "practice ideologies"—or sets of ideas or ideologies that seek confirmation in self-fulfilling prophecies by screening incompatible information and resisting change or reappraisal. The workers select and deal with those clients who will serve their interests—either to confirm their ideologies or comport with the demands of their working conditions, or both. Since technologies and resources are limited, the attributes of the clients who *enter* are important to organizational success. Thus, organizations seek to attract desirable clients and screen out the undesirable. Although public agencies are often limited in their ability to pick and choose, they employ other mechanisms for acceptance and rejection.

Hasenfeld describes the selection and processing of clients as "typification," which is a pervasive feature in the exercise of field level discretion. The organization identifies client characteristics in terms of diagnostic labels, which then determine the service response. Agency perceptions of the client's moral character are often determinative. Is the client responsible for his or her condition and is the client amenable to change? Is the client morally capable of making decisions? Is the client a subject or an object? The answers to these questions, in turn, determine the workers' moral responsibility to the client. The social construction of the client's moral character will have a decisive impact on the treatment that the client receives; thus, the constructed moral character becomes reinforcing.

The mechanism through which the agency delivers the services and gains control over the client is the relationship between the client and the worker. The core of this relationship, according to Hasenfeld, is the nature of the *trust* between the client and the worker. The client has to believe in the desirability of the services and the skill of the worker; the worker has to believe that the client will not abuse the relationship. The worker has to trust the client in order to make the necessary moral commitments. Successful agency intervention depends upon client trust. However, in order for there to be trust, goals and interests have to coincide. There are many barriers to developing a compatibility of interests, but a crucial one, according to Hasenfeld, is the social construction of the client's moral character; in short, is the client a subject or an object?

Hasenfeld's description of power in human service agencies tracks the three dimensions of power. The first dimension is the objective observation of an exercise of power. It is the paradigm of liberal, legal adversarial relations. A dependent person applies for welfare; a condition of aid is a behavioral change—for example, a work assignment—that the person would prefer not to do, but feels that she has to as the price of receiving assistance. The agency is acting either legally or illegally. In either case, it is a direct, observable exercise of power.

Assume that the agency is acting illegally—the woman is legally exempt from the work requirements, the agency has failed to follow required procedures (e.g., evaluation, offers of training, etc.), or that legally required adequate day care is not available. The client knows of the illegality but needs the aid, has no other adequate alternative, and lacks the resources to challenge the agency. Or, the client has available competent legal aid and does challenge the agency. This is the first-dimension of power—there is an objective event—individualized conflict and empirical evidence as to who won what under what circumstances. Power can be defined and measured.

Suppose, however, that the client acquiesces in the condition. Why is there acquiescence? Assume that the client is of the same frame of mind—that is, she would prefer not to work. It may be that the agency is acting legally; in this case, the decision has been made legislatively and the agency is not exercising its discretion but is following a rule. The client is now precluded from voicing her grievance, certainly in this forum, but probably not in any other arena as well. This would be a case of the second dimension of power. There is a grievance—the woman feels that she unjustly has to pay a price for the aid—but she has been effectively precluded from contesting the decision.

There are other ways in which the second dimension of power can also operate. The agency may be operating illegally, the woman feels her grievance, but lacks the resources with which to pursue her remedy or for some other reason feels that it would be either useless or even counterproductive to pursue her remedy. She may, for example, fear retaliation.[49]

---

[49] For a discussion of the barriers to exercising rights to administrative fair hearings, see Handler 1986, chap. 2.

These are examples of the second dimension of power because even though there is no objectively observed conflict, there is a grievance. Moreover, one could empirically verify not only the grievance, but also the reasons for quiescence. Different client behaviors could be empirically established.

There are also several variations on the third dimension of power—a situation in which the absence of conflict is due to the manipulation of consensus, or in which A shapes and determines the very wants of B. The very idea of welfare as an *entitlement* is of recent vintage. Prior to the legal rights revolution of the 1960s, welfare was considered a gratuity, something that was offered on the terms and conditions of the grantor, much as private charity is given today. Given the extremely low level of legal challenges in social welfare programs, one questions even now how far the concept of entitlement has penetrated the consciousness of the disadvantaged.[50] But even if the client thinks she is entitled to welfare, there are competing norms. The work requirement is deeply ingrained in American public values—witness the astonishing consensus on work-for-relief today; many think it perfectly normal and appropriate that an applicant for assistance should work at a public job as the price of the grant; there is very little support for the idea that one is entitled to a minimum level of support without any corresponding obligations.[51] To the extent that the applicant for assistance has internalized these values—the mutual obligations of work, responsibility, and welfare—the dominant group has prevented even the conception of the grievance. As Gaventa points out, this view of power is not individualistic; it is much more institutional, more in the nature of the hegemonic social and historical patterns identified by Gramsci and the subjective effects of power discussed by Edelman; power prevents the manifestation of conflict at all.

The social and historical patterns and the subjective effects are, of course, much more deep rooted, much more pervasive than even the complex example of the work obligation. They are manifest in many of the relationships between the dependent citizen seeking services or trying to avoid sanctions and the officer who controls the resources. Both the powerful and the powerless carry into the relationship their respective characters and self-conceptions, their root values, nurtured through immediate as well as past social relationships. Who they are and where they come from—class, race, childhood, education, employment, relations with others, the everyday structures of their lives, their very different social locations—crucially affect their languages, social myths, beliefs, and symbols—how they view themselves, their world, and others—which pro-

[50] Handler 1986, 2.

[51] See, e.g., Hartmann 1987 and Mead 1986. For a discussion of the current consensus on work and welfare reform, see Handler and Hasenfeld 1991 and Handler 1992.

duce vastly different meanings and patterns in their encounters. How does the staff-professional view herself and the person sitting across the desk in this full, deep context? How does the client view herself and the person sitting across from her in her context? The structures of their social life shape their identities and direct their behavior.[52] There is no agreement, at least in theory, as to how hegemonic these power relationships are. For some, it is no surprise that in social welfare, the vast majority of clients either fail to pursue their grievances or even to conceptualize a grievance. At a theoretical level, one may argue about the degree of hegemony of the three faces of power. In human service organizations that deal with the poor and minorities, official power is, to all intents and purposes, just about all-encompassing. Resistance is often quite feeble and at the margins.[53]

While the three-dimensional view of power may have a theoretical plausibility, it does pose significant methodological problems. A major challenge raised to the two-dimensional view was the empirical difficulty of observing a "non-event." With the third-dimension, "how can one study what does not happen?"[54] How can one tell whether B would have *thought* and *acted* differently under different circumstances? There is a real issue of imputing interests and values to the voiceless. An even more difficult problem comes in empirically verifying the third dimension. When there is acquiescence, how do we know whether the consent is genuine or manipulated? How does the researcher (the dominant group) avoid imputing his or her values, the social construction of meaning, to the quiescent?

In real life, the methodological issues may not, in fact, be that severe in many situations. If there are major inequalities in social relations, at least as a first step, one should not assume that quiescence is natural but seek other explanations. In less obvious situations, Gaventa suggests a number of steps to try to explain the inaction. He would look to the historical development of the apparent consensus to see how the situation was arrived at and how the consensus has been maintained. He would look at the processes of communication and socialization and the relationship between the ideologies and beliefs. There may be comparative examples with different power relationships. However, "if . . . no mechanisms of power can be identified and no relevant counterfactuals can be found, then the researcher must conclude that the quiescence of a given deprived group is, in fact, based upon consensus of that group to their condition, owing for instance, to differing values from those initially posited by the observer."[55]

---

[52] Molotch and Boden 1985. There is a vast theoretical and empirical literature dealing with the problems of lack of rights consciousness. See, e.g., Felstiner, Abel, and Sarat 1980–81; Bumiller 1988; Handler 1986.

[53] Handler 1992.   [54] Gaventa 1980, 25.   [55] Gaventa 1980, 25.

Bargaining as Non-Zero-Sum

Thus far, power versus empowerment has been assumed to be zero-sum—a contest between the agency and the client; what the client gains, the agency has to give up. This is not necessarily true, even in the human service agencies that Hasenfeld describes. The zero-sum assumption does not sufficiently take into account the many situations in which organizations bargain, rather than rely strictly on commands. It is often the case in bargaining that both sides are better off. Indeed, that is the underlying assumption behind voluntary exchange.

In chapter 2, the various contemporary theories of organizations described organizations as collections of competing units and individuals more or less vying with each other for the command over resources. In this struggle, organizational actors seek legitimacy, power, and resources from the environment. Legitimacy is acquired through conformity to dominant cultural norms and belief systems. The institutionalists argue that these norms are very powerful; they are the essence of organizational behavior. They determine an organization's rules and practices. Organizations that conform are more successful in commanding productive resources from the environment—money, legal authority, and desirable clients.

Both the political economy and the institutional perspective emphasize the importance of the organizational environment. Organizational fields are rarely static, especially since there are conflicts and contradictions among many of our basic institutions. Organizations both shape and are constrained by environmental influences. In many situations, organizations are proactive, seeking to strengthen and expand their influence by expanding the power of their interest group constituencies. In other situations, existing organizations seek to defend themselves from newcomers.

In a world of competition and unstable environments, there can be many reasons why organizations will find it in their self-interest to strike deals, to bargain, rather than attempt to secure their position by will. Bargaining, of course, occurs when the regulated subject has something that the agency needs but lacks the ability to command. Regulatory agency bargains with regulated industries are well known. But bargaining also occurs in situations that are not so obvious. A great many police encounters on the street are bargains; cooperation can leave both parties better off. On the other hand, bargaining can also be coercive, as when an agency uses its power to gain even more advantage over a dependent client.

Hasenfeld notes that human service organizations will bargain if clients have desirable characteristics. Organizations may bargain to save scarce resources, to gain a more favorable solution, or to acquire resources that the client controls (for example, valuable information). Similar patterns apply even in stable organizational fields. Bargains are struck, arrangements between the organization and dominant interest groups are solidified. In fact, I will argue that bargaining, or cooperative regulation, is far more common than command-and-control regulation.

In sum, power and empowerment is a relational process, a dynamic process. It has both psychological and material or substantive aspects. Relationships are not stable. Resources and perceptions change; power changes as well. Specifically, all else being equal, we can expect that over time power will gradually shift to the more powerful agency. The agency has the surer command over resources; it has the staying power. This means that empowered clients have to keep struggling to maintain their position. There has to be a continuous structure of incentives; otherwise, energy will dissipate, and clients will become passive and co-opted.

Chapter 6

EMPOWERMENT BY INVITATION

IN THIS CHAPTER, we examine cooperative or bargaining relationships in regulatory settings. Cooperation in regulatory settings is ubiquitous. Why is this empowerment? And why "by invitation?" In the examples that we are concerned with, there are large differences in the power of the parties. If the weaker parties are to engage in genuine participation, they have to be empowered. The contrast is with Hawkins's study of bargaining in water pollution regulation, discussed in chapter 3. There, the regulated companies made a cost-benefit determination to bargain rather than assume an adversarial position. The companies had both knowledge and material resources to pursue either position. In the examples used in this chapter, there are considerable differentials in both kinds of resources. As discussed in chapter 5, empowerment requires both psychological and material resources. Empowerment is a *reflexive process*; the weaker parties gain psychological strength through lived experience. Power and empowerment are *relational*; both the powerful and the powerless have to perceive and experience reciprocal benefits.

Where do the resources necessary for empowerment come from? In part, the weaker parties develop the resources on their own; at the very least, they have to be active agents in appropriating to their advantage whatever resources are available. But it is my belief that in most situations, weaker parties cannot become empowered and *maintain* empowerment on their own—at least in the long term. Over time, the more powerful interests, especially bureaucracies, have too much command over resources. The stronger parties will reassert domination either coercively or by co-optation. Therefore, in order to maintain empowerment, the weaker parties have to get outside resources. In the examples described in this chapter, the resources come from the stronger parties themselves— hence, the expression empowerment "by invitation." In the cases examined in the next chapter, the weaker parties obtain the necessary resources from the larger community. The principal example is a school reform situation in which teachers, parents, and community residents are contesting the established education bureaucracy for control of the schools. Hence the expression, empowerment "through conflict."

Key questions in this chapter are: What leads the stronger parties to invite empowerment? And, then, what is necessary to maintain empowerment? We first consider construction worker safety. Then, we turn to some examples in human services agencies. We conclude with public housing tenants and neighborhood organizations.

WORKER SAFETY

OSHA's Voluntary Protection Program is a system of self-regulation. Companies with exemplary in-house safety systems assume many of the responsibilities of OSHA inspectors and thereby are exempt from regular inspections. The particular programs that Joseph Rees studied were at two large construction sites involved in the California Cooperative Compliance Program (CCP) developed during the early 1980s.[1] These programs were successful in that the three relevant stakeholders—OSHA, management, and labor—worked together and were able to significantly lower accident rates.

OSHA became interested in strengthening private regulatory systems as an alternative to command-and-control regulation. We have already discussed (chap. 3) how OSHA became excessively legalistic in the 1970s. Under its inspection-and-citation enforcement system, two thousand inspectors were responsible for inspecting over six million work places. It turned out that manufacturing and construction sites were inspected, on average, about once every ten years. In the meantime, of course, conditions were constantly changing. Yet, OSHA would use uniform rules to concentrate on identifying well-known hazards common to many work places. Since many hazards are unique to specific sites, it was estimated that OSHA was capable of preventing no more than a quarter of accidents even with perfect compliance.[2] OSHA's decision to experiment with mandated self-regulation was an attempt to strengthen job site safety.

Mandated self-regulation can include both rule making and rule enforcement. A fully mandated program would privatize both rule making and rule enforcement. Mandated self-regulation differs from voluntary self-regulation in that while both are developed by and internally enforced by the firm, with mandated self-regulation, the program is officially sanctioned by government, which also assumes responsibility for monitoring and, if necessary, ensuring its effectiveness. Under the OSHA plan, selected unions and employers were to develop regulatory requirements and compliance mechanisms through collective bargaining. OSHA inspections would be suspended so long as the labor-management safety program proved effective.

---

[1] This example is taken from Rees 1988.

[2] Recent research indicates that OSHA enforcement did result in a lot more compliance than previously thought (Gray and Scholz 1993).

Rees, like Hawkins, was concerned with how cooperation comes about and is sustained in what is normally considered a command-and-control legal structure. A key aspect is what Rees calls "regulatory pluralism." Government regulation is only one of the determinates of firm behavior. Society also has a great many other "private" regulatory systems. There are indigenous normative institutions—in unions, factories, universities, hospitals, corporations—that make rules and induce compliance among group members.[3] State-centered regulation misses this aspect of regulation. One of the questions that Rees was concerned with was the reciprocal influence and the mutual dependence between the "public" and the "private" systems. In the particular case studies, the regulatory environment consisted of a multitude of influences—corporate safety programs, the workers' compensation system, the professional safety movement, union norms, as well as others.

The California Cooperative Compliance Program (CCP), which implemented the OSHA program, assumes that a fully functioning occupational safety program requires cooperation between labor and management. It is self-regulation in that a job site labor-management safety committee acts as the surrogate OSHA inspector. In the particular large construction sites where this program was implemented, there were strong pressures for it to succeed. Even though these particular sites had exemplary safety records, because of worker complaints (the project involved nuclear power construction) there were frequent inspections that were quite disruptive. The companies wanted to reduce this burden. At the same time, the unions felt threatened by competition from open shops. Thus, both management and labor had strong reasons to try and cooperate on a safety program.

There were other important influences at work. Before the voluntary program was implemented, OSHA was important as an enforcement agency. Initially, the firms wanted to comply with OSHA; subsequently, they were able to build defenses against strict, legalistic enforcement. Nevertheless while OSHA's threat was probably always exaggerated, it was used by the firm safety engineers to enhance their authority to stimulate voluntary compliance. This is an example of both a public and a private or firm mandate. OSHA provided the safety engineers with an authoritative source of norms and procedures with which to build the private, internal safety system. The safety departments used the OSHA standards as resources to advance their particular agendas. Thereafter, because the safety programs internalized OSHA's standards, OSHA maintained its influence in the private regime of regulatory standards even though its influence as a public enforcement agency declined. This is

[3] This would be an example of the "new institutionalism" that Power and DiMaggio describe, discussed in chap. 2.

an example of how subunits within large organizations use outside resources (in this, case norms and threats of enforcement) to advance their position within the organization.

Another important "outside" influence was the reform of the workers' compensation system. State benefits increased and states had to upgrade their systems, both of which increased employers' costs. In the highly competitive construction industry, firms began to pay much more attention to safety.

Another source of influence was the professional safety movement, which resulted from the growth of professionalism among the safety engineers. Again, illustrating the internal dynamics of large organizations, the professionalism of the safety engineers was encouraged by management to increase the authority of the engineers and management vis-à-vis the construction superintendents. In time, the safety engineers, with the help of both OSHA and management, were able to develop a corps of safety engineers that had administrative autonomy. Between OSHA and the safety departments, the safety engineers were able to check the construction superintendents' previously sole authority over safety matters. The superintendents had to accept the safety engineers or run the risk of OSHA enforcement.

With these developments—the reform of Workers' Compensation and the professional safety movement—management began to reconceptualize the problem of industrial accidents. Accidents, instead of being viewed as inevitable, were now viewed as a management responsibility and accident prevention an essential element of good construction management. Safety departments argued that accidents were controllable costs, and affected competition. In Hawkins's terms, an accident was a "problem" rather than a discrete act.

It was the combination of all of these developments that induced management to try a new approach to worker safety. But management needed labor support. This was obtained through the establishment of the Labor-Management Safety Committees. One of management's central purposes was to get labor to go the committee for voluntary compliance rather than to OSHA for formal enforcement. Employees were naturally skeptical, especially since construction workers are highly vulnerable to getting fired. To build worker confidence, the labor representative on the committee had to be a seasoned journeyman, someone who was both knowledgeable and respected. Then, the committee had to be sure that employee communications would be listened to and that complaints would be acted upon. The company had to deliver in order to build confidence and increase the flow of information.

The management representative not only had to have construction experience, but also to have real authority with both higher officers and other construction supervisors. Thus, each of the representatives had a distinct role—the safety engineer had professional expertise; the labor representative would make the committee more accessible to the employees; and the management representative would facilitate the abatement process.

Rees found that all sites reported that between 70 and 80 percent of safety-related problems were immediately corrected during the actual committee inspections. This represents a fundamental feature of the construction site environment—namely, that once recognized, most safety problems are not difficult to abate. The safety committee was the surrogate OSHA compliance mechanism. It conducted inspections, reviewed complaints, and assured compliance with CAL/OSHA orders. With easy cases, the committee acted more like a management tool, and most problems were easy. According to Rees, as a result of their shared norms, customary practices, and common experience, labor and management share a broad area of agreement as to what constitutes a "safety problem." This high level of agreement on what is wrong and what needs to be done facilitates quick abatement. There is a strong consensual, problem-solving ethos at the meetings and little appeal to "outside" authorities, that is, OSHA rules.

Rees also observed some harder cases, in which there was disagreement. Even here, with one exception, there was no breakdown in cooperation. In these cases, OSHA rules, as authoritative normative standards, did come into play. In the one instance in which cooperation failed, the failure was due in part to a lack of confidence and communication on the part of the electricians, who had not been part of the process.

CAL/OSHA had the responsibility of monitoring the Cooperative Compliance Program, but the OSHA office in charge of monitoring—the Designative Compliance Officer (DCO)—had a different role than the traditional inspector. Here, he was welcomed as "an asset to the safety program." He combined two roles of cooperative or flexible regulation—a rule-enforcer and a problem-solving consultant. The issue is not *whether* to persuade or to punish, but *when*. As Rees, Hawkins, and others have pointed out, this combination is, in fact, the informal practice. Here, it was officially sanctioned.

In summarizing the study, Rees gives three reasons for the success of the cooperative model. The first has to do with the nature of the regulatory activity itself. As stated, these are legitimate, valued activities. The job is to protect the core activities while controlling the unwanted externalities. In addition, many regulatory violations are, in fact, morally ambiguous. This, too, leads towards cooperation and conciliation.

The second reason for the model's success is that because of adherence to basic norms, peer pressure, influence of customers and employees, a desire to retain a good public image, and so forth, most firms are generally disposed to obey the law. Therefore, regulators should be responsive to the legitimate needs and interests of the firm. This is especially so since regulations tend to be over- or underinclusive, and there is great variety in the field.

The third reason for the model's success is that, winning cooperation is a more effective method of carrying out a regulatory program.

Nevertheless, Rees is sensitive to the limitations of this model. Prior to the legalistic approach of the 1970s, worker-safety regulation was characterized by the cooperative model, and it was ineffective. Enforcement was lax; regulation was co-opted. Labor pressed for strict enforcement, going by the book. Rees's examples were limited to sites where there were strong unions, professional safety engineers, management committed to improving safety as a "management problem," and already good safety records.

In addition, there was the crucial role of the OSHA compliance officers (the DCOs). They had to have a new role, different from the traditional regulatory cops. Cooperative, flexible regulation would not work if the DCO was a strict enforcer or was unfamiliar with the construction industry. At the same time, the DCOs had to be willing to get tough if necessary. They had to be both consultants and enforcers. But, their responses were task driven, rather than production driven. They could perform their roles because the labor-management safety committee performed many of their other responsibilities—review of complaints, inspections, and abatement. Thus, the self-regulation program depends in large part on the effectiveness of the committee, especially in recognizing and abating hazards. This would free up the DCOs to act as consultants. They could concentrate on explaining the reasons for the rules and use the committee for education and training and consciousness raising. At the same time, because they are present and not strangers, and because of the trust, cooperation, and the information sharing, they can be responsive to the concerns of the stakeholders. At times, the safety engineers would seek out the DCOs for a second, professional opinion.

Granted that the cooperative style of responsive regulation was successful in these particular sites—that is, the sites experienced far lower accident rates than comparable sites—what is to prevent enforcement from becoming lax, as happened during the prior regulatory regime? Rees has three suggestions. The first is that construction sites are temporary; therefore, DCOs would rotate rather than build up stable relationships. The second is that DCOs would also be enforcement officers for the other, conventional parts of their job, and thus, would not lose that expertise. But the third, and most important reason, is the presence of a strong union. In other words, in Rees's examples, there were firms with strong commitments to safety, strong indigenous regulatory systems, a regulatory task environment that lent itself to consensual problem solving, and unionized workers that would directly benefit from a strong self-regulatory program. In Rees's view, the presence of strong unions was absolutely crucial; yet, this may be the weakest link in the chain.

There were other construction sites where enforcement of public rules was delegated to private firms. Here, too, regulation, developed as a communicative process between the agency, management, and the employees. Management became convinced that accidents were not just "accidents" but rather a failure of management processes. Employees became convinced that the safety committees would be responsive and that they did not have to file formal complaints with the agency. The agency inspectors, relieved of the constraints of producing enforcement "numbers," were able to act more as consultants and educators than as enforcers. In Rees's cases, there was some enforcement—to maintain credibility—but the agency's role as educator, consultant—a builder of understanding as to what the rules meant and their reasons—was crucial. Regulation became a problem-solving process, a facilitative enterprise rather than one ensuring accountability to rules.[4] Rule making and accountability were still present; but they were not central; rather, they were only a small proportion of the many ways of elaborating policy.[5]

COOPERATIVE REGULATION IN HUMAN SERVICES

If empowerment depends on both *awareness* and *exchange*, then it is easier to imagine empowerment in the business-regulatory context than with human service agencies. With human service agencies, the conditions of empowerment become much more problematic. There is usually an asymmetry of information. In many situations, the client is dealing with a professional, such as a physician, or therapist, or teacher; in other situations, the official or bureaucrat has information that is not normally available to clients—for example, knowledge of the rules about, and the availability of, alternatives. This lack of information alone would contribute to a loss of self-efficacy, even without the other problems that dependent people might have. In addition, moral typification serves to disempower dependent people. Then, there is the asymmetry of resources. Most of the time, the agencies are in a monopoly position, with most agencies having more clients than they can handle.[6]

Thus, in most relationships in human service agencies, it is not surprising that empowerment would be rare. From time to time, there is some bargaining, some exchange at the field level as clients try to manipulate

[4] Hawkins 1984.   [5] Rees 1988.   [6] Hasenfeld 1992a.

the system; and there are also situations in which workers are concerned about client's views. But generally speaking, relationships are characterized by formalism, hierarchy, and domination.

In prior research, I have investigated situations in which there has been empowerment, even with highly dependent clients; these included parents of handicapped children[7] and the frail elderly poor.[8]

Special Education

The first example comes from the public school system. It involves the special education program of the Madison (Wisconsin) School District. The Education for All Handicapped Children Act (Public Law 94–142 [1975], now known as the Individuals with Disabilities Education Act, or IDEA) gave all handicapped children the right to an "appropriate" public education but did not purport to define content. Specific, individual educational programs were to be decided by the relevant participants. School people would be the key decision makers, but the key institutional innovation was the required participation of the parents. Parents of handicapped children had to be notified and had to give written consent before a child could be selected for diagnosis, evaluated, and placed in a special education program. Evaluation had to be done by a multidisciplinary team; there was a conference in which the parent was entitled to be present. If the parent disagreed with any decision, he or she had a right to two administrative appeals (district and state) and judicial review. In sum, the law set the framework for discussion; it specified the relevant participants, but it left it to the concerned individuals to decide the concrete situation.

In some respects, Public Law 94–142 was an improvement over what had gone before. More money was spent on special education, more handicapped children were admitted to the public schools, and many more programs were instituted.[9] What is not clear is whether what is happening substantively in the classroom is that successful.[10] But, in any event, there seems little doubt that the procedures designed to give the parents a participatory role in decisions affecting their children do not work.

Although there was initial resistance on the part of school districts, special education turned out to be a good thing for schools. There were more resources; special education slots were available to relieve regular teachers of troublesome children. Substantively, decisions were made by one or two staff members. The most important information was aca-

---

[7] Handler 1986.   [8] Handler 1990b.
[9] Clune and Van Pelt 1984.   [10] Heller et al. 1982.

demic performance, the students' behavioral or social needs, and the availability of slots. Despite the intent of the law, IQ tests still figured prominently. Once a student was placed, there were strong incentives to leave her or him in that spot; most funding arrangements were based on reimbursement for slots that were filled, and changes would entail a great deal of additional paperwork.[11]

The procedures were also distorted by the bureaucracy. Most parents, especially in the lower socioeconomic classes, do not have the ability to participate. Not only do they have the psychological burdens of coping with a handicapped child, they lack the information and the resources to deal with the school bureaucracy.[12] Both participation in the meetings and the signing of the consent forms are usually formalities only. School districts decide the cases beforehand (called "organizing the data"); consent forms are often signed before the placement meetings; parents are usually presented with staff recommendations, followed by ritualistic certification. Parents are outnumbered; they are strangers confronting a group of people who have worked together and either explicitly or implicitly reached an understanding as to the outcome. The discussion is often in technical jargon, often with the subtle implication that the child or the parent or both are at fault. In large districts, committees spend an average of 2 1/2 minutes per decision. In short, none of the conditions for empowerment are present—most poor parents lack information, self-efficacy, or desirable resources. And the school officials are not interested in communication. This pattern varies by social class. The articulate, knowledgeable, middle- and upper-middle-class parents, pressing for expensive out-of-school placements for severely handicapped children, hold their own. They have a credible threat of litigation.[13]

The Madison (Wisconsin) School District operates differently. Prior to and without regard to the procedural requirements of Public Law 94–142, the district made three conceptual decisions that resulted in a vastly different client-agency relationship. The first was that parents were part of the *solution* to special education rather than the problem. In order for special education to succeed, to prepare children for life in the nonschool world as well as in school, parents had to get involved in the education of their handicapped children; the school could not do it alone. In other words, the parents had resources that the school needed and wanted. The second was a frank and genuine acknowledgment that for most of those labeled mildly retarded, the technology was uncertain; diagnosis and treatment had to be flexible and experimental. This move lowered the level of potential conflict. As long as the two parties genuinely believed in

---

[11] Handler 1986; Heller et al. 1982.
[12] Engel 1993; Heller et al. 1982.
[13] Handler 1986; Heller et al. 1982.

experimentation, one could comfortably concede to the views of the other, confident that the matter was still open for renegotiation.

But what about resources? How were parents *able* to participate, to become part of the solution? The parents had to understand and actively cooperate with the school program. To accomplish this, the district conceived of a *parent advocate*—a lay person who was experienced in the process (usually a parent of a handicapped child)—to help the new parent. In contrast to most cooperative arrangements—where conflict is viewed negatively—here, conflict was deliberately introduced to aid communication. It was not *adversarial* conflict, but *communicative* conflict. The parent advocates helped to build self-efficacy, as Keiffer reported in his study. The parent advocates asked questions in the meetings that the parents were afraid to ask or did not know how to ask. The school people did not want the parents to abdicate to experts. It was through conversation that consensus would emerge. The school people acknowledged the uncertainty of the technology, and they wanted the parents to feel comfortable with the decisions, which were experimental and flexible. Other things that were necessary to build parent self-efficacy were provided, such as parent groups, training sessions, and so forth. The parents needed to have access to their own experts who could participate in the conferences, and school people willing to listen to outside opinion. This was not only consciousness raising, but also provided practical information and reflexive activity.[14]

The Madison system differed from special education procedures in other districts; in the latter, the only changes were in procedure. Since the issue of power was not addressed, dependent people were not able to participate, and the bureaucracy was able to distort and ultimately nullify the legal procedural changes. Something more is required. In the Madison system, there was first, a change in professional norms. The professional task was redefined to include empowerment. This was empowerment not in a zero-sum sense, but empowerment designed to facilitate professional goals. Instead of teachers teaching (disabled) students, with parents in the background, it was teachers, students, and parents working together as a unit.

Second, the technology—in this case, special education—substantively lent itself to flexibility and participation. Participation was not primarily aimed at furthering goals imposed by the general society—for example, norms of procedural due process later imposed by Public Law 94–142. In fact, due process was more than satisfied, but school districts are interested in education, not legal procedures. The procedures of participation were adopted in Madison because they furthered technology and professional goals.

[14] Keiffer 1984.

The third factor was *exchange* of material resources. Under the Madison reconceptualization of the professional task, the parents had something of value to the teachers. In order to accomplish the task, the teachers had to get the understanding and cooperation of the parents; not just the cooperation—all school districts are legally required to get that. They had to get the *active* cooperation of the participants. To get active cooperation, there has to be understanding, there has to be persuasion, there has to be reciprocity. Parents are not able to actively participate unless there is perceived confidence and self-efficacy gained through concrete experience.

Community-Based Care

The second example of empowerment by invitation involves community-based care for the frail, elderly poor. This is an area involving the most intimate, sensitive, fragile relationships. The paradigmatic example is the adult daughter or elderly spouse, often not in the best of health themselves, taking care of the disabled patient. Along with caring activities, there is often great psychological, social, and financial stress.[15] If this informal system breaks down—caretakers can no longer do the work or are not available—then the frail, elderly person will rapidly deteriorate and will have to enter a nursing home. This is not only far more expensive, but, for most people, usually deleterious to their physical and mental health.

Public programs have been developed to help to sustain informal caregiving—either by supporting existing caregivers or by supplying caregivers. The administrative challenges are daunting. The client population is hard to reach; the frail, alone elderly are notorious for their often self-defeating independence; and when reached, they are passive or gratefully accepting rather than complainers or rights-bearing citizens. They are easily frightened and manipulated by aggressive and unscrupulous vendors. In addition, the quality of the product that is delivered is difficult to observe and measure. Distribution, for most services, is in the home by vendors under state contract. How helpful and kind was the home help aide? How long did the physical therapist, in fact, stay, and what kind and how good was the therapy that was given? Is the transportation service patient and supportive, or indifferent, rushed, and abrupt? The style and attitudes of the services are important if they are not to make matters worse by contributing to anxieties, depression, and other forms of disability.

In nursing homes, the state regulatory agencies have to generate all the relevant information, and, as a result, regulation has become oppressive,

15 E. Abel 1987.

clumsy, ineffective, and distorting. Given the nature of the services and the characteristics of the clients, accountability is a serious concern, but how can there be effective accountability in community-based care without intrusive, distorting regulation?

I examined several voluntary and for-profit agencies that are operating community care programs for the frail, elderly poor in the Los Angeles area.[16] First I will discuss the voluntary agencies, and then the for-profits.[17]

There are a variety of programs within each voluntary agency, but basically, what the agencies do is recruit clients, provide case management, and contract services from other agencies according to the needs of each individual client. Quite often case management consists of working with the informal caregivers and supplementing their services. Most help is for the routine, mundane tasks—"assistance in daily living"—such as cleaning, nutrition, bathing, toileting, and transportation. The service most often contracted for is home help, which, in addition to performing specific chores, also provides crucial respite for the informal caregivers. Other services are therapy, adult day care, and health care.

While there are many interesting aspects to this program, what I want to emphasize here is how the active participation of the clients came about. What I found is that in order for the agencies to establish and maintain an effective care system, they had to enlist the clients, and, if available, their informal caregivers. As with the Madison school district, there was a redefinition of the professional task; a suitable technology; and an important exchange.

In part, client cooperation was dictated by the funding source. At the time of the study, Medicaid allowed an agency to spend no more, on average, than 95 percent of what it would cost to have the client in a Medicaid nursing home. It turns out that the agency could not meet the cost constraint without the active participation of the client and the informal caregivers. In other words, the informal caregivers have to share the work. In order to get that active participation, the family must understand and agree with the agency plan. They must work together. For example, if a home aide is needed, the agency must work with the client and/or the family member and train them how to interview, select, monitor, and if necessary, discharge a county-supplied home help aide. If the agency has to do all of this itself, it becomes too expensive administratively. If it is not done, it is difficult to obtain good home help. The agency also has to have

[16] Handler 1990b.

[17] Three voluntary and five for-profit agencies were selected. The agencies were purposely selected on the basis of community reputation for administering exemplary programs. They are *not* representative. My purpose is to see whether client empowerment could occur under real-life situations.

similar cooperative relationships in the other community-based programs, such as those involving transportation, adult day care, recreation, health care, and so forth.

Not only do clients share the work, they also become an important source of information. More information is generated (there is, in effect, continual on-site inspection) and it is of a different quality. There are now personal reports of quality of care rather than those made by an inspector relying on records and interviews. Compare a familiar example—a cooperative day-care arrangement in which parents share teaching responsibilities with the staff. The participating parents have personal quality assurance information.

Clients, then, had something of value for the agencies—they performed part of the work and they were a source of information. Client participation also fit changing professional norms concerning the care of the elderly. The agency and the staff believed that if the frail, alone elderly could take more control over their lives, then in terms of geriatric health and well-being, they would be better off. The technology was suited to sharing. In most of the services, the quality of the face-to-face interactions is crucial. The clients had to have confidence in themselves *and* the agency if they were to do their share competently and be a reliable source of information. Clients had to be confident that honest information would be honestly received and acted upon. This greatly lessened the regulatory monitoring burdens on the agencies. Thus, the clients had a valuable resource that the agency needed especially since the agencies could not do all of the work and stay within the financial cap.[18]

Would the incentives be different in for-profit agencies? If the program has the same professional ideologies as the voluntary agencies, and has a similar structure, then the client-agency relationship should be approximately the same. If the program pays per unit of service, then providers would stay as long as possible, do as much as possible, and the clients would remain passive. If the program is tightly limited per unit of service (e.g., Medicare home help), then the clients will be involved, but in a passive, instrumental manner rather than in joint decision making. In other words, as discussed in chapter 4 on privatization, it is not the form of ownership that matters as much the structure of the program.[19]

For-profit agencies are reimbursed either through Medicare or by the client (out-of-pocket or insurance). At the time of the study, Medicare covered short-term, intermittent care in the home—nursing, physical

[18] Two of the agencies had a fourth structural variable. One agency was strongly rooted in the community; there were extensive personal relationships between staff, volunteers, and clients. The other agency structured community participation in many parts of governance including the important grievance committee.

[19] Donahue 1989.

therapy, occupational therapy, speech therapy, and home health aides. It did not cover homemakers. The home health aide was limited to hourly visits and could only be in the home if there was a representative of another primary discipline providing services (e.g., nursing, physical therapy). Medicare services are highly regulated and strictly limited to only what is necessary to take care of the medical problem. Private pay agencies offer whatever range is contracted for. In the agencies studied, the range went from homemaker to live-ins (some have stayed as long as five years). Some programs include case management.

In all, five agencies were researched. One of the agencies, part of a national chain, which administered a privately financed program, took an "hours and sales" approach; lengthy care was viewed as a benefit to the agency; client education and independence were not encouraged. The client was the "patient"; in contrast, the "customer"—the one who paid the bill—played a larger role in decision making. But this agency was at one end of the spectrum.

All of the other agencies adopted and practiced, in varying degrees, what they called "client empowerment strategies." They permitted clients to take part in the decision-making process and valued client independence. Family involvement was encouraged. All of the agencies, whether paid privately or through Medicare, developed care plans. In most of the agencies, there was some form of case management; in three, staff advocated on behalf of clients with insurance companies. The staff coordinator or case manager monitored the service providers.

In Medicare, strict rules, in effect, preclude much sharing. On the other hand, Medicare does encourage client education. With the exception of the one private pay agency, all of the agencies encouraged family involvement; in part because of the strict program limits, the client and the family had to assist with the care. In the private pay programs, there was more direct client supervision of the providers. With the one exception, all of the agencies stressed the importance of trust and empowerment. They all stressed independence, shared decision making, and dignity as important in their own right and for therapeutic reasons. One example involved a client homebound because of incontinence. Home health services can provide an aide to put in a catheter three times a week. The agency preferred to train the client (or the family) to do this in order to maintain their independence. Other education programs included diet and medication. This was the general pattern, although commitment to empowerment, strategies, and results varied among staff and clients.

One of the for-profit agencies, a hospital, uses multidisciplinary case management and a range of home help services, along with an extensive package of health care and social services. In addition to social workers, the teams include geriontologically trained internists and psychiatrists. The process in the hospital's geriatric program is quite similar to that of the voluntary agencies—multidisciplinary, holistic assessments; joint participation in the development and administration of care plan; extensive reliance on client information, supervision, and complaints. Family involvement is emphasized. The dominating professional norm is "functional independence" rather than the "invalid role," despite the fact that this program is run out of a hospital.

In this for-profit hospital, professional norms have been changed from the medical model; geriatrically trained physicians, using a therapeutic perspective, favor a holistic, empowering approach. The technology encourages client (and family) involvement including the all-important information and monitoring functions. There are also strong economic reasons for the success of this program. It operates at a loss but is supported by the hospital as a method of recruiting geriatric patients. As with all of the programs that are discussed, there is complementarity between professional norms, technology, and economics.

In these two examples, there were good intentions (professional norms) and a compatible technology, that is, the nature of the professional task was consistent with flexibility, negotiation, and sharing. Professionals and clients had something to say to each other. Sometimes this is enough for client empowerment. More often than not, however, when clients are dependent, the conversation becomes distorted. Professionals and staff are usually short of time and resources, working conditions are less than ideal, and there are pressures to get through the day. In these circumstances, the staff begins to listen less, and participation begins to become ritualistic. Social workers frequently complain about the difficulty of maintaining empowerment relationships in the bureaucratic setting. In the Madison school district, the teachers struggle to maintain the active involvement of the parents as well as their own willingness to genuinely listen.

In the two examples, both the parents and the frail, elderly clients performed valuable services for the agencies. By sharing the work and providing information, they considerably eased the professional task. There was an exchange. I have been emphasizing the material base of the exchange, but the exchange was more than instrumental. Empowerment is a moral position. It is a matter of equal moral agency, which we find in these two examples. The parent or the frail, elderly client has to assume large responsibilities in order for there to be success; *passive* acceptance of the professional's orders is not satisfactory. The parent and the client have to have confidence in the professional competence and the good will of the teacher and the case manager; they have to believe that the professionals have the parent's and the client's best interests at heart. The professional is relying on the intelligence and judgment of the parent and the client to absorb the information, to use it properly, and to make intelligent decisions.

When dependent people are performing these roles, there is a change in one's sense of self-efficacy. This is because the change in the social practices of the parent and the client necessarily implies a change in ideologies. The change in power, the ability of the parent and the client to take control of their lives, means that there has been a change in their views about themselves and their relationships with the professionals. Ideology is not separate from action, but is integral to social practices. Ideology defines experiences and social relationships; it constructs reality.[20] As shown in the psychological research on empowerment, changes in self-consciousness are rooted in specific, lived experiences.[21]

But how much empowerment? One must be cautious. These findings are based on stories told by staff and some clients and their families. The clients are sick, old, weak, alone, and poor; they are very dependent. And the case managers and other staff are middle-class professionals employed by powerful agencies. The clients are "success" cases in that they are in the program and have good relations with the staff; they minimize (if not forget) past problems and focus on the present. The staff is attuned to the current professional rhetoric. Thus, we might wonder how much of what is told is ideological construction. How much change has occurred?

Consider the contrast between the clients in the voluntary agencies and the Medicare clients in the for-profit agencies. The former were involved in the full range of decisions from the very beginning. The latter were excluded from most of the important decisions. The doctors diagnosed, treated, and prescribed for the medical problem. The home health aide, under the close supervision of the health care professionals, *instructed* the client (patient) on how to administer the health care during the tightly controlled time that the home service was provided. We would be tempted to say that there was much more empowerment with the voluntary agency client; the Medicare patient, after all, was only instrumentally trained to perform a mechanical task. But do we know this? It may be that for a frail, elderly person to self-administer an injection is an enormously empowering act. In view of the subtleties of the manifestations of power, we need similar kinds of conceptualizations and operational definitions of empowerment. In these selected case studies, we seem to see empowering activities, but there are serious theoretical and empirical pitfalls.

[20] Merry 1986.
[21] Keiffer 1984; Zimmerman and Rappaport 1988.

Nursing Homes

The more one moves away from a major business firm toward groups and organizations consisting of dependent people—such as workers, clients, and patients—the more problematic participation becomes, whether structured or not. As Rees stated, one of the crucial factors for the success of the safety committees was a strong union. Of course, this type of collective strength is absent with most subordinated groups. Nevertheless, there are some prominent examples even among the most subordinate of groups—nursing home residents—although it must be conceded at the outset that these examples are quite rare.

It is difficult to imagine a population less likely to be empowered than nursing home residents. While there is great variation among them—they range from so disabled that they cannot perform the routine functions of daily living—such as eating, toileting, bathing, dressing, shopping—to the gravely ill; they are highly dependent, both physically and often mentally. Even though most nursing home residents need only custodial care, and some medical attention, nursing homes are built on the medical model. They are characterized by formalism and rules. The medical personnel, administrators, and staff dictate every aspect of daily life. The views of the resident are neither solicited or desired. Residents are directed when to wake and when to sleep, meals are offered only at specific times, baths are available only when scheduled by the staff, and there is no involvement in the selection of a roommate. Regulations usually prohibit residents from going outside without supervision, or arranging their furniture in a manner that may be deemed a safety hazard. The lives of nursing home residents are in large part regimented, routinized, and controlled by their care plan. Even though resident well-being requires an environment that addresses psychological and social needs as well as physical ailments, current "medical approaches cast patients in a sick role, one of dependence and withdrawal from ordinary activities."[22] There is general agreement that most of these restrictions are for the convenience of the staff and the institution.[23]

[22] Johnson and Grant 1985, 147.

[23] Wetle 1991, 286. Johnson and Grant (1985), also cite studies that demonstrate that nursing home professionals, bound by the assumption of the medical model, frequently prescribe medical remedies for problems that are nonmedical in nature. One study found that 90 percent of diagnoses were medical when only 38 percent of problems were such; although 23 percent of problems were psychological, only 7 percent were properly diagnosed; and there were no diagnoses for social problems, even though 23 percent of the residents cited inadequate housing as the main reason for their placement. This study is an acute example of typification. The problems of the elderly are summarily categorized to fit the available treatment scheme, and the critical information about psychological and social needs is simply ignored. Because modern medical practice treats the pathologies of more

Moreover, this enclosed, regimented environment does not produce a sense of community either among the residents or between the residents and the staff. Studies have shown that the residents share few bonds or any sense of community. Although a residential setting, the nursing home is primarily a bureaucratic entity. The small supervisory staff spends a great deal of time ensuring compliance with the institutional regulations, and communication with the residents is often restricted. Consequently, the relationships between the residents and staff are distant, and each views the other in terms of stereotypes.

Not surprisingly, passivity and inactivity are common among residents. There is nothing to do, so skills decline. Passive behavior can take the form of complaining, withdrawing, and sitting and watching. Complaining, though giving the resident a sense of assertiveness, is discouraged because it is a nuisance to the staff. Withdrawal is encouraged, at times fostered by the use of tranquilizing drugs. The overall aim of the institution is to create the "good" patient, one who is compliant, passive, and deferential.

There are situations, however, in which the relationship between the nursing home resident and his or her setting is changed. In some situations, families have been able to perform an empowering role. However, it must be stated at the outset, that the relationship of the family to the nursing home, in most situations, is also very problematic. It is not because the families do not care. Quite the opposite. Contrary to popular belief, the elderly, even those who are in nursing homes, have not been abandoned by their families. Families provide the primary source of assistance to the elderly.[24] Often families have postponed placement as long as possible and the placement decision is accompanied by guilt and sorrow. Nursing home beds are scarce, so the family is often grateful as well as relieved; they believe that the nursing home is in the powerful position—if the family does not like the service, they can go elsewhere, but, of course, there often is nowhere else to go.

When the aged person enters the nursing home, families often try to continue in the patterns of involvement that existed prior to placement.[25] From the vantage point of the nursing home resident, there is no question that family involvement enhances both the quality of care and the quality of life. In one study, interviewers were able to determine whether the resident had a family simply by entering a room.[26] Family involvement,

---

common physical illnesses and disease in a uniform and systematic manner, care becomes impersonal, standardized, and routine (Hasenfeld 1992a).

[24] Brody and Brody 1989.

[25] Montgomery 1983; Smith and Bengston 1979; York and Calsyn 1977.

[26] Dobrof 1989.

when successful, also benefits the staff. Simply increasing the number of people available for care is a benefit. Family members can help explain and negotiate changes. They can reduce the sense of isolation on the part of the staff and improve their self-image.[27] These findings have caused many researchers to recommend a model of institutional care of the elderly consisting of shared functions, with the staff performing the more technical and large-scale functions and the family assuming more responsibility for the routine activities of daily living.[28]

Unfortunately, implementation of a collaborative model is made difficult by several organizational and attitudinal barriers between staff and family. The prevalent attitude among the staff is that after placement, the institution takes over, and the family is not involved. The institution is concerned with efficiency and control, and outsider involvement, even by family members, is viewed as interference. The exclusion of the family is not only for staff convenience; it is also part of professional ideology.[29] While families might be frustrated and angered by the care the nursing home provides for their relative, the response, either anticipated or received, will be: "If you're dissatisfied, take your mother home." The family either retreats or retaliates in anger by contacting outside oversight agencies.[30]

Despite the odds, a number of programs have been successful in forging a partnership between the family and staff. A study compared three nursing homes that were operated by a nonprofit management corporation. Home C had the highest staff-family integration as measured by the frequency of family activities and shared functions. This home also ranked highest in family orientation. The staff was regularly informed about resident-family relationships and provided as well as participated in communication training sessions. Family visitation was welcomed and encouraged. Staff members were readily available to family members. Overall, there were more opportunities for family participation and, as a consequence, families visited more frequently, participated in more events, and assisted in a greater number of tasks. Because Home C regarded the family as a "client," care was taken to communicate and efforts were made to meet the family's needs.[31]

In contrast, Home A tended to view the residents as isolated individu-

[27] Dobrof 1989.

[28] Brody 1974; Edelson and Lyons 1985; Johnson and Grant 1985; Litwak and Dobrof 1977; May, Kaminskas, Kasten, and Levine 1991.

[29] Textbooks written for nursing home professionals often lack any reference to the family. Safford (1989) surveyed more than forty textbooks on nursing home management and nursing home care in search of references to the family.

[30] Safford 1989.

[31] Montgomery 1983.

als. Staff members made no effort to involve families but rather treated them as "visitors" and "outsiders." Any family contact was due to the initiative of the family. Although Home B did acknowledge the value of families as useful resources, it did not view them as important clients. Family members were expected to visit and help with technical tasks, and little understanding was shown towards the "irresponsible" family members who neglected their duty. No effort was made to communicate with, educate, or support the family. In both homes, family visitation, participation, and assistance was less frequent. The families in Home B did not visit or provide technical services as often as did those in Home C. In essence, the facility used the family as merely a source of labor.[32] Other researchers have also documented successful family involvement, with positive results for the residents as well as the staff.[33]

Family participation in nursing home care is another example of how empowerment leaves both sides better off. The nursing home administration and staff benefits when residents enjoy a better quality of life. The family provides a link to the community and, potentially, a group of satisfied customers who can create an enhanced, more respectable, public image. And with limited resources and demanding work loads, the family is a welcome source of labor.

Nevertheless, despite these successes, family involvement is the exception. Given the stress, anxiety, and guilt the family experiences upon placement, the absence of programs that foster family orientation, and the institution's standard, depersonalized administration of care, the potential for conflict between staff and family is great. Change cannot come about in these institutions without a change in professional norms and extensive staff development.[34] Successful integration requires that the administrator frame the institution's goals, polices, and strategies in a manner that perceives the family as part of the solution rather than as the source of an irritating and disruptive intrusion. At the same time, the needs of the staff have to be carefully considered.

Sometimes families form more formal organizations to deal with nursing homes. Friends and Relatives of the Institutionalized Aged (FRIA) was founded in 1976 in New York City and at one time, had 2500 total members with 1200 active members. About 10 percent of these regularly visited nursing homes and reported on the conditions.[35] FRIA was concerned with redressing individual complaints, as well as with lobbying for broader change through new legislation. FRIA had a three-tiered approach to dealing with individual complaints. First, FRIA would meet with a complaining resident to discuss a concern and if necessary refer the

[32] Montgomery 1983.   [33] Bowers 1988.
[34] For example see Wells and Singer 1988.   [35] Doty and Sullivan 1983.

complaint to the appropriate regulatory agency or a legal services organization. Second, if possible, FRIA would conduct its own investigation and negotiate with nursing home administrators to resolve the situation. Finally, in the most egregious situations, FRIA would form a chapter to focus attention on a particular nursing home and work for changes in management or ownership. FRIA was most successful when it could rely on persuasion, threats of bad publicity, or its connections with other community resources to achieve its goals. While FRIA itself lacked formal sanctioning powers, the familial connections of its members made it more effective than advocates such as ombudsmen, who are strangers and who rarely visit the same facility often enough to develop relationships with residents and staff.[36]

Kathleen Kautzer[37] describes yet another variation on empowerment structures—Living Is For the Elderly (LIFE). This is a Boston-based advocacy organization composed of both activists and nursing home residents. Great effort is made to involve the residents—even residents who are quite disabled—in organizational activities, including meetings, professional monitoring, and political lobbying. Participating residents attain feelings of self-efficacy and overcome the isolation between residents so often noted in nursing homes. They develop both a personal and a community spirit. Yet, even with a well-functioning chapter, a great deal still depends on the attitude of the local administrator and the staff. The organization depends on the staff for important details—notices of meetings, help in the crucial area of transportation, and a supportive attitude. In some homes, where cooperation is worked out, the administration and the staff see benefits in improved morale and well-being, in better channels of communication, and in these homes, staff volunteer their services to help LIFE. Nevertheless, empowerment on the part of residents always remains problematic. The staff and the home still hold the upper hand. Kautzer thought that in some of the LIFE meetings that she observed, the residents' roles were largely symbolic and the LIFE staff really controlled the agenda; on the other hand, the residents were quite disabled. And, of course, in the political arena, victories for the poor elderly are bound to be incremental.[38]

Another formal organization is the Residents' Council elected by the residents. When Residents Councils work, they became an important source of information when inspectors come to the homes. A representa-

[36] Doty and Sullivan 1983.

[37] Kautzer 1988.

[38] Kautzer 1988. Hubbard, Werner, Cohen-Mansfield, and Shusterman (1992) report on a group of nursing home residents, coordinated by the recreational therapist, who organized, discussed social issues, and became involved in local social and political issues, such as recycling, a food drive for the homeless, a petition for abortion rights, etc.

tive of the council attends the exit conference, participates in the negotiations regarding compliance plans, and publicizes the inspection report to the residents and their families. The councils have the same standing to seek enforcement as the inspectors and have state support and funding.[39]

There have also been programs in which nursing home residents have been trained as peer counselors to help new residents. Senior companion programs used in a variety of settings in addition to nursing homes, provide information, advice, and advocacy in dealing with other agencies.[40]

Efforts have also been made to increase the autonomy of nursing home residents through the ombudsman programs. In 1978, amendments to the Older Americans Act mandated that every state establish and operate a program to (1) investigate and resolve resident complaints; (2) monitor laws, regulations and policies; (3) promote citizen involvement and provide volunteer training; and (4) inform public agencies of problems in nursing home care.[41] States vary in implementing the statute. Some operate the programs directly; others use local governments; and others contract to nonprofits.[42] A recent AARP study reports that typically a state program has an average of three paid full-time staff members, two part-time staff members, and thirty-two active part-time volunteers. Most states mandate some formal training at least for paid staff. Most states require by law that the programs have unlimited access to facilities, and only 10 percent of programs report moderate or extreme difficulty in gaining access. The great majority of local ombudsmen consider complaint resolution and presence in the nursing homes their most important activities. Staff members identified resident care as the most common type of complaint. The majority of complaints were initiated by the residents, families, or friends. Only a small percentage (15 percent) were initiated directly by the ombudsman program itself.

In general, the presence of an ombudsman program enhances the quality of life and the care of nursing home residents. Apparently the mere presence of concerned outsiders increases the staff's sense of importance and motivation. In addition, attention to the needs of the residents enhances their status in the eyes of the staff, which results in greater respect and better care. Presence also brings home to the staff and the administrators the fact of their accountability.[43] However, identifying where ombudsmen are most effective depends on whether one thinks ombudsmen should be concentrating on mediation, advocacy of individual grievances,

[39] Ayres and Braithwaite 1992, 99.
[40] Scharlach 1988.
[41] Select Committee on Aging 1991.
[42] Doty and Sullivan 1983.
[43] Cherry 1991.

or public advocacy. Nevertheless, there does seem to be agreement that the ombudsmen are most effective in protecting patients' rights and establishing complaint mechanisms. The real problem for the programs, however, is the reluctance of residents to express their grievances. One study found that 68 percent of the ombudsmen in New York City believed that the patients "often" feared retaliation. Over half of nursing home residents surveyed had at some point chosen not to express a grievance because of a fear of reprisal.[44]

An example of understaffing is the program in Los Angeles County. The county is divided into six subareas, each with a coordinator who recruits and trains volunteers. The volunteers are committed to work eighteen to twenty hours per month in the facilities. Nursing homes are supposed to be visited weekly, and board and care facilities monthly. The volunteers have reporting power only. Visits are always unannounced and the ombudsmen have total freedom to inspect food and laundry facilities, and to talk to the residents. The Los Angeles city program has a paid staff of only four ombudsmen, all of whom are part-time. Two are responsible for the Los Angeles metropolitan area and two for the entire San Fernando Valley. The program also has twenty-two volunteers. With this staff, the program is responsible for over five hundred facilities. According to the coordinator, they would need about ninety volunteers to adequately monitor all these facilities. In addition to the lack of funding, there is also a shortage of volunteers. Mostly older people volunteer, and there is an attrition rate due to burnout. Because of the understaffing, it is often necessary to dedicate virtually all the ombudsmen resources to the investigation of specific complaints. This, of course, reduces their presence in other facilities. Facilities are required to post notices and provide the 800 phone number for the ombudsman and, at times, residents themselves will act as internal ombudsmen and call the office in the presence of residents who have grievances.

In evaluating the efforts to empower nursing home residents, it must be remembered that these people are the most dependent of all such populations—even prisoners can riot. Empowerment with dependent people will always be problematic. In the final analysis, it depends crucially on whether the professionals or power holders believe that empowerment is a good thing *and* whether the dependent client (resident) has tangible resources of value to the professionals. In the LIFE examples, the administrators and the staff thought that morale and well-being were enhanced and that better communication resulted from empowerment. In other words, their tasks were made easier as a result of the empowerment.

[44] Monk, Kaye, and Litwin 1984.

PUBLIC HOUSING TENANTS

Ordinary citizens are also considered to be relatively powerless when they are in bureaucratic settings. This conclusion is usually based on observation of the citizen participation in the War on Poverty's Community Action Agencies ("maximum feasible participation"), the 1966 Model Cities Act which provided for "widespread" citizen participation, and other programs that followed this pattern.[45] It is commonly assumed that these citizen boards are largely ineffective. The citizens are either token representatives or are simply overwhelmed by the professionals and the experts. This assumption is not necessarily correct. James Morone investigated mandated citizen participation in health planning. This is an area where one would most likely expect co-optation; there is a lot at stake, it is highly professionalized, and subject to domination by experts. Nevertheless, Morone found that in many instances, the citizen groups were effective. While they often did not ultimately prevail, Morone argues that by their active, informed, and insistent presence in these health planning agencies around the country, they did help change the politics of health care. Specifically, it was their willingness to challenge that started the eventual undermining of the medical profession's dominance in the health policy field.[46]

In this section, we consider another example—tenants assuming control over public housing. Tenant organizations are usually thought of in terms of adversarial collective action against both private and public landlords—rent strikes, demonstrations, squatters, electoral politics, and so forth.[47] Here, we consider examples in which tenant organizations, although born in conflict, took control, even ownership, of their buildings in cooperation with public authorities. In some cities, principally, St. Louis, tenant organizations became not only owners, but producers and suppliers of rehabilitated housing and management services.[48]

Starting in the late 1960s and extending through the early 1980s, New York City landlords abandoned rental property.[49] As a result of tax foreclosures, by 1984, the city had become the largest slum landlord, with over twenty-six thousand residential units, accounting for at least one hundred thousand residents. During this period, as a reaction first to private landlord neglect and abandonment and then to the city's inability to manage the properties, tenants in some buildings began to fight back. They organized, made demands, conducted rent strikes, and sued. As the city took over more and more buildings, it responded to both the demands of the tenants and the increasing burdens of property management

[45] Kweit and Kweit 1981.
[46] Morone 1990.
[47] Heskin 1991.
[48] Kolodny 1986.
[49] This section is based on Leavitt and Saegert 1990.

by developing a unique program of tenant management and ownership. Through its Housing Preservation and Development Agency (HPD)'s Division of Alternative Management Programs, tenants' associations, community groups, and landlords were offered the opportunity to manage or eventually buy city-owned property.

Jacquiline Leavitt and Susan Saegert[50] studied three groups of tenants' association: tenant cooperatives that eventually succeeded to ownership; tenant cooperatives that were struggling; and renters that did not succeed. In the first group, the six co-ops that were successful, the tenants' association began with rent strikes in the 1960s. When the buildings were abandoned by the landlords, the tenants joined together to save their homes. They collected the rents, managed the buildings, made repairs, paid the superintendent, and bought the heating oil. During this period, the tenants acquired the skills to run the building. They not only made improvements, but also set up community activities, such as day care, club rooms, painting and decorating clubs, and various committees, such as sickness, fund-raising, and housing, to deal with rent arrears and tenant screening. In 1974, the tenants began working with the Urban Homesteading Assistance Board (UHAB) to gain control of the buildings. As the tenants gained more control, they filled vacancies with people who were active and had skills.

The path was not always smooth. In some of the co-ops, there was conflict during the transitions. Some of the tenants refused to pay the increased costs of the transition; others were asked to leave. The organizations experienced periods of apathy. In some of the co-ops, conflict continued even after ownership. But the distinguishing characteristic of the successful co-op groups was the ability to work together. In part, this was built on a long-standing, stable tenancy that preceded the neglect and abandonment. There was both a memory of, and an attachment to, place. Significantly, although several of the tenants were on welfare, most of the tenants in the successful co-ops were either employed or retired, which reduced the potentially vexing problem of rent arrears. Almost all of the tenants believed that they were better off—both materially and socially— living in the co-op than in a rental building. There was a strong sense of belonging, of solidarity.

But of major importance was leadership and the outside technical assistance and the connection between the two. The differences in leadership between the three sets of buildings—the co-ops that succeeded, the co-ops that were struggling, and the ones that failed—according to Leavitt and Saegert, resulted partly from luck and partly from pure grit. The three sets of buildings varied in terms of problems—locations, tenants,

[50] Leavitt and Saegert 1990.

and the leaders themselves. The buildings that were less successful had tenants who experienced more unemployment, more ill health, and more disability. The buildings were in poorer condition; the neighborhoods were worse. In the buildings where the co-ops failed, there was drug dealing, other criminal activities, vandalism, and many vacancies. Leaders also varied in terms of resources and abilities. Many were heroic, but overwhelmed by either their own personal troubles or the conditions they faced.

The authors conclude that the clearest difference between the three sets of buildings was access to technical assistance. Although the buildings began to decline in the 1930s, the acceleration coincided with the rise of social activism, particularly the War on Poverty (the 1960s), as well as other programs such as Model Cities and Community Development Corporations (CDCs). While these programs were never sufficient to stem the spread of poverty and the decline in housing, many of the tenants (in the successful co-ops) participated; they gained not only benefits (child care, job training, employment) but also organizational and leadership skills. In the mid- and late-1970s, economic conditions worsened in New York. Industries continued to relocate; wages declined and unemployment rose; abandonment of buildings by landlords became even more severe; the demand for services increased but the tax base continued to erode. In an effort to induce landlords to make repairs, the city reduced the time before tax foreclosures from three years to one year. That change only accelerated city ownership.

The beginning of tenant organization in the successful co-ops was the rent strikes. The strikes became legitimated through the 7A program, which authorized the courts to appoint a receiver as a managing agent. In one instance, a judge actually advised the tenants to start a rent strike as a way of initiating the appointment of a receiver. Tenants were often assisted in these efforts by representatives of UHAB as well as other community groups, including churches. UHAB and the these groups not infrequently, became involved in settling tenant conflicts. Organizations provided a range of assistance—information, advice as to strategies, lobbying, negotiating with the bureaucracy, access to lawyers and bankers. UHAB offered required courses for tenants.

Formally structured assistance came through New York City's local community boards. These advisory boards, which came into existence at the time of the first foreclosure law (1977), provided a forum for grassroots organizations. It was the Manhattan Community Board 9 (covering the authors' sites) that led the successful campaign to halt the public sale of foreclosed buildings. Tenants seeking to buy buildings would attempt to gain board approval. The boards varied in terms of the skills of the staff and members. Some boards had difficulty in responding, but others were active in helping organize and steering the group through the 7A management and interim lease programs. Legal Aid lawyers, churches, and politicians were also crucial, from the earliest days of fighting landlords through those of helping with the public programs. From time to time, judges and housing commissioners would advise tenants.[51]

A major impetus for public assistance programs were the increasing burdens of city ownership. City-owned buildings fell into further disrepair; there were horror stories—of shoddy work, irresponsible contractors, and of people freezing to death. Community organizations began to tell the city that they could manage the buildings better and then purchase the buildings when they became available. At first there were direct "as is" sales, followed by the Tenant Interim Lease Program. The public programs not only provided crucial resources, they also strengthened the tenant organizations. In describing the troubles that one tenant association had, the authors say:

> Unlike the more successful co-ops, the tenants' association made little impact on events in the building until they were able to become part of 7A and the tenant-initiated program. The structure of these programs solidified the leaders' position within a shifting tenant population characterized most often by apathy and sometimes destructive behavior directed against the building. If the leaders had not been vested with real control over resources, these factors might easily have overwhelmed the organization and led to its decline.[52]

The authors emphasize just how important technical assistance was in light of the severe poverty and racism:

> Without the existence of city programs oriented to tenants' groups, as well as the help of community boards, churches, and a much smaller but more experienced cadre of community activist groups, the isolation of low-income minority citizens from access to power and resources would very likely have led to their failure. When tenant leaders were asked what they thought would have happened to them without the city's programs, they often could not imagine.[53]

There were a number of ways in which the city programs changed the dynamics. First, the tenants became proactive rather than only reactive. Even the rent strikes were holding actions; the tenants could not define their future. When they ran the buildings, the future was clouded by legal uncertainty. Tenants still had virtually no rights even when the city be-

[51] Leavitt and Saegert 1990, 116–18.
[52] Leavitt and Saegert 1990, 121.
[53] Leavitt and Saegert 1990, 122.

came the landlord. All of this changed with the Tenant Interim Lease Program. Now the tenants could achieve control and even move toward ownership. According to the authors, this program changed the tenants' mind set—now they began to think of the future in comprehensive terms—for example, of renovation instead of emergency repairs and fuel costs. It didn't always happen this way. Sometimes, many tenants preferred not to pay rent at all, and they refused to participate. The tenant groups that struggled or did not succeed often lacked sufficient information about programs or had less support from resource organizations.

The authors emphasize the importance of *both* the tenant groups and the resources. People had to work together—in households, friendships, neighborhoods, blocks, and communities. There had to be locally based leadership and trust. But they could not do it on their own; the odds against them were simply too strong. On the other hand, the outside organizations and the city could not have pulled this off from the top down. In the authors' terms, the bureaucracy had to see the tenants as "agents" rather than as "clients." There had to be "*service-engagement*" rather than "*service delivery.*"[54]

> The distinction between support and bureaucratically provided services is critical. The first builds on the strengths of small social units and relates them to the larger community. The latter takes away the resources of the lower levels of organization and centralizes them in hard-to-affect, distant, and impersonal agencies. . . . Empowerment as a real goal, not the trappings or the rhetoric, . . . has to be central.[55]

In concluding their study, the authors point to other examples in which similar kinds of tenant collective action were successful. They stress the importance of technical assistance—legal aid, local antipoverty agencies, foundations, HUD's Tenant Management Corporations—but especially the technical training of tenants through various cooperative movements. Empowerment needs material and human capital resources.

Leavitt and Saegert are primarily concerned with how community groups become empowered. For our purposes, a crucial ingredient is the role of the city in their story. The city had to get out of the slumlord business. Given the political and economic circumstances of the times, one of the ways that the city could manage its problem was to enlist the tenants in a cooperative relationship. The tenants were brought in not only to benefit the tenants but also to benefit the city—first to manage the buildings, and then, it was hoped, to take ownership. But in order to accomplish this—to achieve the goals of the bureaucracy—the tenants had to be

[54] Leavitt and Saegert 1990, 190.
[55] Leavitt and Saegert 1990, 125.

empowered. They had to have the technical skills and material resources, as well as the desire, to take control over their lives.

There have been other successful public housing tenant management experiences. One of the most prominent is Kenilworth-Parkside, in Washington, DC.[56] The story is similar to what happened in New York. Strong leadership was combined with public support—in this case HUD grants plus technical assistance—with the additional strong incentive to government of being relieved of vexing, politically explosive problems. Kenilworth-Parkside had all of the ills of inner-city public housing. The tenants' offer to take over was eagerly accepted by both the city and the private management company. The tenants formed their own resident management corporation under HUD auspices, and with the help of HUD grants, began making repairs and collecting rents. But they did more. As their confidence developed, the tenants organized day care (restricted to mothers who were working, attending classes, or in training) and started a cooperative store, a snack bar, laundromats, and a variety of other services. When they hired outside contractors, they insisted that the contractors employ residents. They began cooperative efforts with the police and established community watches, as well as substance abuse programs. The crime and drug dealing declined significantly. As the tenant projects took hold, vacancies declined and rent collections increased. As of 1989, it was estimated that resident management in this complex saved the city at least $785,000, and if trends continued, about $3.7 million over six years. It is also claimed that they helped many leave welfare, mostly through employment provided by the resident management corporation.

Another major example occurred in the St.Louis public housing projects.[57] As with most of the tenant movements, this, too, started, in 1969, with a rent strike, protesting, among other things, a sharp increase in rent. The housing authority, already near bankruptcy, was reorganized and as part of the settlement, agreed to explore the feasibility of tenant management. Four years later, and after much on-the-job training, residents in two projects (1,256 units) signed a management contract with the authority giving them management responsibility. The tenant groups were subject to federal rules and regulations, and the authority continued to have overall fiscal responsibility, but annual operating budgets were negotiated with the tenants groups. Three years later, two additional developments signed contracts. The units now totalled almost twenty-seven hundred.[58]

The Tenant Management Corporation (TMC) board, composed of unpaid representatives, sets overall policy. Most of the staff positions are filled by residents. While overall evaluations have not been made, it does

[56] Osborne 1989.   [57] Kolodny 1986.   [58] Kalodny 1986.

seem as though the tenants have mastered basic real estate management skills. However, the tenants organizations did much more. Confronted with a resident population consisting primarily of welfare families, they developed programs in education, recreation, health, social services, child care, care for the elderly, job training, and resident employment. The various components support each other—for example, child care provides employment for some residents and frees other to seek work; food services for both the children and the elderly provide nutrition, training, and employment. By the mid-1980s, the organizations had begun to construct housing, and planned to build a commercial shopping center. Kalodny thinks that these developments would not have happened without the legitimacy gained through successful real estate management and without the institutionalization of the tenants' common interests in the TMC. Nevertheless, he, too, is cautious. A great many of the nationally sponsored demonstration projects in tenant management did not succeed, and even those that did not solve the vast problem of the shortage of affordable rental housing.[59]

Neighborhood Organizations

In the examples above, municipal governments were delegating power to get rid of specific nasty political problems—in this situation, being slumlords.[60] There are many other kinds of delegations of public power to private or citizen groups that have similar purposes—to manage conflict by localizing it. The War On Poverty's Community Action Agencies were used to manage local race and patronage conflicts. The health planning agencies described by Morone represented Washington's attempt to deal with rising health care costs; local citizen groups, it was hoped, would take on the medical profession and allied groups and do the rationing. A much more ubiquitous, long-standing example is the neighborhood associations that are usually spontaneously formed by local residents to protect property values by excluding undesirable outsiders. Formally or informally, they have a large say in local land-use decisions.

Jeffrey Berry and his colleagues examined neighborhood associations in five cities—Birmingham, Dayton, Portland, St. Paul, and San Antonio[61] —that have had a different experience than the usual, parochial neighborhood organizations. The associations that Berry and his associates studied are citywide, long-standing, highly complex, have deep structural relationships with municipal officials, and appear to be quite suc-

---

[59] Kalodny 1986.
[60] This section relies extensively on Berry, Portney, and Thomson 1993.
[61] Berry, Portney, and Thomson 1993.

cessful in exercising real power. The authors claim that there is genuine political empowerment of residents, including those in minority and low-income neighborhoods.

The five cities vary in terms of the structure of their neighborhood associations. In Birmingham, there are more than ninety-five neighborhood associations. They elect officers for a two-year term. The neighborhood associations are organized into broader organizations composed of several associations. Representatives of each of these form a citywide Citizens Advisory Board. The associations communicate to the residents via a monthly newsletter. Each association decides how its community development block grant will be used and works with community staff on neighborhood problems. This three-tiered structure was the first to bring blacks and whites together in Birmingham to work on common problems.[62]

In Dayton, there are seven Priority Boards composed of elected members from each neighborhood. There are monthly meetings between the boards and representatives of major city agencies, as well as a wide range of other meetings on neighborhood issues. The city uses the boards to discuss its plans on the full range of major citywide issues—for example, bonds, employee residence requirements, and so on.[63]

In Portland, more than ninety neighborhood associations are organized into seven District Coalition Boards, each with its own staff. The system provides advocacy, needs reports, crime prevention teams, self-help development grants, technical assistance, citizen mediation, and assistance with individual neighborhood issues and citywide participation issues, including advisory committees for every major agency.[64]

In St. Paul there are seventeen District Councils , elected by residents in each area. The city pays for an organizer and the office in each neighborhood. Other activities are supported by volunteers or funds raised by each council. The councils have jurisdiction over zoning, the distribution of various goods and services, and a significant say in capital expenditures within their areas. A citywide budget committee, composed solely of neighborhood representatives, is responsible for the initiation and priority ranking of most capital development projects in the city. Councils also run crime prevention programs, community centers, an "early notification system for all major city agencies," and a local newspaper.

In San Antonio, the neighborhood organization—Communities Organized for Public Service (COPS)—basically serves the Hispanic sections of the city. The authors claim that over the past twenty years, COPS has developed from a Hispanic group with virtually no political power, to

[62] Berry, Portney, and Thomson 1993, 12.
[63] Berry, Portney, and Thomson 1993, 13.
[64] Berry, Portney, and Thomson 1993, 13.

one that now "arguably has more political power than any other single community group in the nation."[65]

The consensus seems to be that the citizen or neighborhood organizations of the 1960s and 1970s failed; that they had little or no power; and that the citizens correctly judged them as not worth the bother. According to Berry and his associates, elites in those communities wanted the citizen organizations to fail. In the War on Poverty's Community Action programs, for example, the poor had to fight to get included and then they only sat on the boards. Even though individual CAPs provided good training and political experience for urban African Americans, they never were grass-roots programs, and they had little influence in city hall. In contrast, these five organizations, while not trouble-free, have substantial authority over resources and programs; citizens participate, *and elites want them to succeed*. In each of the five cities, groups were organized in every neighborhood; there is extensive communication to and from city hall; there are resources—support staff, training, technical assistance, offices; and, the authority to act on substantive matters.[66]

The five cities are very different in terms of income, education, minority population, economic conditions, and form of government. According to the authors, the common factors that led to the growth of these neighborhood organizations included combinations of grass-roots motivation, vision on the part of government leaders, and federal mandates calling for citizen participation; organization based on small, face-to-face neighborhoods, but conceived as a citywide system; and the exclusion of partisan politics—there was a strict distinction between advocacy on particular issues and electoral neutrality. The neighborhood organizations do not take stands on political candidates. Another important common feature was the development of an extensive, systematic flow of information, neighborhood outreach, and specific mechanisms for communication back and forth between the neighborhood and city hall. The authors emphasize, however, that none of these systems were static. Rather, they evolved over time and experienced major changes. The organizations had resources, including staff supported by the city, which, according to the authors, is really crucial. Then, there was the matter of luck. In each of the cities, the organizations were able to grow strong before they were hit by overwhelming economic and political problems.[67]

The results, of course, vary. Not surprisingly, the neighborhood organizations are most effective on matters closest to home—particularly local land-use decisions—and least effective on citywide matters, such as operating budgets, school budgets, and so on. The organizations are very ef-

---

[65] Berry, Portney, and Thomson 1993, 14.
[66] Berry, Portney, and Thomson 1993, 46.
[67] Berry, Portney, and Thomson 1993, 47–62.

fective in the allocation of resources within their areas, and have achieved dramatic results in poor, minority areas. In both Birmingham and San Antonio, there have been major rehabilitation projects in low-income minority areas that had long been neglected.[68] On the other hand, the neighborhood associations seem better at responding to demands—zoning and development requests, neighborhood complaints—than in initiating projects. They seem to be more interested in local autonomy than in citywide coalitions. In part, this is because they are overwhelmed by local tasks. Nevertheless, the associations do influence the city agenda. City leaders have become attuned to neighborhood concerns.[69]

One difference that the authors noted concerns development. The usual practice in most cities is for developers and their political allies to develop a project in secret and then try to present a fait accompli. These tactics do not work in these cities. The developers know that the neighborhood associations are structured for communication and participation, and, accordingly, they engage the relevant associations early on in the process and seek to work out cooperative arrangements. The authors claim that the data do not show co-optation, and that even though the neighborhood organizations do not always win—the developers have important advantages since the cities want growth and jobs—they do manage to have influence. The associations are able to compete with the developers when matters reach the public agenda.[70]

Continuous efforts are made by the neighborhood associations and city hall to make sure that the organizations are not internally co-opted by the leaders. Each of the cities insists on continuous communication and outreach—newsletters, regular open elections, block clubs, leaflets, door-to-door campaigns, and so on. Both the associations and the cities do this to maintain the legitimacy of the organizations. Survey results show that the organizations are widely trusted in the community and that citizens feel that they can participate if they want to. However, while the organizations seem to do a good job in appearing to be open and responsive, in fact, only a small group participates in the day-to-day matters and participation does vary somewhat with socioeconomic class.[71]

Why do the city halls in these cities support these organizations? In most other cities, city leaders view citizen organizations as a threat or a bother, and they work, usually always successfully, to undermine them. In contrast, in these cities, there are important payoffs to political leaders. Responding to surveys, residents say that they trust their organizations, that they feel that the organizations are effective in resolving differences

[68] Berry, Portney, and Thomson 1993, 65.
[69] Berry, Portney, and Thomson 1993, 108.
[70] Berry, Portney, and Thomson 1993, 146–57.
[71] Berry, Portney, and Thomson 1993, 171–77.

and diffusing community hostility, that channels of communication are relatively open, and that, as a result, they are more likely to accept decisions that they disagree with. The citywide political leaders, in turn, feel that citizen participation, while it often delays decisions, it does build consensus; it brings more people into the decisions, and it de-legitimates the dissatisfied. Political leaders have strong incentives to get along with the associations. Cooperation is the expectation. Open political conflict is damaging.

The authors think that citizens who do participate in these associations feel an increased sense of capacity to affect government. They develop a strong sense of community, a sense of belonging, and a belief that local government is responsive to individuals and their neighbors. They feel that the associations are a reliable source of information that increases their understanding of how politics works and where to go with their problems. As a result, they feel as though their problem-solving skills are enhanced. In short, they feel empowered by their neighborhood associations.[72]

In sum, the factors that make neighborhood associations work, are:

1. The organizations have to have real power over real resources. There can be sharing of power—for example, over development—but the organizations cannot be merely advisory.
2. There have to be real rewards for the city leaders; otherwise, they will try to undermine the citizen organizations.
3. The system must be citywide, not confined only to minorities or the poor.[73]

CONCLUSION

There are common threads throughout these diverse examples. Some of the common themes support the social science literature—particularly the writings of social psychologists who argue that empowerment is not simply consciousness raising in the abstract. Rather, to be successful, dependent people must achieve a sense of self-efficacy through reflexive action. By this, they mean that their lived experiences or practices have to be combined with awareness—information about themselves and their environment.

At the same time, there were cooperative efforts by those who initially held the power—government, regulators, bureaucrats, business. On occasion, there have been dramatic examples of dependent people having organized and seized power through confrontation; but in day-to-day activities, empowerment through confrontation is rare. Quite often confrontation may be necessary to start the process—for example, rent strikes, or lawsuits—but unless the power holders are willing to change

---

[72] Berry, Portney, and Thomson 1993, 279–80.
[73] Berry, Portney, and Thomson 1993, 295.

their ways, in the long run they can usually undermine the groups of dependent people.

In the examples used here, the power holders saw that it was in their interests to share power. This involved, first, a re-conceptualization of their mission. In worker safety, this meant that safety issues and accident prevention were systemic problems that could be solved through joint action based on trust. In special education, it meant that parents were part of the solution rather than part of the problem. I meant that the frail elderly would do better if they took more control over their lives and that tenants could manage projects. Political decisions would be more acceptable if there was early, genuine communication and participation. And so on.

Ideas and good intentions are essential for communication and trust, but they not enough. For both the powerful and the powerless, they have to be buttressed by better concrete results. For the powerless, the *experience* in exercising control over their environment is essential for reflection, consciousness raising, and a sense of self-efficacy. For the powerful, such results in regulation can be achieving legal standards with less cost and agency resources; in special education, they can include better progress for the students; in home-health care, better information on the quality of services and client stabilization at lower costs. In public housing, results can mean better-managed buildings or relief of ownership. And so on.

The importance of a real payoff for the normal power holders helps answer the problem of co-optation. Co-optation with dependent people is a real problem. In the one-on-one situation, the professionals or bureaucrats will begin to stop listening as carefully; they are busy, and after all, they are the experts. There are strong tendencies on the part of the powerless to defer to the professionals. Participation on the part of the dependent person is difficult, often anxiety-producing, and time-consuming. In the Madison School District, parents experienced the good results and began to defer to the teachers, and the teachers began to complain that it became more and more difficult to get parents to challenge them, to express their own opinions.

With groups of citizens, leaders have a tendency to form stable relationships with agencies. The agency provides information and access and gives the leadership symbols of importance and efficacy. The group or organization in turn helps the agency by legitimizing the process, providing political support for the program, and by avoiding negative publicity for the agency and the relevant political leaders. For this kind of partnership to work, there must be a stable leadership that can deliver the members. Depending on the context, there can be strong incentives to form alliances between agencies and organizations.

Over the course of time, two things can happen: the group can grow weak and lapse into irrelevance or the group can develop a stable alliance with the bureaucracy and assume corporatist characteristics. In either event, organizational arrangements that desire or depend on the active involvement of grass-roots members will lose. In other words, although it is relatively easy to co-opt an organization, doing so can be self-defeating. The agency, or the power holders will lose the material advantages that they gained from cooperation. Parents will no longer be able to effectively help educate their handicapped children. The frail elderly will no longer be a reliable source of information. And tenant-managed public housing will no longer help to solve the city's problems. The power holders have to understand the importance of grass-roots participation.

When all is said and done, it must be recognized that the powerless, however they may be empowered in these particular relationships, still remain relatively powerless in other aspects of life. This means that empowered relationships will always be tentative and unstable. They have to be constantly renewed.

Chapter 7

EMPOWERMENT THROUGH CONFLICT: SCHOOL REFORM

Schools as Contested Terrain

Nationwide, we are once again in the throes of school reform. School reform is both cyclical and contradictory. This is no surprise. The education and socialization of the citizenry is one of our most important social functions. Consequently, what schools do or should or should not be doing has always been highly contested. The battles in education reflect conflicts over who we are, what we aspire to be, and how to accomplish those goals. Public schools incorporate powerful, but often competing, legitimating symbols.[1] Thus, school reform is often less about the core technology of schooling—teaching and learning—than contests over ideologies, identity, legitimacy, national security, professionalism, community—in short, status politics—as well as more mundane matters such as local politics, taxes, political patronage, and jobs.

One of the enduring crosscutting issues in school reform struggle is centralization versus decentralization. As "one of America's oldest and most treasured political remedies," decentralization has long been a favorite method of managing conflict.[2] Centralization versus decentralization, too, is cyclical. In one period, local control will give way to more centralized authority, and then there will be a reaction. We return to centralization/decentralization issues, says, James Morone, because of our basic ambivalence about government. We both call on and fear government. We periodically insist on a return to "the people," but what constitutes "the people" is never clear and we have been unable to institutionalize "the people."[3] When school reform turns to decentralization, "the people" are parents and community members or local politicians. With the swing toward centralization, "the people" means a broader, more diffuse community of citizens, including those who are concerned about the more collective results of education.[4]

Today, schools are to be held "accountable" through "restructuring." Accountability through restructuring, as we shall see, can mean anything from standardized measures of performance, to market-determined choice,

---

[1] Peterson 1990.
[3] Morone 1990.
[2] D. Cohen 1990, 337; Weiler 1993.
[4] Elmore 1993.

to teacher or professional communities, to school-site management, to more parental or community involvement ("democratic localism").[5]

For the first half of the twentieth century, the effort of professional educators was to take schools out of the influence of local politics. This meant, of course, restructuring according to their conception of professional public education. They imposed uniform standards, increased the size of districts and schools, centralized financing and state aid. Then, by the post–World War II period, just when the hegemony of the public schools seemed complete, a period of turmoil started. This was the era of civil rights. Minorities demanded not only more access to the public schools, but also more control. As a result of white flight, urban public schools found themselves in competition with the suburban and private schools.[6] In terms of centralization and decentralization, the reforms moved in both directions. There was a demand for both an increased federal and state role, as well as for decentralization and more recognition of diversity. Desegregation, bilingualism, and special education promoted centralization. The dozens of new federal and state categorical programs resulted in an enormous growth in school bureaucracies and nonteaching staff. At the same time, school districts responded to diversity and community demands by increasing student choices through expanded electives, alternative schools, schools within schools, and so forth. David Tyack calls this period "fragmented centralization."[7]

In 1983, the country was stunned by the publication of the U.S. Department of Education's *The Nation at Risk*,[8] a report that documented how the public education system was failing. The "rising tide of mediocrity" threatened the competitive position of the United States. Business and political leaders linked future prosperity to academic achievement. There was a reaction to the laissez-faire curriculum approach of the 1960s. Standardized tests came to be regarded as the principal way to raise the performance of both students and teachers.[9] There was an increased emphasis on improving educational expectations, order, discipline, and stronger leadership. More academic subjects were required for graduation. In many states, teacher requirements were increased, again primarily through the use of standardized tests.[10] Previously, the state had been mostly concerned with minimum levels of resources, personnel qualifications, health and safety, and governance processes. Now, the emphasis broadened into the area of performance. States mandated more measurement outcomes; the new buzzword was "accountability." In many states, there were provisions for the equalization of funding, special

[5] Tyack 1990, 170.
[7] Tyack 1990, 180.
[9] Fuhrman and Fry 1990; Hess 1992b.

[6] Peterson 1990.
[8] U.S. Department of Education 1983.
[10] Witte 1990a.

needs students, technical assistance, and so forth. This resulted in an increased share of state funding and even more state regulatory control.[11]

Despite the rhetoric of state-imposed standardized requirements, both districts and schools seemed to remain quite diverse in practice. Within the schools, there were wide ranges of organization, curriculum, teaching methods, tracking, and so forth. Testing procedures themselves were varied. Comparatively few states instituted statewide testing of any kind, and even those tests that were instituted varied. By 1985, forty states had some form of minimum competency testing, but varied in terms of state or individual district standards, type of examination, grades tested, and purposes—that is, whether the tests were for grade promotion, graduation, special remedial work, and so on. Similar kinds of variation applied to achievement tests.[12] Variation persisted at every level. States continued to provide funds for districts with large numbers of disadvantaged and at-risk students, or for special projects (teen parents, dropouts, etc.). Larger districts, with their own technical assistance, tended to ignore state efforts to encourage curriculum planning, staff development, and evaluation. State oversight agencies tended to pay more attention to districts that were not in compliance or had other, visible problems, such as low test scores or high dropout rates. Districts in difficulty sometimes sought waivers from state requirements—regarding, for example, class size, teacher certification, length of school year, facility specifications— but waivers also brought increased scrutiny. Accountability, itself, also encouraged differential treatment. Technical assistance would be targeted on the basis of performance. Some states intervened more directly with severely troubled districts. There were other pressures to differentiate. State agencies have neither the resources nor the capacity to regulate all the districts. Differential treatment not only sounds reasonable, it also satisfies political demands. Local elites push for reforms in their districts and state political leaders are more anxious to provide local aid than to increase state agency budgets.[13]

That differentiation should persist despite the rhetoric of standardization is no surprise given the structure and complexity of governance in education. As will be discussed in more detail in the next section, a wide range of actors—federal, state, local, unions, interest groups, parents, students, citizens—seek to exercise control or influence over education. Within the districts, the administrators respond to multiple sources of influence. Districts do respond to both internal and external pressures, but, by and large, they cannot control their environments. At the same time,

---

[11] Fuhrman and Fry 1990.   [12] Witte 1990b.
[13] Fuhrman and Fry 1990.

top-down control is varied and uncertain. The result is that the structure and location of control varies considerably.[14]

In any event, the centralized, standardized test approach was barely spreading before the present reaction set in. As this chapter will discuss, many now believe that the central bureaucracy is the problem. Teachers will only improve their teaching and students will only improve their learning if there is more autonomy for teachers to engage in collegial decision making, more attention to getting students to think and demonstrate competence, and more parental and community involvement in learning—in short, decentralization.[15]

David Tyack points out that reform movements seem to come and go, they leave their institutional deposits—usually in the form of another layer of government—but long-term trends in public education continue. Furthermore, these trends are running counter to some of the major tenants of decentralization. In general, school systems are adept at deflecting, if not sabotaging, reform by incorporating some of the symbols but not changing the practice. Decentralization calls for smaller schools, but the long-term trend is for more students per school. Reformers emphasize fewer subjects, more academic subjects, with greater depth in teaching and learning, but this bucks a century of differentiation, a highly diverse curriculum, and extensive tracking, either covert or overt. Reformers seek to reduce middle management, top-down regulation, burdensome paperwork, and to increase the role of teaching; yet, the increase in fragmented centralization has increased the size of the bureaucracy and the increase in the number of principals and nonteaching staff has far exceeded the increase in the number of teachers. Despite the cycles of centralization versus decentralization, there has been a steady growth in state and federal regulation, the size of districts, and the size of the administrative staff. As Tyack says, "with ritualistic regularity, Americans create and then bemoan bureaucracy."[16]

Two crosscutting issues affect school reform in a major way—the perennial mine fields of American policy: race and redistribution.[17] Segregation, by race and class, continues to persist despite decades of attempts at reform. School resources, however measured, are grossly disproportionate depending on location. Despite four decades of attempts at desegregation, a great many urban schools are predominately minority, and in those schools where there has been mandatory integration, internal tracking has been used quite often to reestablish de facto segregation.[18]

As we shall see, there is now a search for more flexible, voluntary, alternative solutions, such as choice and magnet schools, but these, too

[14] Witte 1990b.   [15] Tyack 1990, 183.   [16] Tyack 1990, 185.
[17] Hess 1993a, 85.   [18] Alves and Willie 1990.

raise conflicts. The constituencies of desegregation are minorities, who are disproportionately poor; those who favor choice are more often white, middle-class suburbanites. The former are more inclined toward centralized authority; the latter toward decentralization.[19]

Schools receive most of their funds from the local property tax. Thus, residential segregation produces enormous wealth differences in school districts that may be only a few miles apart. And, of course, the localities in which the poor districts are located have to spend proportionately more for services, crime, public health and safety, and therefore less on schools than the wealthier localities.[20] State aid is insufficient to make up these differences. These inequalities are fiercely defended at the local level; indeed, good neighborhoods, low taxes, and good schools are the reason why people who have the means choose to locate in these areas and why they seek to exclude those of lower social classes. The local property tax system has been challenged, usually in court, but these cases have been bitterly contested. In most instances, judges have not been willing to intervene with what are considered to be traditional local government responsibilities. Even where courts have been interventionists, reform has been exceedingly tortuous and uncertain.[21]

The inability to reform school financing to funnel more resources to those schools most in need creates a continual doubt about the efficacy of school reform. As we shall see, process reforms can help, but they cannot substitute for resources.

PUBLIC SCHOOLS AS ORGANIZATIONS—
DECENTRALIZED CENTRALIZATION

There have been remarkable changes in public education over the last century. At the same time, it is also said that public education bureaucracies are remarkably *impervious* to change. What reforms take hold? What reforms fail? And why? Richard Tyack says that reforms that last usually have the following characteristics: they are add-ons that do not disturb existing ways of doing things; or they develop constituencies (e.g., driver education); or they make work easier or enhance professional status. Conversely, reforms that seek to change what actually goes on in the classroom usually get deflected or ignored. Then, there are attempts at

[19] Tatel 1992–93, 61–72.

[20] Richard Briffault (1990a) reports that in 1986, the tax base in Weschester County, NY, was $221,000 per pupil, while in eight other districts, the tax base was less than $50,000. In Texas, the tax base in the wealthiest district was over $14 million of property wealth per student, while approximately $20,000 per student in the poorest district (20 n. 62).

[21] Clune 1992b; Briffault 1990.

reform that never seem to get settled because they touch issues that are never settled in the larger society. Here, Tyack would include standardization versus diversity, choice versus command, equity among students, integration, and so forth.[22]

The seeming imperviousness of schools to reform efforts raises the question of who controls the schools. In the current reform mode, public education is characterized as a top-heavy bureaucratic monolith, imposing impossible and often counterproductive requirements on teachers and students, sadly out of touch with what is necessary to teach effectively in the classroom. The opposite view is that despite the layers of centralized bureaucracy public education is, in fact, the classic "loosely coupled" organization. Not only is there a great deal of variety in terms of size, composition of the student body, resources, facilities, teachers, and so forth, but there is also a great deal of autonomy as to what happens when the classroom door is closed.[23]

Janet Weiss[24] discusses five kinds of control in education. The first is *professional control*. Professionals define their work through training, credentials, and norms that stress autonomy, discretion, and support. Consequently, teachers may resist efforts to improve efficiency or introduce new ways of teaching, or to work with new types of students. They resist evaluation, not only from nonprofessionals, but even from fellow teachers. As many other professionals feel they do, teachers are more likely to "know what's best" rather than to be willing to listen to clients. Superiors, who have the same training and credentials are expected to be supportive. To the extent that teachers are able to resist outside control, what they do in the classroom, day-to-day, constitutes the work of the organization. While teachers work in isolation, professional organizations, schools of education, and unions are sources of ideas and norms that affect working conditions.

School *administrators* are responsible for setting goals and providing incentives and controls. While they are constrained by organizational structures and technologies, they have varying amounts of discretion over resources, budgets, and personnel. Because the day-to-day work of teaching is relatively immune from direct supervision, administrators rely more on rules of procedures and accepted routines. Administrative control is also affected by the environment. Schools operate within a dense network of social, economic, and political pressures—a world of competing demands and causal indeterminacy. Administrative authority proliferates from multiple levels of government and from categorical programs. School administrators have difficulty in setting priorities or implementing plans. The consensus seems to be that in most situations, administrative

[22] Tyack 1991.   [23] Witte 1990b.   [24] Weiss 1990.

control tends to be very problematic. Administrators seek to control information and deflect criticism. They focus on more easily demonstrable inputs, such as certification requirements, credit hours, and equipment, rather than on improving learning.[25]

Political control is also multiple. Local school boards, most of which are democratically elected, in general, hire and supervise the superintendent, approve the curriculum, provide ancillary services, set the budget, approve capital improvements, and conduct union negotiations. At the same time, schools boards have to deal with other elected officials, other local government agencies (e.g., police, fire, child welfare), the courts, and state and federal officials.

Those involved in political control try to make schools responsive and accountable to the public. At the same time, schools are often subject to multiple, conflicting demands from different constituencies. The threat of litigation can create serious problems. There is often the threat of capture—not only from ideological interests but also from commercial interests (e.g., book publishers, testing organizations). Schools are often a source of patronage. In these political struggles, since school boards represent only a small part of the electorate, they are often weak.[26]

Public schools operate within *markets*. Schools compete for funds, for teachers, and for the approval of parents and students. At the same time, the relevant stakeholders, including the schools, have a differential access to information as well as different abilities to respond.[27]

The fifth source of control that Weiss discusses is *values and ideas*. How people think about their work affects their behavior. Teachers exercise control through their professional and individual ideologies. Other actors exercise influence as well, according to their ideological commitments. What Hasenfeld calls "typification," is a well-known phenomenon in human service agencies; clients are sorted, receive services, and evaluated according to preconceived ideas. Teacher expectations are a powerful influence on student achievement. Professionals process information in terms of their own values and also in terms of expectations generated from the environment. Thus, line professionals are subject to change but changing values and belief systems can be a slow process, especially since most schools find themselves at the center of multiple competing demands.[28]

Weiss says that while the five kinds of control are usually present all of the time, they vary in importance depending on the temporal saliency of different goals. Professional control will be more important when teaching and learning are emphasized; political control when there are de-

[25] Weiss 1990, 103.   [26] Weiss 1990, 109.
[27] Weiss 1990, 115.   [28] Weiss 1990, 118.

mands for public accountability. The different forms of control are usually discussed in zero-sum terms, but Weiss argues that sometimes they are complimentary. In certain situations, strong principals can empower teachers. The reverse is also true. Teacher may lose professional control by resisting administrators.[29]

Education policy is often dictated from the top down but most commentators agree that the top-down approach often runs into difficulty at the district and school level. The proponents of decentralization argue that because schools operate in a casually indeterminate complex environment, a decentralized organization, capable of flexibility, is the most appropriate form of organization. Decentralization puts control in the hands of those who are closest to the problems and therefore more capable of responding to local variation. Weiss says that most educators today agree that smaller, decentralized units are best adapted to the task of improving instruction.[30] On the other hand, local control can also mean domination by local interests, which can be insensitive to minorities as well as to broader community values.

Decentralization is a process that varies with context. As one form of control changes, others will adapt. In one situation, increased parental choice resulted in resegregation that triggered a federally imposed desegregation plan that eliminated choice. Decentralizing choice over textbooks may increase the power of publishers if teachers are overwhelmed. Increased state funding (centralization) may serve to increase school-based improvements. Decentralization involves different actors who may or may not make better decisions. Some schools will improve and others will not.[31]

If the past is any guide, the contest between standardization and decentralization will continue. One can find simultaneous moves toward increased centralized control through standardized tests, minimum graduation requirements, and so forth, as well decentralization through various choice and selection processes and the downward shifting of authority. But what is becoming agreed upon today is the outcome measure—student achievement. The dispute is how this goal is to be achieved and measured. Alfred Hess says that consensus on this goal is in sharp contrast to the traditional approaches to assessing schools, which was on inputs rather than outcomes. The assumption was that good inputs would produce good outcomes, and that if there were differences in outcomes, this reflected differences in students. Hess says that this assumption has been successfully challenged. Schools with similar inputs are producing students with very different outcomes. Differences in school resources and differences in students (socioeconomic background, etc.)

[29] Weiss 1990, 124.   [30] Weiss 1990, 125.   [31] Weiss 1990, 128.

fail to account for differences in achievement. Therefore, differences in outcomes must be related to the ways in which schools function. This is not deny that differences in student backgrounds are not important; it is only to make the point that schools can make a difference.[32]

The idea that schools should be evaluated in terms of outcomes—that is, student achievement—has been resisted by school people—they think that they are being as successful as can be expected, given the resources and the differences in students—but it has been embraced by political leaders and the business community, the voters, and by most academics. Schools are to be held accountable. Thus, the contemporary reform impulse is paradoxical. The demand for accountability in achievement is coming from outside the educational establishment (top-down), but there is also agreement that the implementation has to come from below, at the local level.[33]

School Restructuring as Empowerment

While there seems to be a growing consensus that the way to improve student achievement depends ultimately on a high-quality curriculum that is actually delivered in the classroom, there is, however, no agreement on what kind of reform will deliver substantive, curriculum and teaching changes in the classroom.

Our concern is with reforms that restructure school governance relations in such a manner that teachers, parents, and community members are empowered. There are several kinds of school reform, even restructuring, that are designed to change teaching, but do not necessarily change governance relationships. For example, building on the standardizing restructuring reforms of the 1980s, "curriculum alignment" seeks to control course content by establishing uniform objectives, instructional materials, and student assessments. A single professional agency would have exclusive authority for designing and maintaining a curriculum that is coherent and of high quality.[34]

Similarly, reorganizing the bureaucracy—creating smaller districts, or even delegating substantial power to the schoolhouse—changes power relationships, but not necessarily the relationships between the principal stakeholders at the schoolhouse site—principals, teachers, parents, students, and community residents. Smaller districts or schools under Site-Based Management (SBM) may still be run in the traditional manner, with the principal making the key decisions and teachers and parents uninvolved.

On the other hand, under SBM, there are governance arrangements

---

[32] Hess 1992c.   [33] Hess 1992c.   [34] Clune 1990a.

under which decisions are made communally by principals, teachers, parents, and, depending on the plan, members of the community. Under this approach, SBM, it is argued, would raise staff morale and motivation. There would be quality planning and teaching, and student achievement would improve.[35]

There are a variety of proposals to increase the power of teachers in education decisions, primarily at the school level, and to increase the status of the profession. As previously discussed, teachers have a great deal of autonomy in the classrooms, but they usually have little influence with the principal, and virtually no influence at the district level. Teacher empowerment proposals are designed to increase teacher influence in collective decisions at both the school and district levels. The theory is that this will incorporate teacher expertise and improve work-place satisfaction and teaching.[36]

There are also choice reforms that permit parents, under various conditions, to select the schools to which they send their children. Included here are the magnet schools. In one sense, this is the ultimate empowerment, since parents, as consumers in the market, can then vote with their feet. As will be discussed, many think this form of market competition will improve the product. However, our concern is about parents being formally incorporated into the governance structure. This may or may not occur under choice. Parents may choose to enroll their children in an SBM school that encourages, indeed, insists on active parental participation (e.g., the Comer schools, to be discussed) or parental participation may be minimal. Many magnet schools, for example, are developed internally and professionally, and then offered to the community. Parents who select these schools usually have a stake or commitment to the school, but they may also have very little input into what happens substantively.

Teacher Empowerment

There are two principal arguments for giving teachers greater power over instruction. One, as previously mentioned, is that instruction will improve with teacher expertise and work-place satisfaction. The other is pragmatic: In view of the strategic role of teachers, especially their autonomy once the classroom door is shut, significant reforms ultimately depend on their commitment. However, as Susan Johnson reminds us, teachers vary, and giving more authority to teachers could result in the perpetuation of existing practices or even change in the wrong direction. It is argued, for example, that teachers' unions already have too much

[35] Clune 1990a.
[36] Clune 1990a.

power and teacher empowerment reforms will only further professional self-interest.[37]

There are some notable experiments with teacher empowerment, and, not surprisingly, results vary. The Dade County, Florida, reforms were the joint product of the district management and the union. The proposals were to increase school-based, shared decision-making discretion over budgets, staffing and scheduling, and the delivery of support services. Subject to general standards and guidelines, schools were free to develop their own structures. Initially, 33 of the 300 schools elected to participate in pilot projects for a three-year test period; subsequently, a third of the schools signed on. The pilot schools proposed and implemented a variety of innovations, including different roles for teachers; block scheduling; school-within-a-school; and teachers-as-advisers.[38]

In a study designed to measure the extent to which teachers influenced the outcomes of decision processes traditionally under the control of the principal, it was found that teacher involvement in the innovations varied among the schools, and also according to the stage of the reform. All of the innovations involved additional administrative roles for teachers. Significantly, the teacher roles were more successful when they did *not* involve teaching. For example, collegial hiring and student discipline seemed successfully in place, but not peer evaluation. The reactions of principals varied; many were supportive, but others either retained a veto power or restricted teacher influence to relatively safe areas. In general, the schools were still working out satisfactory solutions to the relationship of the principals to the teachers.[39]

It is not clear whether the reforms can be sustained. They were brought about, in large part, by the strong commitment of the superintendent, who left after the project had been running for five years. The researchers think that the necessary solidarity among the teachers seems to be waning. Within the schools, there is evidence of burnout as well as of continuing conflicts between the traditional teacher norms of autonomy, equality, and privacy and the new goals of teachers as instructional leaders and supervisors. There are also conflicts between activists ("sounding like the principal") and nonparticipants. While the teachers have had more influence, it was "well below the level of determining or changing the direction of a school."[40] The authors say that teacher support for the reform has dropped with the departure of the superintendent.[41]

[37] Johnson 1990; Hess 1991, 199.

[38] Hanson, Morris, and Collins 1992. The participating schools were generally representative in terms of the socioeconomic range of the county; the professional staff was representative in terms of graduate degrees and experience, but somewhat more white.

[39] Hanson, Morris, and Collins 1992, 81.

[40] Hanson, Morris, and Collins 1992, 87.

[41] Hanson, Morris, and Collins 1992, 84.

From other examples, some successful, others not, a few conclusions emerge. One is that reforms have to be supported by both central administration and the local principals. In Memphis, Tennessee, despite significant structural governance changes "on the books," there were prolonged, bitter power struggles between reform-minded teachers and traditional, autocratic principals, who simply refused to engage in consensus decision making.[42] Conversely, in two exemplary districts studied by Jane Hannaway, it was found that teachers were highly involved despite the fact that in one district (A) the curriculum was centralized and in the other district (B) it was decentralized to the individual school. Whereas in District B, the teachers had a collective responsibility at each school, in District A, the teachers developed a common commitment because they felt that they had easy access to the process and there was extensive professional interaction on a well-defined, common purpose. In both districts, the teachers were stimulated to work together. The principal conclusion that Hannaway comes to is that for teacher empowerment to be successful, it must be focused on the central functions of teaching—what is to be taught and how it is to be taught. Curriculum-focused staff interactions organize the schools as schools, provide the frameworks for the classrooms, define expectations, and stimulate peer quality control.[43] Other researchers have come to similar conclusions.[44]

Surveying the field, Johnson says that increasingly one finds joint committees dealing with budget, hiring, allocation of extra staff, administration of districtwide programs, and so forth. Even though many of these decisions are narrow, the fact that teachers participate in final decisions has changed their attitudes concerning their role in school governance. In some schools, teacher peer assistance and evaluation programs have led to the termination of some teachers and, it is claimed, the improvement of many. Teachers, it is said, are more likely to take evaluation seriously when it comes from their peers than when it comes from nonteaching administrators. While unions have opposed merit programs, especially if statewide, they seem to be less resistant at the local level where the teachers have increased responsibility.[45]

As with most restructuring reforms, it is still far too early to evaluate the various teacher empowerment initiatives. The prevailing view is that reforms initiated from the top, especially those that fail to take account of local conditions, are more likely to encounter the most resistance. Statewide programs initiated by political leaders frequently arouse the most intense opposition from the unions and the teachers. Top-down initiatives seem to do better if they establish guidelines and allow for locally

[42] Etheridge and Collins 1992.   [43] Hannaway 1993.
[44] Lee, Dedrick, and Smith 1991.   [45] Johnson 1990.

based negotiations. Reforms that are initiated by teachers in their own school sites insure local commitments, increase morale, and, it is claimed, improve instruction.[46] On the other hand, site-based teacher reforms may run into problems of long-term survival. Programs that are not integrated into the district will be most vulnerable to budgetary cuts and bureaucratic conflicts. In several large urban districts, unions have introduced significant reforms through collective bargaining.[47]

Johnson concludes that for teacher empowerment reforms to work, district officers and principals have to view teacher empowerment restructuring as an opportunity, not a threat. Principals must become collaborators, facilitators, and leaders. Teachers, too, have to change. Traditionally, they have not been trained or prepared to engage in collegial decision making, budget and personnel decisions, or peer assessment. Active decision making requires substantial commitments of time and energy and the ability to collaborate.[48]

Parent/Community Empowerment

The organization of this large, and complex section will be as follows: first, I will discuss the varieties of choice, including the magnet schools. Second, I will discuss "schools as total institutions" where parent and community (as well as teacher) empowerment appears to be at the maximum. And third, I will discuss various other forms of Site-Based Management.

CHOICE

Choice increases the ability of parents, rather than government, to select the appropriate education for their children. In an important sense, there has always been at least some choice for significant portions of the population. Parents who have the resources have always been able to select schools either by paying tuition for private or religious schools or by selecting or changing their place of residence. The proposals today are to expand choice to those parents who lack the resources under the existing system.

Proponents of choice believe that creating parents as consumers will empower them in the exercise of one of their most fundamental concerns—the education of their children. At the same time, they believe that consumer choice will result in responsive, accountable, quality schooling. John Coons and Steven Sugarman believe in the importance and ultimate wisdom of ordinary citizens knowing what is best for their children. They would maximize parental choices through vouchers redeemable for pub-

---

[46] Lee, Dedrick, and Smith 1991b.   [47] Johnson 1990.
[48] Hanson 1992; Johnson 1990.

lic, private, or religious schools. They favor only minimal regulation—dissemination of appropriate information about the various schools, subsidies for poor parents, and the prevention of segregation.[49]

The market approach argues that the public education system has failed because it is a monopolistic bureaucracy. In part, this view started with a line of research showing that school performance (i.e., student achievement) does not seem to be related to traditionally measured school characteristics. As previously mentioned, schools do not seem to matter, as far as student-teacher ratios, expenditures per pupil, material resources, teacher training, and so forth, are concerned. As a result, it was concluded that what matters more seems to be student characteristics. This conclusion was so disturbing that researchers turned their attention away from inputs or production functions toward the schooling process itself—that is, what schools actually do. What they found was that while student characteristics were important, what schools did does make a difference. Research has now focused on school organization. Why are some schools more effective than others in getting students to learn?[50]

The argument now made is that schools that are small and organized nonbureaucratically have improved teacher morale and efficacy and resulted in higher student satisfaction and achievement. These schools have shared community values, strong leadership, strong ties to parents, a strong school culture, and a sense of school community. For schools to be effective, they must be organized more along the lines of communities and teams and less according to hierarchical, large-scale bureaucracies.[51]

John Chubb and Terry Moe press the argument against bureaucracy to its farthest point.[52] They argue that "the most fundamental causes of school failure are the very institutions that are supposed to be solving the problems: the institutions of direct democratic control."[53] The democratic institutions that are supposed to govern schools—school boards, superintendents, the district offices, and local, state, and federal governments—are "incompatible with effective schooling." This is because democratic institutions respond to the various interests and pressures that seek to impose their particular values on the school system and these are often inconsistent with the requirements of effective schooling. Since governing institutions are designed to reflect political interests, "existing institutions cannot solve the problem, because they *are* the problem."[54] Chubb and Moe argue that, all things being equal, schools that are more autonomous are more effectively organized than schools that are more subject to external control. They cite as evidence the differences between private and public schools, and especially between private schools and

---

[49] Coons and Sugarman 1992.
[50] Chubb 1990.
[51] Chubb 1990.
[52] Chubb and Moe 1990.
[53] Chubb and Moe 1990, 2.
[54] Chubb and Moe 1990, 2.

the large urban public schools that are the most bureaucratic. The governing bureaucracies impose goals, structures, and requirements on principals and teachers rather than allowing them to exercise their expertise and professional judgment. Effective education cannot be accomplished unless the potential already present in school professionals is effectively utilized; this potential cannot be achieved within present structures.

Chubb and Moe have little faith in the ability of public institutions to withstand interest group pressure. The institutional alternative to the public bureaucracy is the market. They propose a radical antibureaucratic structure—virtually no higher-level political control—and allow parental choice alone to determine individual school governance. In the market there are no higher-order democratic values that can exercise authority over the schools. Radically decentralized schools would compete for parents and students and, thus, would reorganize to satisfy their customers. The authors point to the generally better educational outcomes of the private schools. Chubb and Moe are sympathetic to the direction of school-based management, but think that these reforms do not go far enough because ultimate accountability resides with upper-level superiors—the superintendent and the school boards—and if problems arise, they will use their authority. The pressure to monitor, they believe, will inevitably result in the imposition of rules and the reassertion of bureaucracy. For similar reasons, Chubb and Moe are skeptical of other forms of decentralization, such as teacher empowerment because teachers are still subject to upper-level bureaucratic control.

Chubb and Moe believe that choice is a "panacea" in that it "has the capacity *all by itself* to bring about the transformation that reformers have been seeking" provided most public authority is vested directly in the schools, parents, and teachers. They propose minimal state criteria for public schools, basically what is set for private schools. All schools—public and private—would be eligible to participate in the system. Schools would be financed according to the number of enrolled students, with more money going to poorer districts. There would be scholarships for students with special needs. Students would be free to choose any school in the state, with transportation provided. There would be parent information centers, and an emphasis on personal contact with the schools. Subject to nondiscrimination requirements, schools would be completely autonomous in making admission decisions. They would define their mission and build their program to attract students. Every student would be guaranteed a school. Every school would decide its own governance system, including tenure, career ladders, textbooks, pedagogy, and so on. The state would hold the schools accountable for the procedural requirements—the charter criteria, nondiscrimination, the dissemination of information—and would oversee the choice process, approve new schools, provide transportation, and monitor legality, but the schools themselves would be accountable for student performance. Chubb and Moe argue that this proposal is not privatization. Rather, it is a public, democratic system with local people and units deciding what kinds of schools they want.[55]

There has been a great deal of criticism of Chubb and Moe. It is claimed, for example, that they gloss over the imperfections of the market; their contrast between educational outcomes of private versus public schools is disputed—there are many excellent public schools and private schools have the ability to select on the basis of student characteristics, and so forth.[56] Advocates of choice are also criticized about their views of the functions of public education. They assume that social purposes are fulfilled when families satisfy their individual tastes and values. Critics contend that while schooling does confer important private benefits, the purposes of schooling are not so limited. Democratic societies rely on public schools to socialize their citizens and to provide a common set of values and the knowledge deemed necessary to preserve and strengthen basic institutions. These requirements suggest that all students should be exposed to a common educational experience. While allowing for choice and diversity, there must be a common language and cultural understanding.[57]

Nevertheless, choice is a powerful reform movement in public education, in part because it taps into basic tenants of American society—both market and democratic values. Choice in public schools is responsive to broader trends toward decentralization: Americans want more local control and choice in public services[58] and believe that because family beliefs and values differ, they should have the right to choose the kind of schools that best fit the particular needs of their children. Matching schools to needs, it is believed, will produce better outcomes. Choice, it is hoped, will shake up the present monopoly, especially for the poor, minorities, and immigrants who cannot exercise choice by moving. Public choice plans provide more alternatives within the public schools, and allow parents to select the school they want. The best-known example, discussed shortly, is the magnet school.[59]

Critics of choice plans raise equity issues—specifically the problems of access to information and of the ability to exercise choice. There are real difficulties in disseminating information. Choice mechanisms are not likely to be neutral. The ability to exercise choice in this complex area will

[55] Chubb and Moe 1990, 218–25.
[56] Carnoy 1993; Elmore 1991b, 687; Hess 1991.
[57] Carnoy 1993; Levin 1990.
[58] Peterson 1990.
[59] Levin 1990.

depend heavily on the institutional structures within which the choice occurs, and the background characteristics and ability of the families to obtain information.[60] Advantaged families will be favored. Transportation
will be an especially serious matter for any choice plan.[61] Elmore reports
that geographical location is the single most important factor in parental
choice, although with vouchers, the importance of location did decrease
over time.[62]

Voice in education, as in other matters of public concern, varies with
socioeconomic class. Higher-educated families provide more school-
relevant experiences to their children before they enter school and more
support to their children while they are in school, and they bring greater
influence on school authorities regarding the decisions that affect their
children.[63] The evidence, thus far, from "low voice" families is not promising. Minnesota has a "pure" choice system—every student is given the
choice of selecting whatever public school he or she wants in the state.
However, no additional funds were provided to implement the program;
no funds were provided to supply information to parents; the school districts did not do any marketing; and many parents did not, in fact receive
any information. After two years of operation, less than five hundred students from a total number of seven hundred thousand participated in the
choice program. Very few transferred to other districts. Word is beginning to get around and participation is starting to increase, but still, as of
the 1992–93 school year (the latest available as of this writing), less than
6 percent of the eligible students chose another district or the Post-Sec-
ondary Enrollment option.[64] In the Sacramento program, parents in the
"choice" school choose the school for safety, not higher academic
achievement. The evidence so far is that a relatively small number of parents would take advantage of high-achievement choice schools unless
those schools were in their own neighborhoods.[65]

Martin Carnoy interprets these findings to mean that for the large
numbers of students who come from "low-voice" families, freedom to
choose may actually worsen their welfare. Most families would send their
children to local schools, not necessarily to higher-quality schools in surrounding areas. Further, the best schools would recruit, select, and demand more from students and parents. Less attention would be paid to
the parents who don't care or who lack the resources. Carnoy thinks that
there is no logical incentive for low-performing schools to compete with
high-performing ones—they have different market niches. Rather, high-
performing schools would compete with each other in the wealthier parts
of the district and low-performing schools would look pretty much like

[60] Elmore 1990a.
[62] Elmore 1990a, 306.
[64] Nathan and Ysseldyke 1994, 2–3.
[61] Levin 1990, 267–70.
[63] Carnoy 1993.
[65] Carnoy 1993, 187.

they do today, since most schools would still be neighborhood schools. Higher achievement, he says, is mainly a *demand* problem, and since demand already varies greatly, choice would only increase that variation, unless provisions were made to increase the level of demand. He has serious doubts whether larger vouchers would be issued for the poor. The more likely result would be to allow the rich to add on, thus, perpetuating existing inequalities. The result would be that the market would privatize the responsibility for failure as much as it privatizes the responsibility for success.[66]

Controlled Choice; Magnet Schools.   Controlled choice, or choice plans within the public education system, is another popular reform measure. It began with magnet schools, and was adopted to deal with desegregation. Within districts, parents can choose schools with a specialized mission. These are the magnet schools—for example, basic academics, art, music, science and math, multicultural enrichment, and so on—that draw from all neighborhoods within the district. Magnet schools or *mini-schools* can exist within the framework of larger, existing schools—an especially attractive option in large, urban schools.[67]

Magnet schools first appeared in the 1970s, and by now, they exist in practically every urban school system.[68] Because magnets were focused on the particular student interest rather than only ability, magnets would enroll a racially heterogeneous student body as well as provide a unique educational experience. As described by Rolf Blank, magnets came to be characterized by (1) specialty curriculum or pedagogy; (2) a way of achieving voluntary desegregation within a district; (3) choice; and (4) access beyond the regular attendance zone. They continue to grow for pretty much the same reasons. They represent an alternative to forced desegregation; they provide diverse curriculum options with the objective of improving educational outcomes; and thus, they meet the demands for both quality and choice by community leaders, business, parents, educators, and politicians. Magnet schools have helped improve racial balance by reducing white flight. They are consistently supported by the U.S. Justice Department.[69]

On the other hand, says Blank, there is concern that magnet schools will increase the disparity in educational quality with traditional neighborhood schools. There is concern about the distribution of these schools and their impact on dropout rates and at-risk students in the remainder of the school system. For example, while the great majority of magnet

---

[66] Carnoy 1993, 188.   [67] Levin 1990, 262–65.
[68] Blank 1990.   [69] Blank 1990.

schools are representative of their districts in terms of racial and ethnic composition, they enroll few at-risk students.[70]

In any event, the number of magnet schools and enrolled students have been increasing significantly, mostly at the middle/junior and senior high schools. They are self-selected and there is competition for a limited number of slots. Data seem to indicate that the better students are applying. Most of the magnets have higher achievement scores than their district averages. Student attitudes and satisfaction are generally high—which is not surprising, since they are attending voluntarily. One study that showed the relationship between magnet school policy and organization and the quality of the educational processes and outcomes revealed that, controlling for student characteristics and school resources, higher outcomes resulted from principal leadership, coherence between the magnet theme and the curriculum and staffing, and district flexibility and commitment. But that study cautioned that magnets cannot be created solely from the top down. While district support is necessary, there has to be a positive local school climate. Teachers have to play an important role in the planning and development of the school. There also has to be high parent involvement.[71]

District 4, New York, known as East (or Spanish) Harlem, is cited as an outstanding example of an "alternative" or magnet school. In 1973, District 4 was about the worst school system in New York City. The district was characterized by both poverty and racial/ethnic isolation. Only 15 percent of the students were at grade level in reading, which placed the district last of the thirty-two community districts in the city.[72]

The new superintendent, with some teachers, created a system of schools—as distinguished from "buildings"—within the schools. In the first year, 1974, three small alternative schools were created. One was for children with serious emotional and behavioral problems, which was popular because it allowed other schools to transfer troublesome students. The others were Central Park East and East Harlem Performing Arts. Students were accepted on the basis of their interest. The schools occupied two floors in regular school buildings. Virtually all of the additional new schools ended up occupying a floor or two in an existing building, and some schools were in three to five different buildings.[73]

The idea of District 4 was to demonstrate that it was possible to offer high-quality education to poor, minority, inner-city children.[74] The program continued to grow as more teachers and principals came forward with ideas. By 1982, there were twenty-three alternative schools. About

[70] Blank 1990, 78–79.   [71] Blank 1990, 97.
[72] Fliegel 1990; Harrington and Cookson 1992.
[73] Harrington and Cookson 1992.   [74] Elmore 1990b.

20 percent of all elementary school students participated, and all junior high school students. Parents rank order their choices, with 90 percent getting one of three choices. Complaints seem to be minimal.[75]

Because of the lack of controlled experiments, it is premature to draw definitive conclusions about the effects of District 4 alternative schools. Nevertheless, the results seem impressive. After nine years, the district was in the middle in terms of grade reading level. In 1982, almost half the students were at or above grade level; by 1987, almost two-thirds were at grade level. Dropout rates from the alternative programs fell to about 1 percent. In 1973, only 10 District 4 students were admitted to New York City's competitive high schools; in 1987, the number was 356. College attendance rose to about 50 percent. Specially recruited teachers were retained and staff morale was high. While the outsides of the buildings were indistinguishable from the rest of the neighborhood, the insides were clean and well maintained. There were computers, performing arts materials, and student work displayed throughout.[76] Applications have risen to the point that the alternative schools are selective, and students from outside the district are applying. About 4 percent of the student body were transfers from white, middle-class neighborhoods.[77]

Despite District 4's apparent success, the pace of development has been deliberately slow and cautious. Twenty-three alternative schools were established, but over a sixteen-year period. There were never more than three programs per year, and in some years, none were established. One program was "refocused" after it was determined that it lacked sufficient quality, and one was closed. While principals and teachers in the district are encouraged to come forward with proposals, and support will be available in the initial period when enrollments might be low, the clear message is that the programs have to be educationally sound and be supported by the faculty and the parents.[78]

Throughout its development, District 4's program encountered significant problems. There was recurrent friction with principals, with other teachers, parents, community activists, and administrators. The idea was challenged as elitist, exclusive, and too specialized. The district never had more than token support from the citywide school administration; the program was tolerated, initially, because the district was in such bad shape that anything was worth trying and, later, because it did not stir up trouble outside the district.[79] District 4 survived through patience and persistence and good leadership. It moved slowly, incrementally, anticipating problems and opposition, making accommodations.[80]

[75] Elmore 1990b; Fleigel 1990.   [76] Elmore 1990b.
[77] Elmore 1990; Harrington and Cookson 1992.   [78] Elmore 1990b.
[79] Elmore 1990b; Fliegel 1990.   [80] Elmore 1990b.

District 4 has been cited as an example of how parent choice can improve quality.[81] Harrington and Cookson, however, argue that the opposite is more accurate—namely, that it is quality that makes choice work, not the other way around. There are important differences between alternative schools and schools of choice. A school of choice is chosen, but is not necessarily different from other schools; in fact, it is usually only another regular school. Alternative schools, on the other hand, are *alternative* to *regular* schools. Choice was important in District 4. Parents, students, and teachers choose, and then have a stake in the success of the school. But they were choosing something different. Harrington and Cookson think the most important innovative ingredient was school size. Small size gives each child the opportunity to know and be known by adults, and this, in turn, connects the adults to the community. Other factors producing success were leadership, imagination, expectations, and time. The district superintendent not only encouraged, but expected, a climate of innovation. No one expected every experiment to succeed, but the superintendent nurtured teacher professionalism. He pushed, trusted, and encouraged teachers. As the authors put it, the teachers "owned" their schools. Within each of the schools, extra funds were found for new ideas to support school themes. Finally, there was time to work out the ideas. School reform takes time. Perhaps District 4 was successful because it was able to keep its distance from citywide administration. But the ingredients for the success of District 4 may also be its weakness. Harrington and Cookson say that when the superintendent left, most the creative energy seemed to go as well. School reform, as is too often the case, is too closely tied to particular individuals rather than being institutionalized. More attention needs to be paid to permanent staff appointments and appropriate teacher empowerment.[82]

Richard Elmore says that while District 4 shows a generally positive picture of choice, thus reinforcing the general consensus that choice can improve the conditions of teaching, learning, and student achievement, the evidence is not sufficient to support the general proposition that choice does in fact produce these results. Without proper controls, there is no way of knowing whether increases in alternative school enrollments increased achievement or whether achievement was going up independently. Learning, says Elmore, depends on what and how students are taught. One cannot say how much choice improves learning without knowing how choice systems influence what is taught. While a choice plan requires parents to choose, it cannot force parents to be engaged. Choice can have considerable effects on the quality of schooling but Dis-

---

[81] Chubb and Moe 1990.
[82] Harrington and Cookson 1992.

trict 4 also significantly regulated what was offered. It was the combination of both demand and supply changes that made the difference in District 4. Parents did become engaged.[83]

Magnets and Desegregation.   Choice, as an alternative to court-ordered desegregation, grew out of the idea of magnets. Called "controlled choice," this strategy essentially "magnetizes" the whole school system, giving all parents the right to choose, while controlling for racial balance. In the usual plan, parents make multiple school selections, in rank order. No student is guaranteed first choice and all final assignments ensure that both majority and minority students have proportional access to all schools and programs of choice. The actual enrollment within each school and program reflects the racial composition of the system as a whole. Additional elements include upgrading the whole system by replicating successful schools and requiring unsuccessful schools to improve. Controlled choice, it is claimed, is especially well suited to the large urban schools that have been unable to desegregate all their schools, or whose neighborhood-based desegregation plans have been continually defeated by population shifts.[84]

Two of the more famous examples are Milwaukee, Wisconsin, and Cambridge, Massachusetts. In 1976, Milwaukee, under a court order to desegregate its schools, developed a controlled choice plan for its entire urban school district. In 1977, all parents were required to select a school. Approximately one hundred eight thousand choice requests were processed for the 150 schools. Ninety-five percent of the first choices were granted.[85] Subsequently, the program was refined, but remained remarkably successful in not only meeting, but even exceeding, the court-ordered requirements—85 percent of students attend a racially balanced school. It is said that this success in meeting desegregation goals has been replicated in other districts. Moreover, the controlled choice plans have proven to be stable. For ten years, Milwaukee has been able to maintain its racial balance despite an increase of 23 percent of minority students. The principal reason for the success, argues Bennett, is that choice plans, in contrast to traditional plans, allow year-to-year flexibility.[86]

The Boston controlled choice plan grew out of the 1975 school desegregation case. The plan provided that no student would be mandatorily

[83] Elmore 1990b, 24.

[84] Alves and Willie 1990; Clune 1990a; Tyack 1992.

[85] Bennett 1990, 127.

[86] Bennett 1990, 135. The basic plan is first to run the magnet school selection, then start over for attendance area schools, followed by requests for transfers. The initial enrollment priorities are capacity and racial balance; then such factors as distance, siblings, and gender are taken into account.

assigned to a school on the basis of residence and that all parents would be given the opportunity to select schools by rank order of preference. All the schools would be included but procedures were established to prevent re-segregation.[87] Three zones for elementary and middle schools, and a citywide zone for high schools were established. The assignment zones functioned as semiautonomous school systems for education planning. The zones were large enough to encompass heterogeneous student populations, but small enough to make transportation reasonable.[88]

Within each zone, there were Parent Information and Student Assignment Centers that conducted informational meetings, prepared and distributed informational packets, brochures, notices, etc., and processed all final assignments. Parents were to be given sufficient time to acquire information, visit schools, plan changes, and so forth. Zone supervisors certify the instructional capacities of each of the schools; this includes the availability of special services (e.g., special needs, bilingualism, etc.) as well as the amount of available space. Each zone was to offer an equivalent range and quality of educational opportunities. The centers were monitored by the Department of Implementation.[89]

There were Zone School Improvement and Planning Councils. Membership on the councils were drawn from diverse, local interests, for two-year renewable terms. Each school was responsible for attracting students; thus, educational planning and decision making were decentralized to the school building. Principals, teachers, parents, and students fashioned the educational mission and the learning environment.[90]

All space was initially allocated on the basis of the proportions of white, black, and other minority students residing in the particular zone in order to guarantee proportional access. If space was oversubscribed, there were procedures for selection, for example, consideration of siblings and distance, a random lottery, or waiting lists. With undersubscribed seats, there was redistribution to minority students within the racial guidelines. There were also hardship provisions.

Charles Glenn reports that 88 percent of elementary, 86 percent of intermediate, and 91 percent of high school students received their first choice. A very small percentage received their second or lower preference. Parents were *not* counseled out of expressing their first preference, but *were* encouraged to rank order. As it worked out, "safety" schools were not needed in the great majority of cases. It was also clear that many minority parents want their children to attend schools outside of their

[87] For example, final assignments could not deviate more than 10 percent from the proportion of white/minority students in the eligible zone.
[88] Alves and Willie 1990.
[89] Alves and Willie 1990, 44.
[90] Alves and Willie 1990, 48.

neighborhoods. In 1991, more than half of the applications were to non-neighborhood schools. And there was no evidence that parents were manipulated during the process.[91]

Schools that were undersubscribed were targeted for immediate technical assistance and improvement initiatives. For the first year, the responsibility was with the principal, the teachers, and the council. If progress was insufficient, the school came under the scrutiny of the zone superintendent. If sufficient progress was still not made, the zone superintendent could take whatever steps were necessary.[92]

Alves and Willie conclude, from the Boston experience, that school desegregation through a voluntary, controlled choice plan, is a political as well as an educational process. Planning has to be public. There have to be numerous small, group meetings, the sharing of information, learning of preferences. There has to be open access. The goal should be to try to present the plan as a community consensus. The community process requires both horizontal (between the political and education systems) and vertical (between schools and the community) linkages. Educational change needs the support not only of political leaders but also of families and the community. Controlled choice, if properly thought through and executed, empowers families, but schools have to learn how to reach out, to gain power through allies.[93]

While Alves and Willie speak optimistically about the Boston controlled plan, David Tatel points out that there are potential conflicts between the goals and supporters of desegregation and those of school reform through choice.[94] The two movements, he points out, have different constituencies. Desegregation is supported by minorities, whereas school reform is supported by white, middle-class parents who want improved education in the city. There is also a structural conflict. Desegregation is centralizing; it focuses on student reassignment, busing, and so forth, which can conflict with school reform flexibility, afterschool programs, and so forth. Uncontrolled choice can lead to re-segregation, and courts have blocked plans relying on voluntary attendance at magnet schools. They have also refused to order plans to create neighborhood schools that would promote re-segregation. Similarly, there could be problems with other reforms that have a disproportionate impact on minority students and faculty—for example, new tests, higher standards, merit raises, and so forth.[95]

There are other issues with magnet schools. While many have been re-

[91] Glenn 1992, 47–49.   [92] Glenn 1992, 51.

[93] Alves and Willie 1990, 55. For one of the most insightful studies of the importance of social groups for the democratic process, see Cohen and Rogers 1992, 393–472.

[94] Tatel 1992–93.   [95] Tatel 1992–93, 62–64.

markably successful both in attracting students and in changing racial balances, they have been charged with elitism, with substituting socioeconomic status for racial isolation. There will always be some parents disadvantaged in the selection process, thus raising fears and opposition from poor and minority parents. And there is always the concern about the quality of the students in the nonmagnet system.[96] There is still a lot of opposition to magnet schools; surveys show that a majority of school board presidents, superintendents, and principals oppose public school choice. Teachers in nonmagnet schools feel that they have been demoted. Parents who complain about the education of their children are blamed for making poor choices.[97]

The controversy over magnets and choice continues despite the fact that great disparities already exist under the present system, and magnets may not be creating greater inequalities. Furthermore, as Mary Metz argues, access to magnet schools is far more open than access to suburban schools; in magnet schools, after all, there are racial quotas, free admission (although it is biased and may favor the more affluent and well-educated parents). In fact, magnets are generally more diverse in race and class than the majority of neighborhood schools and certainly more so than most suburban or inner-city schools. Metz argues that the inequalities in the present system are papered over by the myth of standardization.[98]

At the present time, magnet schools are playing an increasingly larger role in urban education. Both their numbers and the demand for them continue to grow. Some observers, such as Blank, think that the magnets will continue to be a "primary method of educational innovation" primarily because they appear to satisfy the demands for improved educational quality, opportunities for diversity and choice, and appropriate levels of racial balance. The major issue is the impact on the district as a whole, and whether a two-tiered system will develop.[99]

What is not known at this time is the impact on the support for magnet schools of the recent U.S. Supreme Court decisions sharply restricting, if not outlawing in fact, the use of racial preferences and limiting court-ordered desegregation.[100] As discussed, magnets are not without opposition, and, without the threat of forced desegregation and with the probable illegality of racial preferences, the support for magnets may weaken.

[96] Bennett 1990.
[97] Tyack 1992.
[98] Metz 1990.
[99] Blank 1990, 101–3.
[100] Adarand Construction, Inc. v. Pena, 115 S. Ct. 2097 (1995); Missouri v. Jenkins, 115 S. Ct. 2038 (1995).

On the other hand, in many areas, magnets have been so successful in reducing social conflict and improving education, that they may continue to be supported. There are notable examples of adverse court decisions having actually galvanized social movements.[101]

The idea that each individual school should be viewed as a total institution in which all the stakeholders are empowered is usually attributed to James Comer, a Yale psychologist. For more than twenty years, "Comer schools" have been spreading, especially in deprived areas.[102]

Comer's basic idea is that sharing responsibility will enhance the stakeholders' engagement with and commitment to the educational process. A governance team of the principal, the teachers, and the parents collectively decides on the goals of the program. It is then up to the team to enlist the support of all the teachers, staff, and parents. The ultimate success of the program depends on obtaining that support. Parent members have the responsibility to reach out to other parents to make sure that they are expressing representative views. Individual parents are encouraged to volunteer to work in the classrooms or in other school activities, especially those that are designed to improve the school climate. Parents not only engage in social activities, but also, since they are in the classroom, interact with teachers over pedagogy. The program assumes that sooner or later most parents will want to hear about the curriculum and learn about practical ways to help their children with their schooling. Parent committees provide interested parents with skills to help their children, general parenting skills, and, if needed, adult literacy. Enlisting the activity of noncommittee member parents is considered critical for the ultimate success of the program, since it demonstrates a willingness to consult widely and to develop a cooperative spirit. The goal is to provide "a sense of direction in the school, to create the feeling of shared ownership and responsibility for the school's program, to promote implementation of the plan, and in general to create a cohesive local community which values educational performance and expects it of children."[103]

The Comer program lays great stress on the decision-making climate. There has to be mutual respect and willingness to listen to others; there must be closure on all issues so that they will not be avoided or left unresolved and allowed to fester. All decisions are by consensus rather than vote, and while the principal has management responsibilities, he or she must share power. Committee members "must feel empowered *by the*

---

[101] Handler 1990b.

[102] The following discussion of the Comer schools relies extensively on Anson et al. 1991.

[103] Anson et al. 1991, 9.

principal."[104] The students, parents, and teachers "own the program they participate in."[105]

Other interpersonal relation issues are emphasized, especially those dealing with race, gender, and generations. Comer started with the belief that many educational problems stemmed from a lack of understanding between schools and the homes of poor African American children. Many of the parents of these children view the schools with hostility, as institutions that betrayed them, whereas the teachers see unprepared and uninterested children. These problems are to be confronted, but in the context of the committee meetings. There has to be communication and trust between the school and the parents, especially with parents of color of low socioeconomic status.[106]

The Comer model looks to adult incentives. Teachers will not go along unless their needs are met. Foremost among those needs is a disciplined environment, one that is safe and orderly, where learning can take place. Comer believes that discipline cannot be imposed from the outside, but can only develop from within, when the students have the skills and incentives for self-discipline and control. The social climate can be changed when the whole adult community sets consistent standards of behavior and agreed-upon strategies. But Comer believes that all the adults in the enterprise—not just those on the committees—need collaboration, mutual support, and positive feedback and guidance, and that better relationships will make jobs more rewarding and schools more effective. It is in this kind of environment that teachers have the necessary structure and support, and if these needs are met, then teachers will feel important and efficacious. All the adults in the school will feel that they have a genuine role and will be able to see the results of their efforts as the school changes.

The Comer school student has to believe that he or she can learn in order to be successful, and that self-efficacy can be enhanced through the school environment. This means being sensitive to individual capacities, the need for extra help and for other programs, such as art, athletics, and social activities, so that children who are not strong academically can experience a sense of accomplishment. The schools must respond to student strengths, rather than weaknesses so that competency and self-efficacy become part of one's identity.[107]

A great deal of learning develops out of interpersonal attachments, especially trust and bonding, with significant adults. Students feel comfortable in asking for help. Both teachers and parents are needed for the process of endorsing mutual values, goals, and expectations. This climate of

---

[104] Anson et al. 1991, 11.

[105] Elmore 1990b.

[106] Anson et al. 1991.

[107] Anson et al. 1991, 19–20.

mutual respect and trust ought to also affect relationships between students; those who feel competent have less need to prove self-worth by competition; instead, they are urged to cooperate, paralleling the adult process in the school community. The Comer program assumes that in addition to developing inner resources, children from minority groups need special group-based affirmation. School programs should encourage students to express their specific cultural identities, the achievement and history of minority groups, and the social and economic realities of their world. It is important for children to feel that at least one mainstream institution cares about them. The Comer program assumes that academic performance will improve because attendance, achievement, and respectful, orderly behavior are goals that all the stakeholders in the school desire.[108]

Another similar prominent example of schools as total institutions is the *Accelerated Schools* program developed by Henry Levin, a professor at the Stanford University School of Education. The goal is to restructure elementary schools to ensure that *all* students are educated. Disadvantaged students—those who come from homes that are disproportionately poor, minority, single-parent, and so forth—begin school with a learning gap. Existing models of intervention assume that these children will not be able to maintain a normal instructional pace. They are placed in less demanding instructional settings to give them time to catch up. While this approach appears both rational and compassionate, in fact, it has the opposite results and these students remain marginal. Effective schools, argues Levin, have to reverse this approach by creating high expectations for all the participants.[109] The goal should be that every student performs at grade level by the end of elementary school. To do this, schools must be completely restructured so that there are high expectations for all students on the part of teachers, parents, and students.

According to the Levin model, schools have to be reorganized from the bottom up. Each school has an overall steering committee and task forces composed of the principal, the teachers, other staff, and the parents who work together to set up a program that fits the needs of the school and builds on the strengths of the district and the staff. The assumption of this model is the establishment of a unity of purpose among all the participants, all of whom have a responsibility for the outcomes. Parent involvement is central. They are part of an agreement that affirms the goals and responsibilities of the participants. Parent obligations include such things as ensuring that children go to bed at a reasonable hour and attend school regularly; they must affirm high educational expectations, talk to their

[108] Anson et al. 1991, 26–27.   [109] Levin 1991, 3.

children regularly about the importance of school, and take an interest in their activities and the materials that they bring home. The purpose of the contract is to emphasize the importance of the parental role, along with the obligations of students and the staff.

Parents also play an important governance role. They are members of the steering committee and the various task forces. Parents also interact through the school's "open door" policy. There is a parents' lounge. Training to help parents help their children and to understand what the students are learning is available.

The heart of the process, says Levin, is the responsibility of the individual school for the educational processes and the outcomes. The various governance structures, composed of the principal, the teachers, aides, staff, parents, and student representatives, approve of all major decisions concerning curriculum, instruction, and the allocation of resources that have schoolwide implications. The principal is responsible for coordinating, facilitating, and obtaining logistical support. The principal is a listener, a participant, who keeps the school focused on its goals. Levin says that often it is necessary to train principals, teachers, and staff to make group decisions. They usually do not have this experience. Special attention has to be paid to group processes, the sharing of information, and working toward decisions.

Accelerated schools start slowly. They first establish a baseline of information to begin the process of self-examination and then construct a vision of change that will work for their particular students. The transition process from the baseline to the vision, Levin estimates, is usually about six years. The full accelerated process must be supported by all—the principal, the various governing committees, the district, and the staff.

Accelerated Schools established two pilot schools in the San Francisco Bay area in 1986. By 1994–95 there were over seven hundred elementary and secondary schools in thirty-seven states. So far parent participation has increased dramatically, discipline problems have declined significantly, and attendance has improved. There has been a substantial improvement in staff morale. New programs have been selected and scores are beginning to rise. There is evidence of reduced grade retention.[110] Levin points out that other similar models also seem to be working—the Comer schools; Success for All;[111] Higher Order Thinking Skills;[112] and Reading Recovery Program.[113]

[110] Levin 1991, 12.
[111] Slavin 1991.
[112] Pogrow 1987.
[113] Clay 1990.

DEMOCRATIC LOCALISM: CHICAGO

The challenge to Chicago's "democratic localism" is whether it can combine the elements of choice and schools-as-total-institutions with large-scale public reform. Democratic localism is designed to give more power over local schools to the parents and citizens of the attendance area surrounding the school. One of the main purposes is to displace the centralized bureaucracy. However, democratic localism is different from parental choice in that here, the parents and community members are incorporated into a formally recognized governance system. The idea is that the locally based, democratic governance system will reorganize the school to harmonize local needs with overall goals of student achievement.[114] The most prominent and radical example underway is the Chicago public school system.

Background

As the third largest district in the country, the Chicago public school system experienced all the familiar urban problems: white flight, segregation, declining enrollments, and declining budgets.[115] The school system was closely linked with the Democratic political machine that controlled city government. Approximately twenty-thousand nonteaching positions derived from patronage. The highly segregated school system came under civil rights pressure. In 1980, under the threat of a desegregation suit, the district began to expand magnet schools to increase desegregation through voluntary means. Subsequently, these magnets formed the core of the current choice system.[116]

In the meantime, the district endured recurring fiscal crises and strikes. A number of reforms were tried—voluntary desgregation, alternative schools, a standard citywide curriculum to improve math and reading (which was repealed), increased high school standards—but with no additional funds, the reforms failed.[117] The Chicago school system was labeled one of the worst in the country.

Local reform groups began to form. "Designs for Change," a parent-student advocacy group, organized low-income and minority parents for a school system independent of city politics and for school-level improvements. Several reports documenting poor school performance were is-

[114] Hess 1994a.
[115] The history of the Chicago reform effort relies extensively on Moore 1990, 1992, Moore and Pandya 1992.
[116] Moore 1990.
[117] Moore 1990.

sued, and these received wide publicity. In 1981, the business community began to organize around school reform. After several rebuffs from the school board, which convinced the reformers that nothing short of fundamental restructuring would improve the public schools, a coalition of various reform groups formed CURE (Chicago United to Reform Education) and worked out a program designed to place control of the schoolhouse in elected parents and community representatives, limit the tenure of principals, reduce the size of the central administration, and increase choice, but with safeguards. A bitter teacher's strike galvanized business elites, parents, and community groups around fundamental reform and the fight moved to the state legislature. The restructuring proposals were extremely controversial, but with the credibility of both the school system and the teachers union damaged because of the strike, business leaders and citizens groups mounted an intensive lobbying campaign, and the Chicago School Reform Act was signed in 1988.[118]

The Reform Act

Under the 1988 reform act, each school is governed by a Local School Council (LSC), composed of six elected parents; two elected community residents; two teachers elected by the school staff; and the principal. Neither the parents nor the residents may be school employees. The elections are for two-year terms. The LSC appoints the principal to a four-year performance contract. Principal tenure is abolished. At the end of the four-year term, the LSC decides whether to renew.[119]

LSC members must receive thirty hours of training annually; this is supplied either by the central administration or by an independent organization selected by the LSC. The LSC develops and approves the school improvement plan, which addresses increasing student achievement, reducing truancy and dropout rates, and preparing students for employment or further education. The LSC develops and approves the school budget and has substantial flexibility.[120]

The authority of school principals is significantly increased. They can fill vacancies without regard to seniority. Teachers rated "unsatisfactory" by the principal can be dismissed (with some protections).[121] The principal is responsible for school management, for implementing the improve-

---

[118] Moore 1990.　　　[119] Moore 1990.　　　[120] Moore 1990.

[121] Teachers at a given school have the right to stay on, but must apply for open positions at other schools. After the twentieth day of the school year, teachers cannot be dismissed because of the reduced enrollments. Teachers who lose positions because of declining enrollments or changes in the curriculum, must be provided employment in the school system while they seek a new position (Moore 1990).

ment plan, and for the budget. The teachers have enhanced authority through their two positions on the LSC and through the Professional Personnel Advisory Committee (PPAC), which advises the principal and the LSC on curriculum, staff development, the contents of the improvement plan, and the budget. Subject to citywide objectives and standards, the principal, in collaboration with the PPAC, has the authority to develop the methods and content of the curriculum. Since curriculum is determined at the school level, teachers have an increased role in both curriculum development and in selecting materials and methods. Thus, at the school site, there is both participatory decision making and professionalism.[122]

The reform act provides for subdistrict councils (composed of elected members from each LSC) and superintendents (again, on four-year performance contracts) who promote coordination and supervision for schools failing to take the necessary steps to improve; they can intervene through a prescribed process. Ultimately, the central board can remove an LSC, the principal, or the staff, or even close the school for nonperformance. There are other provisions in the act, including state compensatory funds for low-income children that are allocated to each school according to the proportion of low-income students. This supplementation is to be used at the discretion of the LSC. The act also directed the state board of education to complete a study of strategies for increasing school choice, to be implemented in 1991–92. Admission was to be by lottery (but consistent with the desegregation consent decree) and transportation for low-income students was to be provided.[123]

Implementation—the Record So Far

As provided by the reform act, the existing central board of education was replaced by an interim board for a limited term. The new central board was to specify systemwide curriculum objectives and standards, supervise special education and bilingualism, provide transportation and school meals, develop a systemwide disciplinary code, and manage construction. The board was also to be in charge of protecting civil rights, enforcing the civil and criminal law, and taking final action with nonconforming schools. The systemwide reform goals and objectives were to be approved by the School Finance Authority. The central board selects the

---

[122] Hess 1993a.

[123] Moore 1990. After the statute was passed, the principals brought a lawsuit challenging the right to terminate their contracts and the election of the LSCs. The principals lost their claim, but the election procedures were declared unconstitutional by the Illinois Supreme Court. The election procedures were amended, and the reform proceeded.

general superintendent for a three-year performance contract. The act provides for an expenditure cap on the board that is intended to result in substantial savings to be passed on to the local schools. The School Finance Authority approves and monitors the implementation of the systemwide education reform goals and objectives plan. It can block central board contracting that is inconsistent with the reform plan; has wide data-gathering and investigative authority; and can direct the board to take specific actions, and impose sanctions, including suspension and removal, on board members and system staff.[124]

The social movement organizations remained active. They organized task forces, engaged in parent and citizen training and community organization, and monitored school implementation. Business groups organized a nonprofit organization to support school reform implementation. The reform was supported by the mayor. The school choice plan proved very controversial, and was delayed until 1994–95. The plan that was adopted affords most students a substantial number of options, including alternatives to their neighborhood elementary and high schools.[125]

The Consortium on Chicago School Research issued an interim report in 1993. The report cautioned that the reform was still in its early stages. The first year (1989–90) had been devoted mostly to structural issues and governance process—that is, elections, training councils, writing by-laws, and so forth. Half of the schools were required to evaluate their principals and make a decision on retention; the other half made this decision in 1991. This meant that by 1993, only half of the schools had three years experience under the reform, and the other half, only two years. The consortium reminded its audience that comprehensive education reform restructuring, especially in a system of over four hundred thousand students and twenty-five thousand teachers, takes a long time—at least five years—and that the "bottom line of student achievement" is one of the last things affected.[126]

The report focused on the elementary schools, where the average student achievement was substantially below national norms. This was 86 percent of the system, and the primary target of the reform.[127] Needless to say, the consortium found an enormous range on almost every aspect of the reform.

The reform act reconceived local school politics from a process involving traditional self-interested stakeholders to one centered on redefining the purposes and mission of the schools to serve all the children. To do

[124] Moore 1990.
[125] Moore 1990.
[126] Consortium on Chicago School Research 1993, 3.
[127] Consortium on Chicago School Research 1993, 4.

this, there had to be sustained conversations at the community level that would lead to a better understanding of how to advance the well-being of the school community. For this kind of conversation to take place, there had to be regular productive interaction among the three sites of power—the LSC, the PPAC, and the principal.[128]

There were multiple opportunities for leadership. The principals could facilitate or block collaboration; they could encourage or discourage change. While the consortium found complete variance—from "engaged constructive collaborative activity" to perfunctory collaboration, to contests based on narrow self-interests, 46 percent of the principals displayed "inclusive leadership" in that they were "active promoters of broad participation within their schools."[129]

Teachers had to be involved from the beginning in the planning stages, to have regular opportunities to function as a group, to feel comfortable, and to have a sense that their ideas had influence. They had to, in fact, spend time in these activities. The consortium found that 18 percent were highly engaged in collective faculty action, and an additional 33 percent were moderately engaged.[130]

Active LSCs have to meet regularly, establish structures for advancing work outside of meetings, and engage participation from the broader community. The consortium found that only 19 percent of the LSCs were "nonfunctional."[131]

The consortium found four types of local school politics: The most prevalent type (46 percent) was characterized as "consolidated principal power," under which neither the parents nor the community nor the teachers were able to sustain active involvement. The principal either acted autocratically or commanded deference paternally or maternally.

[128] Consortium on Chicago School Research 1993, 5.

[129] Principals gave strong positive responses to three or more questions dealing with personal professional development and teacher/staff development; working with parent and community groups; a broad teacher role in budgeting and hiring; and the ideas that conflict is necessary for change and that committees can be used to resolve conflict.

[130] Teachers were asked whether they felt safe in expressing their opinions; have influence over a range of decisions; know about and are involved in the School Improvement Plan; have an opinion about the role of the PPAC in developing new programs and ideas; work on committees; participate in PPAC; and whether the principal reports that the PPAC plays an important role in developing new programs and ideas and whether the teachers coordinate their work.

[131] Indicators included meeting at least once per month; having at least one subcommittee; averaging three or more guests per meeting; having four or more stable parent/community members since the second election; having had 5 percent or more of parents voting in the second election; having at least as many parent/community candidates in the second election as positions were available; and having a principal who does not strongly agree with the statement: "I am able to get the LSC to do what I want" (Consortium on Chicago School Research 1993, 6).

The next largest group (32 percent) was "strong democracy." In these schools, there was sustained debate over dissatisfaction with current operations, and shared interests emerged, at least some of the time, to promote school improvement. In some of these schools, the principal played a key role in initiating strong democracy. In others, it was the teachers searching out new programs and curricula, and in others, it was parents or community members in the LSCs.

The next group (24 percent) was pretty much satisfied with the status quo. The principals were usually involved in placating competing interests.

In only a small number (9 percent), was there sustained, adversarial conflict—usually over control and power, personalities, allegiances, and so forth, and rarely about substantive matters.[132]

The elementary schools varied substantially in terms of the proportions of low-income students, race and ethnicity, size, and student mobility rates, yet each of the four types of school politics could be found in schools with any combinations of these characteristics.[133]

The major problem for most schools was convincing parents and students that their neighborhood school could be different and that parents and students could have an effective voice in improving their schools. The first step was to establish the schools as a "safer and more caring place." Many schools focused their efforts on strengthening ties to the parent community and local neighborhoods to draw in outside resources. Teachers, too, had to be convinced that the reforms would improve their working conditions. Structures had to be created for teacher participation. Buildings were in disrepair and there were insufficient teaching materials. Many schools used their discretionary funds to upgrade the libraries and basic instructional programs while other's focused on visible signs of improvement as strategic first steps in building community participation.[134]

Ideas for improvements varied. Sometimes add-ons, such as for example, tutoring, adult mentoring, an expanded preschool, and an extended school day, were very important. The challenge, though, was to take a more systemic approach to school reform, to look at the entire program. Such an approach, it was felt, was not inconsistent with a focused mission, such as an Afrocentric curriculum, or a bilingual environment. It was hoped that decentralized governance would result in distinctive schools.[135]

The consortium identified five different types of initiatives.

[132] Consortium on Chicago School Research 1993, 7–8.
[133] For an update on the consortium report, see Easton and Storey, 1994.
[134] Consortium on Chicago School Research 1993, 13.
[135] Consortium on Chicago School Research 1993, 14.

1. *Environmental Order.* Establishing a safe and orderly work environment was the first order of business for many schools. Among other things, these schools worked with parents to start new disciplinary and attendance programs, and to seek other ways to motivate children.
2. *Peripheral Academic Changes.* Here, add-ons were haphazard, and did not affect either the core instruction or classroom practice. The improvement process had not yet developed.
3. *"Christmas Tree" Schools.* These schools were the same as the peripheral ones, only more expansive. They garnered more resources, but did not engage in a systemic analysis of their program.
4. *Emergent Restructuring.* In these schools, a lot of time was devoted to discussing improvements, trying new ideas, involving faculty, parents, and community members, as well as outside expertise. Subgroups of faculty engaged in professional development to improve classroom practice. Teacher leadership began to emerge. Groups of parents with long-term commitments developed, actively recruiting other parents.
5. *Sustained Systemic Activity.* This would be the maturing of emergent restructuring. Schools became essentially new organizations. New norms of collaboration became institutionalized. Relationships were collegial rather than hierarchical. Teachers had leadership roles, and time was structured for planning and professional development. In these schools, principals, teachers, and parents worked together.[136]

The consortium found that during the first year or two of the reform, most schools spent most of their time on the environmental order and on improving relations in the communities. Then, virtually all of the schools moved on to the next categories. Here, the major differences were between unfocused improvement activities (2, 3) and more systemic ones (4, 5). In the unfocused approaches, principals preferred traditional roles. The involvement of the teachers, parents, and the community was limited. The teachers, in these schools, did not connect failures in student achievement with classroom practices; hence, they saw little need to revise the core instruction. With the systemic approaches, there was a strong emphasis on broad participation in improvement planning. Teachers as well as parents were involved. A great deal of time was spent in both developing and implementing the School Improvement Plan and community relations, and in communication with parents, with LSC members, and with teachers. There was active collaboration and a sense of collegiality. In these schools, principals reported high levels of teacher commitment and influence in decision making. The teachers reported that their instructional practices had changed as a result of the School Improvement Plan.

[136] Consortium on Chicago School Research 1993, 16; Hess n.d.

The consortium found the following distribution: Between 26 and 35 percent of the schools were "unfocused"; between 36 and 45 percent were "systemic"; between 15 and 25 percent had features of both; and 11 to 13 percent were not classifiable. Again, both unfocused and systemic improvements were found in a wide array of schools. Neither socioeconomic status nor prereform student achievement was related to systemic reform; systemic reform was present in the poorest as well as the relatively more advantaged schools.

Democratic governance turned out to be a key ingredient. This was the basic logic of the reform act—that local participation leads to systemic reform efforts and sustained attention to instructional improvements. The consortium found that systemic improvement was strongly related to those schools that were governed by strong democracy. In those schools that engaged a broad base of stakeholders in sustained discussions over educational issues, two-thirds engaged in systemic improvement; an additional 16 percent displayed some features of systemic improvement, and only 9 percent remained unfocused. In contrast, 80 percent of those schools that engaged in adversarial politics were unfocused. In schools characterized by consolidated principal power, there was little collective discussion. Forty-three percent of these schools were unfocused. Even well-intentioned principals, says the consortium, cannot reform schools on their own.[137]

Does school improvement lead to instructional change? About two-thirds of the systemically improved schools report a moderate or significant use of what the consortium characterizes as "authentic learning practices"—that is, a deep engagement of the subject matter, students actively participating in the learning process, emphasis on the student production of knowledge. This proportion is twice as high as in the schools that were unfocused. More than a quarter of the systemic schools report that almost all of their students participate in innovative teaching and curricula approaches, including cooperative learning. Only 6 percent of the unfocused schools make similar claims. Sixty percent of the unfocused schools report that less than half of their students experience cooperative learning. Twice as many systemic schools as compared to unfocused schools report that writing runs throughout the curriculum. The consortium cautions that it is too early to tell whether these innovations will result in greater student achievement, but it does seem that systemic restructuring does foster instructional change.[138]

The consortium then took an in-depth look at the process of change in six of the most active schools in a study entitled the Experiences of Ac-

[137] Consortium on Chicago School Research 1993, 21.
[138] Consortium on Chicago School Research 1993, 24. For a more skeptical view, see Hess 1994a.

tively Restructuring Schools (EARS). Three of these schools were among the worst in the Chicago system prior to the reforms. Each of the principals displayed a commitment to the students and the parents in the community. The LSCs played an active role in improving parent and community involvement, enlisting parents to support home learning, improving the physical plant, improving order and safety, and generally focusing attention on local needs. The principals and the teacher leaders took the initiative in school improvement planning, budgeting, and instructional activities. In all of the schools, however, the key feature was principal leadership. The principals developed good working relationships with the LSCs, were sensitive to local needs, and were committed to an inclusive process of open communication. All the principals were enthusiastic, optimistic, and passionate in their commitment to the restructuring. While each principal had a distinctive vision for the school, the commonalities were changing the relationships of parents and to the local community to the school and to a total commitment to the students.[139] The principals sought to create a "sense of agency" among the parents and the teachers, to instill in them the idea that they could make a difference—"together we can make this place better."[140]

The principals worked hard at staff development. They sought to build a team that was compatible with the collaborative vision of the school. There were efforts to engage the whole faculty in teacher improvement. Teaching behind closed doors was no longer the norm. Time was created for the teachers to meet, consult, exchange ideas, and assume the responsibilities that the reform plans called for. Since much of the collaborative activity occurred during the nonworking parts of the day, discretionary funds were used to provide at least partial compensation. In each of the schools, most of the faculty eventually became engaged in at least some manner.

In each of the schools, what the consortium called a "professional community" developed. A professional community develops when the whole school engages in important conversations concerning education issues, when the teachers individually and collaboratively examine their teaching behaviors, when there is sustained attention to what students are actually learning, when there is concern for students both in and out of school and a commitment to the idea that every student can learn and that all are of equal value.[141] Much of the task of getting a professional community going in each of the EARS rested with the principals. The principals had to change the climate, to convey the message that "we must work together" to improve the school and to create a professional com-

[139] Consortium on Chicago School Research 1993, 27.
[140] Consortium on Chicago School Research 1993, 28.
[141] Consortium on Chicago School Research 1993, 30.

munity, and to sustain that community in its initial stages. In short, the principals had to use their power to empower the teachers.

While each of the schools developed external connections to support their improvement programs, the newly available discretionary funds were key.[142] While amounts varied, they were substantial. Some of the funds were used to meet basic educational needs, for example, textbooks and art and music materials. Significant funds were spent for additional teachers, aides, teachers for after-school programs, social workers, and psychologists. The funds played an important role in creating a new image for the schools. The consortium thinks the funds were crucial to whatever progress was made.[143]

The consortium then examined the classroom to see whether there were changes in the nature of the teaching, social relations, and opportunities for student learning.[144] In three-quarters of the classes, across the six schools, students were actively engaged in the learning process in comfortable classrooms with teachers who were open and supportive. There was a wide range of teaching activities. In some classes, teaching was responsive to linguistic and cultural backgrounds and incorporated multicultural understandings. Others built on student experiences. There was some cooperative learning, and some inclusion of special education students. Mostly, though, the teaching could be characterized as "thoughtful didactic instruction," occasionally with innovative methods. On the other hand, in a quarter of the schools, the teaching was uninspired, the academic content was minimal, and there was little energy in the classroom.[145]

Virtually all of the teachers were positive toward the reform; they liked their school, their colleagues, and their classes. They reported increased cooperation, communication, and teamwork. There were opportunities for increased parental and community involvement. The teachers were involved in the development of the improvement plan and said that it was a positive experience. They spoke in "glowing terms" about their work, their colleagues, and their students, a "key indicator of a sense of personal well-being."[146]

The researchers were impressed with the atmosphere in both the classrooms and the hallways—pleasant and cheerful. Students who lived in bad neighborhoods emphasized the safety of the school (in four of the

[142] Rosenkranz, 1994.

[143] Consortium on Chicago School Research 1993, 31.

[144] Observations were made in reading and math classes in the first and third grades; social studies and math in the sixth and eighth grades. Observations were made of forty teachers performing fifty-two different lessons (Consortium on Chicago School Research 1993, 32).

[145] Hess thinks that there has been little change in classroom practices (Hess 1994a).

[146] Consortium on Chicago School Research 1993, 33.

schools, the streets were so dangerous that the students had to stay indoors after school and on vacation). The students were appreciative of teachers who "really listen." They felt comfortable with other students and engaged in a wide range of extracurricular and after-school programs. Most students reported that the teachers had high expectations, that the teachers cared about them, and that success was rewarded. Parents were informed about successes, honor rolls were prominently displayed, there were ceremonies for high achievers, and exemplary work was on display. The majority of students were very satisfied with their teachers, and appreciated their support and care and the value placed on the commitment to academic learning.

At that time (1993), the consortium cautiously believed that the Chicago school reform was working. This is not to say that the goal of the reform—all schools reaching national norms within five years—would be met; no plan, in the opinion of the consortium, could ever meet that goal.[147] But the major premise of the reform act was that enhanced democratic participation at the schoolhouse level would bring about systemic restructuring that would improve teaching and learning. And there was enhanced democratic participation in many schools. At least a third of the schools most in need of reform developed strong democratic participation focused on a systemic approach to whole-school improvement, and perhaps another third shared some of these characteristics. Many of the schools were moving through the developmental process consistent with the theory of the reform act. In this sense, the reform was succeeding.[148]

Despite the accomplishments, the consortium believed that the reforms were still very fragile. Even though more and more teachers were assuming important roles, the reforms all relied to a great extent on the leadership of the principals. In a 1992 survey, the consortium reported that in their opinion while the majority of principals were generally supportive of the reforms and said that local governance was working well in their schools, the principals were working very hard with insufficient resources and authority, raising concerns as to how long they could maintain their efforts,[149] Indeed, subsequent to the report, several of the schools experienced principal turnover frequently admidst controversy.

The schools relied a lot on the support and encouragement of parents and the community. All of this could change, cautioned the consortium, with changes in leadership, loss of resources, and changes in staff.[150]

---

[147] Apparently, achievement scores in Chicago have not shown much improvement, at least as measured by conventional standards, and this has produced great controversy. See Hess 1994a; Bryk et al. 1994.

[148] Consortium on Chicago School Research 1993, 36.

[149] Consortium on Chicago School Research 1992.

[150] Consortium on Chicago School Research 1992, 37.

Much remains to be done. A major effort is needed to improve teacher expertise, both as to subject matter content and pedagogy, and it is not clear whether new materials and techniques will generate new types of learning. The professional community is a new concept for teachers and principals, and new skills are required. A serious issue is the constraints on teacher time. Schools cannot continue to rely on good will and volunteer time.

Decentralization has created the need to develop new infrastructures that can support individual school development. While central control was obviously inadequate, a hands-off approach is also unsatisfactory. Schools need support, but how to accomplish this while valuing individual initiative and recognizing the need to develop a wide range of expertise, knowledge, and skills, has not been thought through. As to the quarter of the schools that have not changed, it is unlikely that much will happen if they are left on their own. The system has to figure out a way to intervene in the most troubled schools. In the opinion of the consortium, reform and improvement is most likely to come in the small schools. But the real threat to the current progress is the current fiscal crisis in Chicago. Advocates of the reform act contemplated that reducing the central office staff would produce large sums of discretionary money for the schools, with disproportionately larger amounts going to schools with high numbers of low-income students. However, the interim board increased the compensation of the teachers, with no new resources. As a result, the base level of funding for all the schools had to be cut, undermining much of the discretionary budget power of the LSCs. This could have a disastrous effect on the whole effort.[151] Then, there was a hard-fought political compromise over the 1993–94 budget that, in the opinion of the Chicago Panel on School Policy, was particularly devastating to the reform efforts (1993).[152]

In the most recent development, as the present temporary school board ceases to exist, the Illinois legislature decided to turn complete control over the school system to the mayor. The goal is to streamline central management and fix accountability. The mayor will have the sole right to select the head of the city schools, the members of a "superboard"—a scaled-down panel of five members to run the system—and every other top decision maker. The mayor's powers are to last for four years, after which the board is to expand to seven members. In addition, the legislation curbs the teachers union. Collective bargaining is to be restricted to salaries and benefits (class size will be decided by the board) as well as tenure issues for jobs that are abolished. The union is prohibited from

[151] Consortium on Chicago School Research 1992, 40; Hess and Easton 1992.
[152] For further accounts of the fiscal crisis, see Rosenkranz 1994.

striking for eighteen months (the union has already filed a lawsuit contesting these provisions). But the legislation does not disturb the 1988 reforms concerning control over local schools; in fact, the authority of individual principals has been strengthened. However, no additional state funds are to be provided to the school system, which continues to be in serious financial straits.[153]

Another study of the Chicago reform, by Alfred Hess and John Easton,[154] is not quite as sanguine as the consortium is. They note the continuing conflicts between the central administration and the LSCs. From the very beginning, there was controversy over the authority of the LSCs and the opposition, both within and without the school system, has sought to undermine them. Hess and Easton studied governance in ten elementary and four high schools, representative in terms of race, size, and location. The patterns varied. In some schools, the LSCs made decisions, in others, they appeared to do little more than agree with the principals. Although average attendance varied, most of the councils did have a core membership that could be counted on. The chairs (parents) and teachers had high participation rates; the community members and parents attended less. Members differed in influence in terms of issues, but the principals and the chairs, followed by the teachers, participated frequently. Community members and other parents spoke less frequently. In general, the principals provided information and the chairs were facilitators.[155]

The reform act was based, in part, on the conviction that effective schools would be led by effective principals. However, the authors found that not all the principals were that enthusiastic about the changes. While they like their increased discretionary authority in terms of staff and discretionary funds, overall, the principals were negative. They complained about the increased demands on their time, the need to constantly supply information, engage in public relations, and worry about their jobs. They were concerned about the LSCs exceeding their authority (for example, evaluating teachers) and that they, the principals, would be evaluated by teachers. The principals had a somewhat negative view of the capabilites of their teachers.[156] At the same time, the principals complained that they had the ultimate responsibility.[157]

Contrary to the expectations of critics, the LSCs did not engage in political wrangling or patronage, but instead focused primarily on substan-

153 Don Terry, "Chicago's Mayor Gains School Control That New York's Mayor Would Envy," *New York Times*, June 29, 1995, A6; G. Alfred Hess, Jr., telephone interview by the author, June 29, 1995.
154 Hess and Easton 1992. See also Hess 1994a.
155 Hess and Easton, 1992, 164.
156 Hess 1994a, 259–60.
157 Hess and Easton 1992, 167.

tive school issues. Problems as well as discussions varied by school. Some discussions were brief and decisions were routine, but others were long and protracted. While in most cases, decisions were made by votes, most votes were one-sided.[158]

While all the schools adopted school improvement plans, some were cursory and did not address curriculum or instruction; others were extensive and far-reaching, and most were in between. The authors reported that most of the plans would not result in radical changes in education. Rather, they were small increments—for example, remediation, extra study, tutorial time for students below grade level. Hess and Easton say that this may be the most that could be expected in the early years, although it may not be enough to meet the statutory goals.

The reform act resulted in an outpouring of energy and enthusiasm. Sustaining that interest will be a major challenge. Already, the LSCs are experiencing frustration because of the teacher compensation decisions made by the central administration. The authors report that there have been other kinds of conflicts with the central administration over school personnel. Nevertheless, despite these difficulties, major new decision-making authority has been delegated to the local schools, and many new actors are participating in school governance. The fact that there is near unanimity on most LSC decisions indicates that the councils are working collaboratively, and the willingness of parents and teachers to work together was a major concern of some critics of the Chicago reform.[159]

Donald Moore, who was centrally involved in the Chicago restructuring, summarized what he believes are the lessons learned so far concerning the role of parent and community involvement.[160] He argues that while research does show that, in general, when parents are involved, children do better in schools, and go to better schools, the broad generalization is misleading. "Parental involvement" covers a variety of activities, ranging from regular parent-school contacts, helping with homework, volunteering at school, to more controversial activities, such as involvement with decision making, advocacy, and choice.

The conceptual model for Chicago's Designs for Change focused not only on the classroom, but also on the school itself, and on the larger school community—the family, peer groups, and the neighborhood. The school was reconceived as not just a social institution that provides narrow classroom instruction, but as a resource that encourages attendance and graduation, minimizes internal sorting, and creates a decent humane environment that can facilitate and provide high-quality instruction. With the expanded concept, a wider range of productive parent and com-

---

[158] Hess and Easton 1992, 170.   [159] Hess 1993b; Hess and Easton 1992.
[160] Moore 1992.

munity involvement becomes relevant—encouraging students to attend, eliminating rigid tracking, pressing for school upkeep, improving discipline, and so forth.[161]

Moore says that the various forms of parental involvement, such as communication with the school, home support, involvement with decision making, tend to be mutually supporting. The important thing is to allow for a range of involvement and planning, and to have the involvement extend over a long period of time. The basic precondition is regular contact. Moore claims that several studies show that frequent parent-school contact is associated with higher levels of student achievement and more positive school staff attitudes. There is, of course, variation among schools serving different populations, even at this basic level. Parents helping at home—communicating high expectations, having regular conversations about school, encouraging completion of homework—are also related to achievement, including that of low-income children. Parent and community member volunteers at schools have also been associated with higher student achievement, but this usually only involves a small number of parents.

Far more controversial is parent and community involvement in decision making, especially if it is real participation rather than just the giving of advice. Moore says that this form of participation has not been studied that much, and the results so far are inconsistent. Chicago has the first large-scale urban reform effort that clearly envisages real decision-making authority on the part of parents and the community. While the experiment is based on careful analysis and research, it will take years to see its results.[162]

On the basis of the Chicago experience thus far, and what research there is, Moore offers the following "critical conditions for effective decision-making involvement:"[163]

1. The school must be the key unit. If the units are too large, then parents cannot participate and the community boards will be dominated by the established political interest groups. In contrast, each Chicago school was governed by its own council. Parents would be motivated because the particular schools with which they were involved were the ones their own children attended. In 1989, more than fifteen thousand parent and community members ran for council seats; moreover, participation was fairly consistent across the schools.

2. The school-site governing bodies must include all the stakeholders, but the parents must be in the majority, otherwise they will be dominated by the professionals. It was predicted that the Chicago scheme would heighten

[161] Moore 1992, 139–40.   [162] Moore 1992, 144–45.
[163] Moore 1992, 146.

conflicts between parents and educators, but, in fact, 65 percent of the teachers on the councils report that staff-parent relations have improved since the elections.

3. The governing bodies must have significant decision-making authority within those areas that are critical to school improvement, such as staffing, budget, and spending priorities. The governing bodies set policy rather than engage in day-to-day operations. In addition, the Chicago councils have authority to select principals on four-year performance contracts.

4. There have to be incentives that focus the governing bodies' priorities on the quality of the educational experiences and student performance. There must be targets for attendance, graduation rates, achievement, transitions to college, and so forth. The principal's performance contract and the school budget must be focused on improving education.

5. Because these tasks and responsibilities are new, the members of the governing bodies and the staff must have ongoing training and assistance.

6. The authority of the central administration and of the board of education has to be reduced and restructured in light of the changed responsibilities. Otherwise, the central bureaucracies will thwart local initiatives.[164]

Moore notes that when school-site management schemes are dominated by educators, they bring, at most, only limited changes. This is because professionals are too often constrained by existing routines and frames of reference, as well as by political bargains. Principals and teachers typically avoid putting problems on the agenda that will run counter to traditional professional norms. This is especially true of practices that would require teachers to evaluate each other or that require aggressive initiatives. Instead, they will focus on problems and issues that are relatively straightforward or noncontroversial, for example, encouraging independent student reading. Parents, on the other hand, are not bound by organizational routines or political bargains. Moore reports that in the first years of the Chicago reform, parents placed on the agenda new problems, such as persistent teacher absences, lack of sufficient substitute teachers, and safety in the bathrooms, playgrounds, and while traveling to and from school. Furthermore, parents used their political and community networks to help the school get particular problems solved. Moore says that even though the reforms are just underway in Chicago, there were hundreds of individual examples of new problems brought by parents.[165]

Parent and community advocacy is, of course, very controversial. Moore reports that here, too, the record is mixed. Some efforts have been highly effective, while others have been either harmful or irrelevant.

[164] Moore 1992, 146–48.   [165] Moore 1992, 148–51.

Moore found that those that did result in significant improvements had the following characteristics: The groups developed an increasingly precise understanding of exactly what changes they wanted to pursue, pressed for the changes, developed an accurate "map" of both the formal and informal systems, built a well-organized, committed constituency capable of mobilizing political power, intervened at multiple levels, and engaged in vigorous monitoring. The Chicago reform, he says, would not have happened without this kind of sophisticated advocacy. To give one significant example, the year after the reform, the superintendent was prevented by the advocacy groups from reinflating the size of the central administration budget by taking $80 million of the discretionary funds from the schools.[166]

CONCLUSIONS

The range and scope of school reform illustrates many of the major elements of the politics of structure. It is hard to imagine a more intense controversy involving the full range of symbols, values, and material resources. At stake are some of the most important issues facing contemporary America—race, redistribution, socialization, community, let alone education of the citizenry.

Most reform efforts, therefore, are the result of mixed motives and multiple aims. Magnet schools, for example, can viewed as reforms aimed at increasing quality education through concentration and focus, or a method of acknowledging the worth of diverse cultures and traditions in America, or a method of furthering parental choice, or a device to further the advantages of elites and disfavor the ordinary urban population, or a form of decentralization designed to defuse intense conflicts over mandatory racial desegregation.

School restructuring can be viewed as a move designed to break the corruption and inefficiency of centralized bureaucratic control, or as a way to defeat the union protections for teachers, or as a device to increase neighborhood advantages. School restructuring—ranging from the radical democratic localism of Chicago to the magnets to the various choice plans—claims to be focused on improving student achievement. A critical element in most of the restructuring plans is empowering various stakeholders previously left out of the decision-making process—teachers, parents, and, sometimes, community residents. The methods of empowerment vary from market-based choice, to choice within the system, to incorporation into the governance system.[167] It is no wonder that the landscape is not only extremely varied but also in flux. As Terry Moe

---

[166] Moore 1992, 151–53.   [167] Hess 1993b.

points out (chap. 2), victories in bureaucratic struggles are rarely complete; too much is at stake. We already see that major restructuring efforts, such as those in Dade County and perhaps in District 4, seem to be losing momentum. If the history of education reform is any guide, we know that current reforms efforts will not be the last word.

The specific concern of this book is with the empowerment of dependent people. The democratic localism of Chicago is the most radical, far-reaching attempt to empower teachers, parents, and community residents. In the next chapter, we focus more specifically on the empowerment issues, using Chicago as our principal example.

Chapter 8

CONCLUSIONS

THE CONTEXT OF EMPOWERMENT

Decentralization, deregulation, and privatization continue to enjoy increasing favor in American politics. As discussed in the introduction, whether viewed as the reallocation of authority between state and market or state and lower units of government, these ideas resonate along different ideological dimensions. For conservatives, decentralization, deregulation, and privatization have traditionally meant (1) reducing the public sector in favor of the private sector; (2) reducing the regulatory burden on the private sector; and (3) bringing those government functions that remained public closer to the people. Gains would be efficiency, effectiveness, and citizen freedoms traditionally associated with liberal capitalism and local democracy. While less government and more markets are commonly associated with conservatives, liberals have also championed decentralization and, increasingly, deregulation as well. The most notable recent example was the War on Poverty's Community Action program. Town governments, neighborhood associations, and community empowerment, both historically and today, are the sole province of neither the Right or the Left. The same is true for flexible, cooperative-style, environmental, health, and safety regulations, and school reform.

While there are many ways of examining decentralization, deregulation, and privatization, in this book we have looked at these issues from the perspective of the ordinary person. Both conservatives and liberals argue that, depending on the circumstances, these reallocations of authority will (can, or may) increase the freedom of the ordinary person, whether that person be citizen, client, patient, or consumer.

The key phrase, of course, is "depending on the circumstances." It would be nice if one could reach some firm generalizations—that privatization will increase client choice, that choice will increase patient control over the delivery of social services or parent control over schools, that decentralization to local governments will enhance the voice of the citizen. But the world of power and politics does not favor the ordinary citizen or parent or dependent client, and, as we have seen, whatever labels, whatever the slogans or symbols, decentralization, deregulation, and privatization are contests over the allocation of power. Procedures designed to give voice to the voiceless are always threatened by underlying inequalities in wealth, resources, influence, and information.

The experience of privatization, and especially contracting, is sobering. As distinguished from the relatively powerless patient or client, here, the stakeholders have information and resources. However, as Donahue, and the examples from New Jersey and Massachusetts have shown, the benefits from contracting only accrue when there is competition; and competition is indeed rare. In these major examples, the important actors—both public and private—are able to reconstruct the contracting system to perpetuate the mutual, reciprocal benefits of organizational survival. Private suppliers, whether profit or nonprofit, come to resemble public monopolies. In time, there is little competitive bidding, contracts are sometimes renegotiated, but rarely terminated. Services may very well be increased—indeed, contracting strengthens the lobbying resources of the private sector—but both efficiency and consumer choice are submerged.

We note similar disturbing trends in the nonprofit sector. Government revenues, in the form of contracts, make up the bulk of payments to charities. Responding to the new environment, the successful charities have become large, hierarchical, and dominated by the entrepreneurial chief executive. Concerns about the effects of privatization in the delivery of health care are illustrative of more general trends in the nonprofit field. Among scholars, there is a difference of opinion as to who is controlling whom—the government contracting officers or the nonprofit as the ultimately indispensible provider—and whether nonprofits are more or less efficient than for-profit providers. Opinions also differ as to whether the consumer of charitable services are (or will be) better or worse off with the bureaucratization of the nonprofit sector. There is, however, no evidence that clients have more voice under the new contracting arrangements.

Similar results are often present with delegations to lower units of government. As far as the ordinary citizen or client is concerned, local government can be just as bureaucratic, just as unresponsive as state or federal government. Indeed, the near universal protest against public education is testimony to the unresponsiveness of local government.

On the other hand, we have discussed situations in which there did seem to be cases of genuine participation by ordinary people. These examples were from a wide variety of fields—worker safety, special education, home health care, public housing, neighborhood associations. While each of these examples had different histories and characteristics, the common threads were the importance of context, and, therefore, the inherent, underlying instability of relationships. If a generalization can be made, it is that the concept of *process* has to be taken seriously. Empowerment involves the reallocation of power to subordinate or relatively powerless people. Empowerment does not have to be zero-sum—indeed, I argue that empowerment should be looked at as the sharing of power, where both sides benefit—but even as sharing, empowerment involves altering power relationships. Because underlying inequalities are not disturbed, and because underlying inequalities shift over time, empowerment is never permanent. The politics of structure are continuous.

Granted the importance of context, in a world of instability, what can we say about when the conditions are favorable, or necessary, for empowerment? By definition, the starting point is an initial unequal distribution of power. In the water pollution regulation example (chap. 3), the parties were roughly equal in terms of power. Each of the parties knew their own position, probably had a pretty good idea of the other's position, and made a cost-benefit calculation as to whether to cooperate or to fight. In the cooperative relationships, they exchanged material benefits—forbearance in return for information and cooperation in changing practices. The question is how can this kind of cooperative relationship apply when power is unequal.

In chapter 6, I explored empowerment by invitation. While there were conflicts of interests, the principal stakeholders voluntarily came together and agreed to work out a cooperative relationship. Where the parties are unequal, the weaker party has to be empowered; otherwise the cooperation is a sham. In order for there to be cooperation in unequal relationships, I have argued the following:

1. There has to be a change in professional norms on the part of the power holders, that is, they have to come to believe that the dependent clients are part of the *solution* to their professional task.
2. The technology has to be appropriate to participation. By this I mean that the contribution of the dependent client to the professional task has to be real, it has to be valued—for example, parents helping to educate their handicapped children, or the frail elderly supplying valuable information to the home health care agency. This leads to the third element.
3 There has to be an *exchange of material resources*. The dependent client contributes something of value. This is important for a number of reasons. It helps continue the willingness of the power holders to listen. Good intentions (changes in professional norms) are crucial, but they are not sufficient. Teachers, social workers, physicians, psychologists, administrators, and managers are busy. The material incentives keep them listening. At the same time, exchanging something of tangible value is important for the powerless. They have evidence, real evidence, that they are important. This is the lived experience that Keiffer emphasizes. In education, home-based care, and worker safety, there was a sharing of expertise and resources from teachers, agencies, and management; in return, parents, clients, and workers per-

formed essential tasks. The New York City housing tenants relieved the city of the politically burdensome task of administering rental property, but the tenants could not have done this without critical resources from the city. In the neighborhood organizations, citywide political leaders benefitted from the decisions reached by the local organizations.

In all of these examples, changes in power were not zero-sum. There were not winners and losers; rather, both sides benefitted. I think that because cooperative relationships are so fragile in hierarchical bureaucracies or where power otherwise remains so unequal, that these kinds of reciprocal, material benefits are essential to sustain genuine bargaining. Otherwise, even with beneficient motives, there will be gradual cooptation.

Material resouces have to be exchanged, but dependent people, again by definition, lack resources. This means that the less powerful have to have outside sources of support to sustain their end of the relationship. They can't do it on their own. In the chapter 6 examples, much of the crucial resources came from the power holders. This is what I mean by "empowerment by invitation." To be sure, the clients, parents, patients, and workers have to be able to seize the opportunities and become empowered through their efforts as well. Empowerment is a reflexive process. Nursing homes are the most problematic example. Nursing home residents are so dependent, so vulnerable, and, so increasingly disabled, that virtually all the exchange has to come from outsiders, such as families or advocacy groups.

The inherent instability the cooperative arrangements with dependent people returns us to the analysis of the nature of organizations and the politics of bureaucratic design. As Moe reminds us, bureaucratic design, in general, is the struggle over money, resources, influence, and symbols. Organizations, whether public or private, struggle for survival by gaining allies, acquiring resources, seeking legitimacy, and fending off rivals. Decentralization, deregulation, and privatization are aspects of these processes. The allocation and reallocation of authority, either between units of government or between government and the market, is a principal method of managing conflict. It is not surprising that the more important stakeholders will prevail. Thus, whether or not the organization serves the interest of dependent clients depends on whether client interests coincide with the interests of the more important stakeholders. We have seen, for example, that human service agencies will select and sort clients to further agency goals of acquiring legitimacy, political support, and resources. Nonprofit agencies become large, bureaucratic, and more oriented to the government funding source than to their clients. Privatization, it seems, more often than not establishes a private monopoly rather than consumer choice. In these situations, decentralization, deregulation, and privatization, from the perspective of the dependent client, only means the substitution of one hierarchical regime for another. There is no significant change in consumer voice.

None of these tendencies is foreordained. Indeed, there are examples in which privatization does lead to efficiency and consumer choice. There are examples in which delegation to lower units of government results in improved services and greater client satisfaction, especially if choice is allowed. Examples here include magnet schools, many of which appear to be quite successful. But the most important point is to recognize that *none* of the relationships discussed in this book are stable. This is the lesson of the politics of structure. Relationships depend on context, and the context is always changing. Even when the parties are equal, as in the water pollution example, cooperative relationships will change when one party thinks that it will be better off by becoming more adversarial. Changes can be internal to the process, for example, an increase in the cost of correcting conditions, or exogenous, such as political demands for strict enforcement. Similarly, in the worker-safety cooperative relationships described by Rees, much depended on the cost of worker's compensation and the strength of the unions, both of which could change over time. In the Madison, Wisconsin, special education example, parents seemed to become passive and co-opted despite the efforts of teachers to keep them actively involved.

Hierarchical bureaucratic relationships may appear to be stable, but here, too, stability is only relative. The new institutionalists (chap. 2) saw isomorphism, stability, and the inability of organizations to adjust to environmental change. Others saw organizations situated in fields of ideological contradiction and change. Recall the discussion of the nature of the education bureaucracy in the previous chapter. Some view public education has monolithic and impervious to change; others view it as a constantly shifting coalition of interests. In any event, we know from the examples in the last two chapters that empowerment in normally hierarchical relationships is unstable.

When empowerment is born in conflict, the inherent instability and the importance of context of the politics of structure become even more self-evident. Our major example, school restructuring, involves intense, enduring conflicts over values, power, jobs, influence—just about every issue one can think of. The conflicts continue as long as there is something important at stake, and with public education, there is always something important to fight about. In Chicago, some of the most dramatic aspects of struggle involved the mundane ones of municipal politics—money, jobs, patronage, central control, unions, compensation. The reform act came about as a result of a protracted, intense political fight that mobilized both the business community and citizen reform groups. As Moe points out, victors realize that the struggle continues; they therefore try to neutralize the losers, in the event that they may come to power. The Chicago School Reform Act did this by legislatively limiting the size, jurisdiction, and most important, the amounts of funds that could go to the central board. The reformers knew that the board would never give up. And one year after the reform went into effect, the board tried to seize $80 million from the all-important discretionary funds. The board was thwarted because the reform groups remained vigilant. The law was not enough; there had to be staying power on the part of reform groups to preserve gains. In the meantime, the central board is still not reconciled to the LSCs and is constantly trying to undermine them. In the latest round, the reform groups were not able to prevent the union from obtaining substantial funds, and this may turn out to be a crippling blow. Observers believe the absence of discretionary funds will undermine the LSCs and eventually the reforms.[1] Chicago is a dramatic example of the context of continual struggle.

Empowerment by conflict is the hardest test. School reforms, in most instances, seem to have been born out of controversy, out of profound dissatisfaction with the existing state of affairs, and as a result of political struggle. Chicago, of course, clearly fits this pattern. But even seemingly more benign examples, such as District 4 or many of the magnet schools, have different origins and live in different political climates than the empowerment by invitation examples in chapter 6. District 4, it will be recalled, achieved its results largely on its own; it constantly had to deal with a central administration that oscillated between suspicion and grudging tolerance, if not hostility, and clearly opposed any expansion to other city schools. Similarly, most traditional school people are suspicious of magnet schools; they worry about elitism and the diversion of scarce resources. Most school people are opposed to magnet schools and school choice. The current wave of charter schools seems more like a reluctant acceptance of decentralization to diffuse conflict than a warm embrace of innovation. In the school reform examples, perhaps with some exceptions, even in the best situations, reformers may be on their own; and in many situations, there is continuous, open warfare. The possible exceptions are magnet schools that have been used as alternatives to court-ordered desegregation. At least prior to the recent U.S. Supreme Court decision casting doubt on court-ordered desegregation, school reform did have something to give the central administration and the polit-

[1] Hess 1994a; Rosenkranz 1994.

ical leaders.[2] Whether that bargaining chip will remain available to maintain existing magnet schools or provide for new ones is uncertain.[3]

Where there is no support from the powerful stakeholders, then the less powerful have to depend on charismatic leaders and/or powerful social movement organizations. District 4, Dade County, probably the Comer Schools, and the Accelerated Schools rely on the former. They build parent organizations and some local community groups, but they seem to depend primarily on very unusual leadership. And, indeed, the reforms in District 4 and Dade County seem to be waning with the departure of the leaders. Fatigue has become a real problem. In Chicago, in the schools that appear to be succeeding, there are strong leaders (principals) in the individual schools and powerful social movement groups struggling to keep the reform going. Moreover, these groups are not formally connected with the school system. They are composed of business leaders and concerned citizens. This is not to deny the importance of parent and resident participation in the local schools—indeed, that, too, is essential. But the important distinction in Chicago is the key role that the outside reform groups played not only from the very beginning but also as the process continued, as continual monitors. It will be recalled that it was the citizen and business groups that rallied and prevented the Chicago central board from trying again to reappropriate for itself the crucial discretionary funds that were to go to the local schools.[4]

We have described the conditions of empowerment—changes in norms, an appropriate technology, and an exchange of material conditions—as well as the context of instability. But how do we know empirically that there is empowerment in the particular relationship? The usual test is to examine the decision-making process. Indicators would be attendance, participation, control of the agenda, how the decisions are made (for example, voting, consensus), who prevails, how often, for what kinds of issues, and the substantive decisions that are actually made. If the dependent participants scored "high" on the indicators, then we would say that there is empowerment. We have seen, however, in the discussion of power and empowerment in chapter 5, that this kind of objective standard may miss critical elements of the process. There are both substantive and process issues. In the home health care examples, a contrast was drawn between a frail elderly person who actively participates in the hiring and supervising of the worker and the person who was taught to administer her own injections by the Medicare nurse. The former would be empowerment, but the latter raises doubts. It could be argued that all the

[2] *Missouri v. Jenkins*, 115 S. Ct. 2038 (1995).
[3] Handler 1990a.
[4] On the importance of support groups, see Cohen and Rogers 1992.

major medical decisions were made without the patient's participation and that administering her own injection is only one small act. On the other hand, it could be that this act constituted an extremely important issue of efficacy for this particular patient.

The process issues usually concern acquiescence. As will be discussed more fully in the next section, in the neighborhood associations cases that Berry and his associates researched, citizen participation was, at best, very spotty, despite considerable efforts at outreach and the dissemination of information. Yet, the citizens thought that they were empowered by their associations. They felt that they were reasonably informed, that their leaders were responsive, and that they could have access to the process whenever they wanted. The researchers agreed with these assessments.

Both the substantive and process issues of empowerment remain elusive; they involve not only judgments by the participants, but also by the researchers. In the remainder of this chapter, we examine more closely the substantive and process issues of empowerment by returning once again to Chicago. Chicago school reform is not only important in its own right, but, as we have seen, it has produced an unusual amount of high-quality scholarly analysis.

EVALUATING CHICAGO: SUBSTANCE

School reform is not necessarily about democratic governance; rather, it is substantively driven. Nationwide, and in Chicago, the current reform is about improvements in student achievement. Empowerment is a means to that end. Those who favor parental and community participation at the schoolhouse site view these reforms as a way to improve instruction and learning. The premise of the reform act was that enhanced democratic participation at the schoolhouse level would bring about systemic restructuring that would improve teaching and learning.

But empowering teachers and parents is only one of several routes to improving achievement. Many school reformers, for example, take the opposite approach; they believe that the way to improve instruction and learning is through a centrally imposed curriculum. But even reforms that emphasize decentralized governance, do not necessarily embrace parental participation.[5] For example, despite the fact that the Chicago program has been called the most radical school reform experiment in the century, a recent volume titled, *Designing Coherent Education Policy: Improving the System* does not even discuss parent participation in school governance.[6] William Clune argues that while governance restructuring can be justified on other grounds—increasing attendance, discipline, graduation

[5] Clune 1992b.   [6] Fuhrman 1993.

rates, democratic rights of parents, promoting desegregation, political legitimacy, shifting blame, consumer sovereignty, or what not—the *only*
governance changes that are likely to improve student achievement are
those that focus substantial attention on a high-quality curriculum that is
actually delivered in the classroom. In Clune's view, school improvement
has to be content-oriented. Restructuring reforms have to be focused on
improving the supply side of education.[7] Clune argues that the evidence
thus far shows that school achievement is accomplished through curriculum alignment and content-oriented school improvement, that is,
through a high-quality curriculum that is actually delivered to students of
all abilities in the classroom. Clune contrasts the Chicago reforms with
District 4. In the former, the reforms are primarily concerned with remov-
ing the negative influences of the central administration bureaucracy;
the latter illustrates a strong theory as to how to design educational
improvement.[8]

Many other researchers have come to similar conclusions, namely, that
restructuring, by itself, does not necessarily lead to either improvements
in process or in academic achievement. Bryk, Lee and Smith, for example,
state categorically that "the principal determinant of academic achievement is course-taking."[9] Yet, in their view, many current reform efforts
do not take the curriculum as the organizing focus. Similarly, they argue,
it is hard to think of parental choice, by itself, as a remedy for many of the
problems that the urban inner-city schools face. In fact, increasing choice
may increase inequities. Reforms based on "shared values" or a "sense of
ownership," while touted as promoting excellence, in a prior age, they
remind us, promoted intolerance and exclusivity, and, even today, are
used by the religious right to seize control of local schools. What is important is how social values and individual commitments become manifest in
the organization of the school.[10]

The empowerment proponents, for the most part, are also substantively focused. They argue that the professionals and administrators—the
central administrators, most of the principals, and most of the teachers—
are the "problem." The problem is not necessarily democratic governance, but poor-quality education. It is only through sustained, constructive conversations with the local stakeholders in the community—residents as well as parents—that a better understanding of how to advance
the well-being of the entire school community would be reached.

Much of the evaluation of the Chicago reforms hinges on the connection between empowerment and the substantive schooling outcome. As
noted, the Consortium on Chicago School Research looked at the rela-

---

[7] Clune 1990b, 395; 1990a, 14.   [8] Clune 1990b, 396.
[9] Bryk, Lee, and Smith 1990, 187.   [10] Bryk, Lee, and Smith 1990, 190.

tionship between "strong democracy" and systemic restructuring leading to improved teaching and learning along with student and teacher morale. Even the evaluation of empowerment itself—that is, of whether or not the less powerful stakeholders participate meaningfully in school governance—seems to depend on the substantive reform in instruction and learning. Lewis and Makagawa,[11] for example, not only define empowerment in zero-sum terms, but then draw their conclusions as to whether or not there is empowerment on the basis of the substantive outcomes in the schools and the degree of satisfaction of the parents with those outcomes. The authors make the following distinction. The "empowerment" model, they say, assumes that parents can fix schools. The alternative view—which they call the "enablement" model—is that schools can fix parents. In the former, the impetus for change comes from the parents; in the latter, from teachers and bureaucrats. It's not that professionals in the enablement model do the same old thing. Rather, to further the goals of education, they have to change to be able to overcome the alienation of the family and the community and bring them into the schooling enterprise. "Parent involvement is mostly about parents helping the school with the educational endeavor or supplementing the schooling process. Parents should be taught how to help their children learn better and support what the school is doing educationally. . . . Educational professionals can make this happen through enlightened programming and innovative leadership."[12] Lewis and Nakagawa say that this is basically Comer's approach. Teachers will bring in parents when teachers have higher levels of commitment, caring, and understanding.

The authors say that the "enablement paradigm" is different from the "empowerment paradigm" because with the latter, the participation is for political ends—to control the schools—whereas the former is "participation for educational ends."[13]

> If transferring power is the key to the empowerment approach, then cooperation is the key to the enablement approach. The first assumes that the interests of professionals and parents are opposed while the second assumes a convergence of interests around the goal of educating the child. . . . While power is to be shared [in the enablement paradigm], it is to be done with professionals in charge. The parent gets involved when she feels respected and wanted. In contrast, for the empowerment paradigm, the parent gets involved because he or she feels ignored and taken for granted. Satisfaction with the school leads to participation in the enablement approach, whereas dissatisfaction draws parents into participation in the empowerment approach."[14]

---

[11] Lewis and Nakagawa 1992.   [12] Lewis and Nakagawa 1992, 5.
[13] Lewis and Nakagawa 1992, 5.   [14] Lewis and Nakagawa 1992, 6.

The authors draw normative implications from the two approaches. The "enablement paradigm focuses on more traditional educational participation."[15] For this reason, they hypothesize that enablement participation would be associated with school satisfaction, higher school quality, and higher socioeconomic status of the parents. The empowerment paradigm would be associated with dissatisfaction, but also involvement with community organizations. Parents would be dissatisfied but they would care and would not feel powerless.

The authors interviewed Chicago parents during the second year of the reform. They found that over 80 percent of the parents who were elected to the LSCs were of the enablement mold; that is, they "did not see themselves in conflict with the *professional* leadership of the school" (authors' italics). Following the normative dichotomy, the authors view this result as co-optation:

> If the empowerment reforms were hoping to see a radical transformation of the school based upon democratic decentralization they are going to be disappointed. The majority of parents who were empowered by the reform do not seem interested in taking control of the bureaucracy. These findings suggest that empowerment strategies may not be the best way to radically transform schools."[16]

The authors did find that community involvement was a major predictor of political participation—those parents who cared about community values also cared about participating in school reform. However, these same parents also have a basic level of satisfaction with the school.-Moreover,

> this complacency is reaffirmed by their experiences in the policy arena. The parents may well be critical of certain aspects, but they act in a supportive or supplemental role. While this form of participation will increase the legitimacy of the schools, it will not result in any radical transformation. Paradoxically, then participatory reforms will, in the final analysis, increase the control of the professionals and the bureaucrats.[17]

Malen, Ogawa, and Kranz[18] take a similar approach. While the central assumption of site-based management (SBM) is that formal changes in decision-making arrangements will alter "influence relationships," they argue that influence means more than inclusion or even the legal authority to decide. Rather, the test means the ability to affect important outcomes. While it is extremely difficult to determine empirically whether decision making is altered in fact, even with so-called "exemplary examples," in their view, the evidence thus far shows that although SBM in-

---

[15] Lewis and Nakagawa 1992, 6.   [16] Lewis and Nakagawa 1992, 18.
[17] Lewis and Nakagawa 1992, 19.   [18] Malen, Ogawa, and Kranz 1990.

creases involvement, in general it does not appear to substantially alter the decision-making influence of the site participants. There is more communication and consultation, and more participants are on governing bodies, but, they conclude that these reconstituted governing bodies are mostly advisers or endorsers rather than decision makers. While they do address important issues, such as discipline, fund raising, improvements, and so forth, they rarely address the central issues of teaching and learning. The same is true, they say, with principals and teachers. The principals control the agendas. In joint meetings, they rarely focus on budget, personnel, or program. Rather, principals use SBM as a buffer to diffuse divisive issues and maintain existing relationships.[19]

There are many factors that inhibit SBM councils from altering traditional relations, but clearly one of the more important ones is the staying power of the participants. The initial bursts of enthusiasm are followed by increasing demands on time and energy, the anxieties and stresses of new roles and expectations, the inevitable conflicts and frustrations, and only marginal change, all leading to burnout. In the opinion of the authors, participants often feel more overburdened than empowered. In the final analysis, the participants lack the resources, time, skills, and funds to engage in the continuous, coordinated planning that is required to improve schooling.[20]

Why, then, is SBM so popular? Because, say the authors, it is a political response aimed at restoring order and legitimacy by conveying the impression that the schools will now respond to dominant social values in the community. The response is deliberately kept ambiguous to avoid deciding among the competing interests. Instead, exemplary schools are emphasized and SBM spreads as the appropriate response.[21] In other words, SBM, as a form of delegation, is used to manage conflict.

Alfred Hess also seems to base his skepticism of empowerment on normative outcomes. So far, he says, there is little evidence that either teacher or parent empowerment efforts can be directly linked to improvements in student achievement. In exemplary schools—for example, Cambridge, East Harlem—one does not know whether improved scores are due to expanded choice in enrollment or program differentiation. But the principal reason for the confusion is that the restructuring changes are still too new. It takes a long time to see whether elementary school reforms improve attendance rates, grade retention, test scores, and high school graduation rates.[22]

Hess says that the two major restructuring strategies—use of teacher

---

[19] Malen, Ogawa, and Kranz 1990, 307–8. For a more optimistic view of the work of LSCs, see Easton and Storey 1994.

[20] Malen, Ogawa, and Kranz 1990, 313.

[21] Malen, Ogawa, and Kranz 1990, 326.

[22] Hess 1992c, 232; Hess 1994a.

empowerment or of parent, student, and community representatives—
represent two halves of the same apple. Teacher empowerment focuses on
relationships among teachers and between teachers, principals, and district administrators, while downplaying relationships to parents and
largely ignoring relationships to community members who do not have
children in school. Thus, teacher empowerment tends to remain a school-
bound strategy. Parent or client empowerment focuses on parents and
community members and their ability to hold teachers and principals accountable for their performance. In many inner-city neighborhoods, public schools are seen more as colonial outposts of a hostile mainline culture
than as community institutions. Still, maintains Hess, the two restructuring strategies are not necessarily hostile to each other and not necessarily
mutually exclusive.[23]

In the final analysis, Hess is skeptical whether professionals will know
what to do to improve schools. On the basis of his personal experiences
with school-level educators, he does not detect the radical vision and
ideas about organization and processes, curriculum, teaching, student assessment and parent participation necessary to bring about significant,
long-lasting change. The case studies, he says, show the need for really
strong leadership.[24]

EVALUATING CHICAGO: PROCESS

If we take the view of empowerment offered in chapter 5, perhaps the
Chicago experience, as well as other examples of school restructuring,
look a bit different. Commentators on empowerment do not usually
focus on substantive outcomes; rather, they are concerned with the effects
on the participants. Some emphasize material effects. Do the less powerful, in fact, exercise more power in decisions affecting their lives? Others
emphasize psychological impacts. Is there personal growth, a sense of
self-control over one's environment? Keiffer, as well as other commentators, emphasizes the interaction between material or context and psychological development. Empowerment is a developmental process whereby
people gain a sense of self-efficacy by dealing with their environment. The
powerless combine changes in ideology and self-perception with experience and reflection, and eventually become more confident in their ability
to control their environment.

As defined by Keiffer and others, empowerment has a psychological
base—a developing sense of self-efficacy. How do the participants feel
about themselves and their environment? To what extent, though, is empowerment also materially based? To the extent that a powerless person

[23] Hess 1992c, 235.   [24] Hess 1992c, 236; Hess 1994a.

can, in fact, influence the environment—for example, persuade a case-worker to make a different decision—then it is easy to see the combination of the psychological and material aspects of empowerment. There were plenty of examples of this in the Chicago schools that were on the path toward basic, systemic restructuring through "strong democracy." In these schools, parents, community residents, and teachers influenced the agenda, assumed responsibility, and substantive changes in curriculum and instruction were being made. There were also examples of the opposite—in which principals retained autocractic control and LSCs and teachers were passive. In these polar cases, whether or not there was empowerment is a relatively straightforward observable issue.

The question of whether or not empowerment exists becomes more complicated when the oberserved behavior becomes more ambiguous. First, we will discuss the more simple cases, again where the behavior can be readily observed, even though the meaning is unclear, and then move to the more complicated forms of behavior.

School choice—or exit—is assumed to be a form of empowerment. Indeed, as we have seen, the more radical proponents of choice view exit as one of the most important forms of empowerment, as well as the most powerful mechanism for school reform. Recall the position of Chubb and Moe in the previous chapter. Coons argues that overall, and certainly as compared to politicians and bureaucrats, families are wiser consumers; moreover, by exercising choice, families develop a stake in the school. Furthermore, one could argue that exit is also a material form of empowerment as long as this is what the empowered person decides for herself, even if an outside observer thinks that the decision is unwise. For example, a family might prefer a neighborhood school to a more distant magnet school, and that decision might be based on factors other than the child's education. Or a family might simply make the "wrong" decision, but, I would argue, that is still empowerment.

A key issue in choice, of course, is the amount and quality of information that is made available and that the parent utilizes. In Minnesota, it will be recalled, virtually no information was made available. At least during the initial years, few parents exercised choice.[25] But because of the lack of information, "no choice" is hardly an empowered decision. The contrast is Cambridge and Milwaukee. In these situations, a great deal of effort did go into making information available and large numbers of parents did exercise choice, which tends to confirm the view that Minnesota families remained disempowered even though choice was formally offered. The problem of information is particularly serious in view of the evidence of class effects—"low" voice families, may have even less voice

---

[25] Word does seem to be picking up in Minnesota. Nathan and Ysseldyke 1994.

than they do now. Resources are likely to follow the demands of "high" voice families, further exacerbating educational inequalities.

Several of the Chicago schools, as well as other sites of parent and teacher participation, were faulted on the basis of the subject matter of the decision making. That is, there was a division of labor. Parents, for example, would focus on attendance, discipline, home learning, fund raising, and the physical plant, leaving budget, personnel, curriculum, and instruction to the professionals. This was called "enablement" rather than "empowerment" in the sense that the parents were being used to enable the professionals to carry out their tasks rather than exercising "real" power.

There are three issues involved in this position. First, since empowerment is a developmental process, LSCs will proceed at different rates. It may be too soon to pass judgment on an LSC that is first getting organized by tackling environmental rather than core problems. It is entirely possible that these LSCs will move on to more core issues as they gain confidence and improve working relationships with the professionals. On the other hand, since empowerment is a dynamic process, some LSCs may reach a particular stage and then retreat into co-optation. Or, they may never get beyond environmental issues.

Second, it does not necessarily mean that these LSCs are not empowered, just because they choose particular issues that are *important to them* rather than issues that are important to outside observers. Again, we return to the example of a Medicare patient learning to administer her own injections. To an outsider, this may seem like a minor act; to the elderly woman, it might be an important matter of self-control and dignity. Issues of school safety and order, as well as fund raising, and other kinds of social activities, are important in their own right, and could be very important to the parents and community residents, even though improvement in these areas does not result in the kinds of curriculum and teaching reforms that the reform act supporters envisage. Johnson, it will be recalled, in surveying teacher empowerment, concluded that even though many of the decisions were narrow, the fact that teachers did participate in them changed their attitudes concerning their role in school governance. The important point—which will be repeated throughout this chapter—is that empowerment is the power to make one's own decisions; it is not the power only to make wise decisions.

Granted that some LSCs may be empowered as to environmental issues, this still leaves the issue of acquiescence in the role of the professionals over the core issues of schooling. In the two situations above, the LSCs were exercising observable power—either with the professionals on the core issues or by a division of labor on the environmental issues. But in both cases, decisions were observable. How, though, do we interpret

LSC behavior in cases in which they *appear* not to be engaged in the core issues of curriculum and teaching? Is this by choice or as a result of manipulation?

In the discussion of the three faces (aspects) of power (chap. 5), it was pointed out that power is exercised not only in a direct, observable manner, but also by structuring the agenda so that certain issues are not even on the table, or through indirect, cultural socialization, so that the powerless are not even aware that power is being exercised. The critics of many of the LSCs argue that either the second or third "face" (aspect) of power is manipulating the LSCs—either the professionals are not bringing the core issues up for discussion or the parents and community members have been socialized into believing that these are matters best left to the professionals. Recall the discussion of the consortium's in-depth look at six of the most active schools—EARS. While the Consortium on Chicago School Research talks of the active involvement of the parents and the community, most of the discussion of substantive changes in teaching and learning involves the principals and the teachers. The parents supported home learning, improving the physical plant, improving order and safety, and focusing on "local needs." The principals and the teacher leaders took the initiative in school improvement planning, budgeting, and instructional activities. What does acquiescence on the part of the parents and community members in the division of labor mean? Is this a lack of empowerment in this critical area of school reform? This is the position of those skeptical of parent involvement. At most, parents are "enabling" the professionals.

The skeptics' view of empowerment is based on a theory of governance that Jane Mansbridge[26] calls "adversary democracy." It assumes that that there are conflicts of interests among the stakeholders (or citizens) and that when the less powerful willingly go along with the more powerful members of the polity, it is either the result of direct exercises of power or manipulation ("false consciousness"). Mansbridge studied democracy in two small entities—Selby Township (pseudonym), composed of 350 adults, and a participatory crisis center called Helpline. Mansbridge says that when she started her study, when the less powerful in Selby Township seemed to accept inequalities, she attributed this to "false consciousness." Yet, when the less powerful said the same thing in Helpline, that they trusted the more powerful, she believed them. The puzzle began to disappear, or at least diminish, when she focused on the interests of the participants. The difference was that in Selby, there were conflicting interests, and in Helpline, more common interests, which meant that in Helpline, the less powerful could rely on the more powerful to represent

26 Mansbridge 1980.

their interests. This led Mansbridge to draw the distinction between "adversary" democracy and "unitary" democracy. The latter assumes a high degree of common interests and an equality of respect—more like friendship—among its members. Thus, unitary democracy is characterized by face-to-face assembly and consensus. In contrast, adversary democracy is associated with large-scale politics, where one assumes conflicting interests. The emphasis is on equal protection of members' interests rather than on equal respect. It is a system of secret ballots and majority rule.[27] Most political scientists, Mansbridge says, assume that interests conflict and think in terms of large governments rather than small groups. She argues that democratic organizations take on different forms depending on whether interests conflict or coincide. Mansbridge is careful to point out that every polity contains elements of both adversary and unitary democracy, and therefore every polity needs appropriate institutions to make appropriate decisions. One of the more interesting conclusions that Mansbridge draws—for our purposes—is that with unitary democracy, participation is sometimes "unnecessary and irrelevant."[28]

In the case of adversary democracy, whem members disagree, they vote, and the majority wins. Under unitary democracy, people come together as friends and reach consensus on the basis of face-to-face discussion. Mansbridge argues that both conceptions of democracy often exist within the same polity. They are not contradictory because interests coincide as well as conflict. The distinguishing features of unitary democracy are equal respect, consensus, and face-to-face meetings that encourage members to identify with each other and think of the group as a whole. When this happens, interests can be protected even if power is unequal.[29]

"Friends are equal," says Mansbrige. "They expand in each other's company."[30] There are four components of friendship: equal status or respect; consensus; common interests; and face-to-face contact. When democracy is based on friendship, the participants are of equal status; they share a common good, and are thus able to make decisions unanimously. "The pleasure of the collective experience outweighs individual preferences," whereas voting accentuates individualized differences.[31] Interests, says Mansbridge, are not confined to "objective" interests. Rather, they can include altruism, ideals, tastes, and so forth. Altruism can produce common interests, especially when there is empathy for other members or concern for the welfare of the group as a whole. Then, the other's welfare or the welfare of the group as a whole becomes one's own goal as well.[32] Equality of respect preserves the bonds of friendship and makes

---

[27] Mansbridge 1980, ix.   [28] Mansbridge 1980, xii.   [29] Mansbridge 1980, 3–6.
[30] Mansbridge 1980, 9.   [31] Mansbridge 1980, 10.   [32] Mansbridge 1980, 27.

empathy easier.[33] Common experience, in turn, reinforces a shared sense of equality.[34] Mansbridge thinks that elements of unitary democracy are quite prevalent, and that majority rule is the exception. She points to the fact that in a great many decisions votes aren't taken. Rather, a consensus is reached. This is especially true when there is face-to-face decision making.[35]

On the other hand, Mansbridge observed that face-to-face conflict could suppress participation. In the situations that she observed, the less powerful felt intimidated. They were afraid of appearing foolish or of criticism, and thus, even more powerless. Thus, there are costs with unitary democracy when there are conflicting interests.[36] At the same time, it is hard for groups to shift from unitary democracy to adversary democracy when conflicts do appear. There is the desire to remain friends and to avoid formalism and conflict. But consensus, when interests conflict, suppresses the less powerful.[37]

The crisis center that Mansbridge studied was not a simple, small communitarian-style organization in which consensus would be natural or automatic. Rather, Helpline was a complex organization, composed of different units, some of which were located in different parts of the city (and one unit was rural). There was turnover. There were conflicts of interest, but they were small because the organization worked hard at generating a strong sense of common purpose.[38] To be sure, there was some suppression, especially among newcomers, those who worked away from the central location, and some based on age, race, gender, and class.

Nevertheless, the members were committed to reaching decisions by concensus. In fact, the formal rules dictated that decisions involving the organization as a whole could not be made if there was not agreement. Moreover, each of the subunits had a similar decision rule. Mansbridge observed that to reach closure on important decisions (and there were many), a concept of "live with" or "second-order consensus developed." As the names imply, members who disagreed would go along in the interests of the group as a whole. In practice, "live with" was a form of majority rule. Every organization, Mansbridge points out, that is governed by majority rule, has a "live with" process; otherwise, the dissenters would leave.

In face-to-face groups, especially where friendships are strong, the desire for harmony creates informal pressures to reach unanimity. The norm of consensus drives the group to consider the common good, to draw the dissidents into the group, to encourage listening and empathy,

---

[33] Mansbridge 1980, 28.   [34] Mansbridge 1980, 30.   [35] Mansbridge 1980, 34.
[36] Mansbridge 1980, 71.   [37] Mansbridge 1980, 75.   [38] Mansbridge 1980, 147.

and the development of moral bonds.[39] As distinguished from discussions under adversary democracy, where face-to-face interaction can be anxious, fear-producing, and ultimately suppressive, discussions at Helpline, where everyone expected eventual agreement, were more in the nature of a joint search than a competitive struggle, according to the staff. Since opponents could not be overriden, it was necessary to find out what they wanted. "The need to include everyone promoted caring and listening,"[40] while the face-to-face contact made it more likely that the more powerful would represent the interests of the less powerful. Mansbridge says that the more powerful wanted to maintain the respect of the less powerful; they wanted their approval for their own self-esteem.[41] However, Mansbridge notes, there was no guarantee of unity; not infrequently, majority rule in the form of second-order consensus was used to reach decisions.[42]

There were inequalities in Helpline, but the staff was not particularly disturbed because they felt that on most issues, common interests would prevail. The trust in others allowed the group to live with a certain amount of inequality.[43]

We can see elements of Helpline in the six EARS that the Consortium on Chicago School Research looked at in depth (1993). Three of these schools were among the worst in the Chicago system prior to the reforms. Each of the principals displayed a commitment to the students and the parents in the community. The LSCs played an active role in improving parent and community involvement, enlisting parents to support home learning, improving the physical plant, improving order and safety, and generally focusing attention on local needs. The principals and the teacher leaders took the initiative in school improvement planning, budgeting, and instructional activities. In all of the schools, however, the key feature was principal leadership. The principals developed good working relationships with the LSCs, were sensitive to local needs, and were committed to an inclusive process of open communication. All the principals were enthusiastic, optimistic, and passionate in their commitment to the restructuring. While each principal had a distinctive vision for the school, the commonalities were changing the relationships of parents and the local community to the school and to a total commitment to the students.[44] The principals sought to create a "sense of agency" among the parents and the teachers, to instill in them the idea that they could make a difference—"together we can make this place better."[45]

The principals worked hard at staff development. To repeat, they

---

[39] Mansbridge 1980, 165.　　　　[40] Mansbridge 1980, 174.
[41] Mansbridge 1980, 231.　　　　[42] Mansbridge 1980, 175.
[43] Mansbridge 1980, 234.
[44] Consortium on Chicago School Research 1993, 27.
[45] Consortium on Chicago School Research 1993, 28.

sought to build a team that was compatible with the collaborative vision of the school. There were efforts to engage the whole faculty in teacher improvement. Teaching behind closed doors was no longer the norm. Time was created for the teachers to meet, consult, exchange ideas, and assume the responsibilities that the reform plans called for. Since much of the collaborative activity occurred during the nonworking parts of the day, discretionary funds were used to provide at least partial compensation. In each of the schools, most of the faculty eventually became engaged in at least some manner. In each of the schools, a professional community developed in which all the principal stakeholders engaged in important, sustained conversation. The goal was to work together to sustain the community. The principals used their power to empower the teachers and the parents.

It will be recalled that the consortium found that virtually all the teachers had positive attitudes toward the reform, their colleagues, and the school, that there was increased communication and collaboration with parents and the community, and that the majority of students were very satisfied with their teachers, and appreciated the commitment to learning.

It was predicted that the Chicago scheme would heighten conflicts between parents and educators, but, as Moore points out, in fact, two-thirds of the teachers on the LSCs report that staff-parent relations had improved since the elections.[46] Hess, too, while quite skeptical of parent participation, reports that contrary to the expectations of critics, the LSCs did not engage in political wrangling or patronage, but instead focused primarily on substantive school issues. Problems varied by school and discussions varied. Some were brief and decisions were routine, but others were long and protracted. While in most cases, decisions were made by votes; most votes were one-sided.[47] The fact that there was near unanimity on most LSC decisions, says Hess and Easton, indicates that the councils were working collaboratively, despite the fact that the willingness of parents and teachers to work collaboratively had been a major concern of some of the critics of the Chicago school reform.[48]

These descriptions of most of the Chicago LSCs sound like those of Mansbridge's unitary democracy in Helpline—small groups, face-to-face discussions, the emphasis on working together, and consensus decisions. The Comer schools have not been systematically evaluated, but at least in theory, they, too, sound like examples of unitary democracy. It will be recalled that Comer's basic idea is that sharing responsibility will enhance the stakeholders' engagement with and commitment to the educational process. The initial governance team is composed of principals, teachers, and parents; they then enlist the support of other parents, and this step is

[46] Moore 1992.   [47] Hess 1992c, 170.   [48] Hess and Easton, 1992.

considered to be critical to the enterprise. There is a commitment to develop a cooperative spirit, to create a sense of shared ownership and responsibility, a cohesive community. Comer strongly emphasizes the decision-making climate. As in the case of Mansbridge's Helpline, there has
to be mutual respect and a willingness to listen. Significantly, closure
must be reached on all decisions, and all decisions must be decided by
consensus. The governing members must feel empowered by the principal
and there must be trust and bonding among the principal stakeholders.

Another similar example in the Accelerated Schools program. The
basis of this model is the establishment of a unity of purpose among all
the participants. All are responsible for ensuring the educational goals of
the school.

One could argue that in all of these examples it is very likely that common interests develop and that the elements of equal respect, empathy,
and all of the other characteristics of face-to-face governance that
Mansbridge describes may be present. They seem to resemble the description of Benjamin Barber's strong democracy:[49]

> In this realm [strong democracy], citizenship is in a dynamic relationship
> among strangers who are transformed into neighbors, whose commonality
> derives from expanding consciousness rather than geographicaly proxim-
> ity. . . . [T]he civic bond under strong democracy is neither vertical nor lat-
> eral but circular and dialectical. Individuals become involved in government
> by participating in the common institutions of self-government and become
> involved with one another by virtue of their common engagement in politics.
> They are united by the ties of common activity and common conscious-
> ness—ties that are willed rather than given by blood or heritage or prior
> consensus on beliefs and that thus depend for their preservation and growth
> on constant commitment and ongoing political activity. . . .
>
> The political style that emerges from this dialectic of common association
> is one of activity and cooperation, and the civic virtue that distinguishes that
> style from other styles is civility itself. Strong democracy promotes reciprocal
> empathy and mutual respect, whereas unitary democracy promotes recipro-
> cal love and fear and thin democracy promotes reciprocal control. Civility is
> rooted in the idea that consciousness is a socially conditioned intelligence
> that takes into account the reality of other consciousnesses operating in a
> shared world. . . . [C]ivility assumes free agents who are roughly equal, not
> necessarily by nature or right but by virtue of their shared consciousness. . . .
> The ideal . . . of strong democracy is *creative consensus*—an agreement that

---

[49] Barber (1984) distinguishes "strong" democracy from "thin" democracy or "unitary"
democracy. Thin democracy is liberal, representative. Unitary democracy is governance
through blood. His definition of "strong" democracy is the same as Mansbridge's "unitary
democracy."

arises out of common talk, common decision, and common work but that is premised on citizens' active and perennial participation in the transformation of conflict through the creation of common consciousness and political judgment.[50]

The most careful empirical examination of the actual workings of local political groups is the study by Berry and his associates of neighborhood organizations in five cities, discussed in chapter 6. The authors devoted considerable attention to how much actual power was exercised by these organizations and found that, in general, it was significant. While the organizations did not always prevail, the authors did not find evidence that they were co-opted either by their leaders or by city hall. The authors went on to point out while the organizations appeared to be open and responsive, only a small group of citizens actually participated in the day-to-day affairs; moreover, variation in participation seemed to be based on socioeconomic status. Nevertheless, surveys showed that the organizations were widely trusted in the communities; that most people were aware of the mechanisms and procedures under which they could participate; and that they felt that they could participate if they wanted to. And they did participate when particularly salient issues arose. In Mansbridge's terms, this was another example of unitary democracy.

Furthermore, it is not even clear that adversarial relations must apply when schools are viewed as organizations. It is true that many organizations house competing coalitions of interests, that authority is negotiated, and that individuals and groups exchange a variety of incentives. As applied to schools, this conception would fit the analysis of empowerment skeptics. There are conflicts of interests between the principal stakeholders. Therefore, a division of labor under which the parents and community members are consigned to peripheral issues would indicate an exercise of power on the part of the professionals.

It is true that a great many organizations, including schools, fit that description. But other organizations do not, and Philip Selznick[51] argues for organizations as moral communities. Formal systems operate through people, and it is the people that create the social reality. The individuals in the organization bring their own personalities, values, and interests, which may be constrained, but are not confined, by the formal rules. Over time, organizations develop into what Selznick calls "institutions"— created of values, ideologies, rituals, symbols, and purposiveness. This process, in turn, strains toward community as the organization takes on a distinctive identity. To sustain the enterprise at a high level of commitment, more is needed than obeying directives; rather, attention must be paid to incentives, multiple interests, and "the dynamics or cooperation

[50] Barber 1984, 223–24.   [51] Selznick 1992.

and conflict." In this process, there is a transition from managing the organization to what Selznick calls, "*governing* communities."[52] He thinks that a sense of institutional identity and an ideal of community will most likely develop in organizations in which values are more important than goals, and in which goals can accommodate a broad range of interests, in contrast to organizations that are more narrowly and instrumentally focused. Schools, universities, hospitals, churches, and government agencies are more like the former.[53]

Governance, in an organization as a community, takes account of all the interests that affect the moral character of the enterprise. The basic commitment is to the participants "*as persons.*" This commitment may or may not be altruistic; it may only reflect the need for cooperation. But, says Selznick, "*the broader the organization's goals, the more leeway it has in defining its mission, the more requirements there are for winning cooperation, the more fully the lives of participants are lived within it, the more important does governance become.*"[54] Schools, in particular, are communities. Selznick points to the importance of schools beyond formal learning. Rather, they are settings for interaction, communication, and growth—"a center for life as well as learning." Students are "whole persons." Accordingly, education is concerned with freedom as well as discipline.[55]

The moral community that Selznick urges is one in which a framework of shared beliefs, interests, and commitments unites different groups. Some of the interests are peripheral, and some are central, but all are connected by bonds that establish a sense of common purpose, of belonging, and a supportive structure. Community, says Selznick, is a variable. It can evolve out of special-purpose institutions, but "happens most readily when purpose is not very rigidly or narrowly conceived, when participation is an important part of the individual's life. *The emergence of community depends on the opportunity for, and the impulse toward, comprehensive interaction, commitment, and responsibility.*"[56] The community is largely supported by the experience of interdependence and reciprocity, which goes beyond personal exchange. Community contemplates continuing relationships and high stakes. Selznick contrasts community with contract, which is a relationship of *limited* obligations. The realities of association in community may require "*unequal* contributions." With community, mutuality extends beyond exchange to "enduring bonds of interdependence, caring and commitment. The transition is from reciprocity to solidarity to fellowship."[57] Among the important virtues of community, "persons are equal as moral actors and as objects of moral

---

[52] Selznick 1992, 237.   [53] Selznick 1992, 237.   [54] Selznick 1992, 291.
[55] Selznick 1992, 295.   [56] Selznick 1992, 360.   [57] Selznick 1992, 362.

concern," which involves "deference, constructive self-regard, concern for the well-being of others." These foundational principles guide "the development of a living community."[58]

Community does not mean unanimity. Selznick argues for the moral worth of diversity. Pluralism is an "essential aspect of communal democracy." But he calls for "participatory pluralism rather than oppositional pluralism." At the same time, he recognizes that participatory pluralism can also be corporatist, undemocratic, and unresponsive.[59] The foundational component of the moral community is civility—which protects autonomy and fosters tolerance, dialogue, and respect for individuals; where the effort is to listen, understand, and appreciate.[60] Civility, says Selznick, includes "concern for the common good. More particularly, civility signals the community's commitment to dialogue as the preferred means of social decision."[61]

> [C]ivility presumes diversity, autonomy, and potential conflict. . . . [The] norms of civility are predicated on a regard for the integrity and independence of individuals and groups. Reconciliation is a keynote, and much attention is given to narrowing differences and encouraging communication. There is no question, however, of extinguishing interests or denying rights. In civility, respect, not love, is the salient value. . . . In truly civil communication . . . an effort must be made really to listen, . . . to understand and appreciate what someone else is saying. . . . We discover and create shared meanings; the content or substance of the discussion becomes more important than its form. The outcome is often a *particular* community of discourse and a *unique* social bond. A foundation is laid for affection and commitment.[62]

What Selznick is describing seems to fit the goals of Comer, the Accelerated Schools, as well as the process goals of the Chicago School Reform Act. From both an organizational and a political perspective, there is a different vision of what is happening in the Chicago schools. Quiescence, consensus, a division of labor can easily fit within concepts of empowerment; or, as Mansbridge and others readily concede, can also mean repression or unconscious socialization. As Gaventa reminds us, interpreting quiescence on the part of relatively powerless people is the most difficult problem to solve. This is the "third face" of power (chap. 5). Gaventa asks, "how can one study what does not happen? How can one tell whether B would have *thought* and *acted* differently? . . . [H]ow do we know whether the consent is genuine or manipulated?"[63] The danger, of course, is the researchers imputing their values to the quiescent. Gaventa makes a number of research suggestions, such as examining the his-

---

[58] Selznick 1992, 480–83.   [59] Selznick 1992, 517–18.   [60] Selznick 1992, 387.
[61] Selznick 1992, 391.   [62] Selznick 1992, 391–92.   [63] Gaventa 1980, 25.

tory of the relationships and the processes of communication and socialization. In the end, however, he says, if no evidence of power or relevant
counterfactuals can be found, the conclusion must be that the quiescence
is.in fact based on values that are different from those of the observer.

Reviewing the observed data from several of the Chicago schools, it
seems that community interest in the schools is reasonably high, that participation in the LSC meetings is reasonably active, and that many agenda
items are brought forward by parents and community members. All of
this would be evidence of at least some forms of empowerment. The kinds
of decisions that parent members engage in vary, but consensus on divi-
sions of labor and on decisions would not, by themselves, indicate co-
optation. In view of the fact that the most important decision that the
LSCs make is the selection of the principal, one would expect deference,
at least initially. The fact that many parents may go along with the professionals may be regrettable, in the view of at least some of the Chicago
reform community, but democratic governance does entail the risk of
making bad decisions.

At the time of this writing, the Chicago public school system is in a
state of flux, and the outcome is still very much in doubt. As always with
large urban school systems, there are serious problems of money, and the
reformers have to fight both the unions and a central administration determined to regain power.

For those who seek the empowerment of the powerless, the basic point
of instability, context, and struggle is both one of hope that change can
come about and despair that there is no end. So much depends on dedi-
cated leaders. When they leave or become exhausted, decline seems to set
in. Critics say that the reforms have to be "institutionalized." Rees thinks
that strong unions were a key factor in the development of the worker-
safety committees. Unions were instrumental in teacher empowerment in
Dade County. But institutions are made up of people. They are variable,
changeable, and, to say the least, are not necessarily supporters of citizen
empowerment. Around the country, and certainly in Chicago, the teachers unions, in general, are not allies of reformers.

In the final analysis, empowerment rests on a basic contradiction—it
envisages a democratic process of equality between participants who are
unequal in terms of power and resources. It is for this reason that I emphasize the importance of outside resources. In empowerment by invitation, the powerful deemed it in their own interests to have the empowered
participation of the powerless; and the powerful supplied resources to
make sure that empowerment developed and survived. When the powerful failed to maintain the outside resources, participation began to decline; the clients or parents could not maintain the engagement on their
own. In Madison, for example, the social movements (the parent groups)

were allowed to wither, and individual parents, on their own, began to be co-opted. Co-optation was not necessarily the work of the individual teachers, even though they admitted that they were not listening as carefully. Rather, it was the creeping, insidious general reluctance of the parents to keep challenging the institution *on their own* without outside support. Similar, Rees thinks that even though management wants cooperation, and provides resources, the unions are still critical. In these, as well as the other examples, the dynamics of power differentials in society will undermine the process. Despite the efforts of the Madison educators, most parents of handicapped children are, or feel, dependent. Most construction workers, especially without union protection, are vulnerable. They can participate under favorable conditions, but the relationship is unstable. Because the parents and workers still remain dependent in fact, it is difficult for them to continue. Empowerment is a developmental process; it can regress as well as progress.

The powerless have to be in a position to contribute something of value. In most of the examples, this was true. They contributed to professional or enterprise goals. When they cannot make a meaningful contribution, empowerment becomes problematic. The differences between the home care for the frail elderly example and the nursing home patients example was instructive. In the former, valuable benefits—primarily reliable information—were supplied to the agencies and help in meeting therapeutic goals was obtained. Significantly, the agencies could not fulfill their contractual obligations without the help of the clients. With nursing home patients, particularly as they become more disabled, there is less that they can do for the staff. Families and support groups are viewed more as adversaries than participants; and cooperative relationships are increasingly hard to find.

Despite the challenges, one can see progress with empowerment by invitation. There is continuing interest in moving away from command-and-control regulation, and there are a variety of examples from which one can extract various principles. This means that replication is possible as long as there is the desire. Other construction companies and unions could replicate Rees's worker safety committees, especially if it can be demonstrated that both management and labor will be better off. This becomes a cost-benefit calculation. It is similar to the water pollution control example, only here, the additional mechanisms for empowerment have to be understood and implemented. With "softer" human services, professionals have to come to realize that empowerment is not a zero-sum proposition, but rather that *their* professional task will be accomplished better with empowered clients. This sounds easier than it is in practice. After all, in medicine, genuine informed consent—as distinguished from merely obtaining the patient's signature on a form—is still the exception

rather than the rule. Still, it somehow seems easier to try to persuade officials and professionals when the task starts from the proposition that they
will be better off.

Empowerment becomes much more problematic in situations of conflict. As school reform—especially in Chicago—shows there will be real
losers when power is transferred. Students and teachers may be better off,
but central administrators, traditional bureaucrats and teachers, and job
holders will not be. Here, there will be raw struggle, and, it will be both
contentious and continuous. The Chicago experience is very instructive.
There was a titanic effort to get the reform legislation enacted. It took
incredible perspicuity on the part of the outside social movement groups
to try to prevent the central administration from subsequently resurrect-
ing itself by reappropriating always scarce public funds, and yet, the fight
goes on continuously. One can safely predict that if the outside support
groups begin to decline, the Chicago school system will recentralize.

Democratic governance asks a lot of dependent people. Constitutions
are usually written by well-off, well-meaning people. They too often assume that if opportunities to participate in matters that are important to
them are given to citizens, then these citizens will participate. We know,
and have known for a very long time, that this is simply not true. There
are so many reasons why dependent people cannot participate, at least in
a meaningful way. People who are poor, who lack resources, who are
vulnerable, cannot be expected to challenge bureaucrats and professionals. This is not to say that dependent or subordinate people are helpless;
in many situations, they do display surprising resilience and strength. Empowerment does require the active role of the participants. But in the day-
in, day-out encounters, especially where the relationship is long-term, as
in many human services, then resources have to be supplied either from
the inside or from the outside.

REFERENCES

BOOKS AND PERIODICALS

Abel, Emily. 1987. *Love Is Not Enough: Family Care for the Frail Elderly*. Washington DC: American Public Health Association.

Abel, Richard, ed. 1982. *The Politics of Informal Justice*. Vol. 1. New York: Academic Press.

Ackerman, Bruce, and Richard Stewart. 1985. "Reforming Environmental Law." *Stanford Law Review* 37:1333–65.

Alves, Michael, and Charles Willie. 1990. "Choice, Decentralization and Desegregation: The Boston 'Controlled Choice' Plan." In *Choice and Control in American Education*. Vol. 2, *The Practice of Choice, Decentralization and School Structuring*, ed. William Clune and John Witte, 17–76. New York: Falmer Press.

Anderson, Terry, and Donald Leal. 1991. *Free Market Environmentalism*. Boulder, CO: Westview Press.

———. 1992. "Free Market versus Political Environmentalism." *Harvard Journal of Law and Public Policy* 15:297–310.

Anheier, Helmut, and Martin Knapp. 1990. "Voluntas: An Editorial Statement." *Voluntas* 1:1–12.

Anson, Amy, Thomas Cook, Farah Habib, Michael Grady, Norris Haynes, and James Comer. 1991. "The Comer School Development Program: A Theoretical Analysis" *Urban Education* 26:56–82.

Aranson, Peter. 1990. "Theories of Economic Regulation: From Clarity to Confusion." *Journal of Law and Politics* 6:247–86.

Atlas, John, and Peter Dreier. 1986. "The Tenants' Movement and American Politics." In *Critical Perspectives on Housing*, ed. Rachel Bratt, Chester Hartman, and Amy Meyerson, 378–97. Philadelphia: Temple University Press.

Axelrod, Robert. 1984. *The Evolution of Cooperation*. New York: Basic Books.

Ayres, Ian, and John Braithwaite. 1992. *Responsive Regulation: Transcending the Deregulation Debate*. New York: Oxford University Press.

Ayers, William. 1992. "Work That Is Real: Why Teachers Should Be Empowered." In *Empowering Teachers and Parents: School Restructuring Through the Eyes of Anthropologists*, ed. G. Alfred Hess, Jr. Westport, CT: Bergin and Garvey.

Bachrach, Peter, and Martin Baratz. 1962. "The Two Faces of Power." *American Political Science Review* 56:947–52.

———. 1970. *Power and Poverty: Theory and Practice*. New York: Oxford University Press.

Bachrach, Peter, and Aryeh Botwinick. 1992. *Power and Empowerment: A Radical Theory of Participatory Democracy*. Philadelphia: Temple University Press.

Barber, Benjamin. 1984. *Strong Democracy: Participatory Politics for a New Age*. Berkeley: University of California Press.

Bardach, Eugene, and Robert Kagan. 1982. *Going by the Book: The Problem of Regulatory Unreasonableness*. Philadelphia: Temple University Press.

Barzelay, Michael. 1992. *Breaking Through Bureaucracy: A New Vision for Managing Government*. Berkeley: University of California Press.

Bendick, Marc, Jr. 1989. "Privatizing the Delivery of Social Welfare Services: An Idea to Be Taken Seriously." In *Privatization and the Welfare State*, ed. Sheila Kamerman and Alfred Kahn, 97–120. Princeton, NJ: Princeton University Press.

Bennett, David. 1990. "Choice and Desegregation." In *Choice and Control in American Education*. Vol. 2, 125–52. See Clune and Witte 1990b.

Bennett, R., and Eisdorfer, C. 1975. "The Institutional Environment and Behavior Change." In *Long-Term Care: A Handbook for Researchers, Planners, and Providers*, ed. Sylvia Sherwood, 391–454. New York: Spectrum Publications.

Bergthold, Linda, Carroll Estes, and Augusta Villanueva. 1990. "Public Light and Private Dark: The Privatization of Home Health Services for the Elderly." *U.S. Home Health Services Quarterly* 11:7–33.

Bernstein, Susan. 1991. *Managing Contracted Services in the Nonprofit Agency*. Philadelphia: Temple University Press.

Berry, Jeffrey, Kent Portney, and Ken Thomson. 1993. *The Rebirth of Urban Democracy*. Washington, DC: Brookings Institution.

Blank, Rolf. 1990. "Educational Effects of Magnet High Schools." In *Choice and Control in American Education*. Vol. 2, 77–110. See Clune and Witte 1990b.

Blumm, Michael. 1992. "The Fallacies of Free Market Environmentalism." *Harvard Journal of Law and Public Policy* 15:371–89.

Boggs, Carl. 1986. *Social Movements and Political Power: Emerging Forms of Radicalism in the West*. Philadelphia: Temple University Press.

Bosanquet, Nick. 1984. "Is Privatisation Inevitable?" In *Privatization and the Welfare State*, ed. Julian Robinson and Ray Robinson, 58–69. London: George Allen and Unwin.

Bowers, B. J. 1988. "Family Perceptions of Care in a Nursing Home." *The Gerontologist* 28:361–68.

Boyte, Harry. 1980. *The Backyard Revolution: Understanding the New Citizen Movement*. Philadelphia: Temple University Press.

Bratt, Rachel, Chester Hartman, and Ann Meyerson, eds. 1986. *Critical Perspectives on Housing*. Philadelphia: Temple University Press.

Briffault, Richard. 1990a. "Our Localism: Part I—The Structure of Local Government Law." *Columbia Law Review* 90:1–115.

———. 1990b. "Our Localism: Part II—Localism and Legal Theory." *Columbia Law Review*. 90: 346–454.

Brizius, Jack. 1989. "An Overview of the State-Local Fiscal Landscape." In *A Decade of Devolution: Perspectives on State-Local Relations*, ed. E. Blaine Liner, 51–80. Washington, DC: Urban Institute.

Brodkin, Evelyn, and Dennis Young. 1989. "Making Sense of Privatization: What Can We Learn from Economic and Political Analysis?" In *Privatization and the Welfare State*, 120–54. See Kamerman and Kahn 1989b.

Brody, E. 1974. *A Social Work Guide for Long Term Care Facilities.* Rockville, MD: National Institute of Mental Health.

Brody, E., and S. Brody. 1989. "The Informal System of Health Care." In *Caring for the Elderly: Reshaping Health Policy,* ed. C. Eisdorfer, D. Kessler and A. Spector, 259–77. Baltimore, MD: Johns Hopkins University Press.

Brown, Mary Jo McGee. 1992. "Rural Science and Mathematics Education: Empowerment through Self-Reflection and Expanding Curricular Alternatives." In *Empowering Teachers and Parents.* See Hess 1992.

Brunet, Edward. 1992. "Debunking Wholesale Private Enforcement of Environmental Rights." *Harvard Journal of Law and Public Policy* 15:311–24.

Bryk, Anthony, Paul Deabster, John Easton, Stuart Luppescu, and Yeow Meng Thum. 1994. "Measuring Achievement Gains in the Chicago Public Schools." *Education and Urban Society* 26:306–19.

Bryk, Anthony, Valerie Lee, and Julia Smith. 1990. "High School Organization and Its Effect on Teachers and Students: An Interpretive Summary of the Research." In *Choice and Control in American Education.* Vol. 1, 135–226. See Clune and Witte 1990a.

Bumiller, Kristin. 1988. *The Civil Rights Society: The Social Construction of Victims.* Baltimore, MD: Johns Hopkins University Press.

Carnoy, Martin. 1993. "School Improvement: Is Privatization the Answer?" In *Decentralization and School Improvement: Can We Fulfill the Promise?* ed. Jane Hannaway and Martin Carnoy, 163–201. San Francisco: Jossey-Bass.

Carroll, Thomas. 1992. "The Role of Anthropologists in Restructuring Schools." In *Empowering Teachers and Parents.* See Hess 1992.

Chicago Panel on School Policy. 1993. *Panel Update: Legislative Action Finally Keeps School Doors Open* 9, no.1 (fall).

Cherry, Ralph. 1991. "Agents of Nursing Home Quality of Care: Ombudsman and Staff Ratios Revisted." *The Gerontologist.* 31:302–8

Chubb, John. 1989. "U.S. Energy Policy: A Problem of Delegation." In *Can the Government Govern?* ed. John Chubb and Paul Peterson, 47–99. Washington, DC: Brookings Institution.

———. 1990. "Political Institutions and School Organization, Commentary." In *Choice and Control in American Education.* Vol. 1, 227–34. See Clune and Witte 1990a.

Chubb, John, and Terry Moe. 1990. *Politics, Markets, and the American Schools.* Washington, DC: Brookings Institution.

Chubb, John, and Paul Peterson. 1989. *Can The Government Govern?* Washington, DC: Brookings Institution.

Clarke, Lee, and Carroll Estes. 1992. "Sociological and Economic Theories of Markets and Nonprofits: Evidence from Home Health Organizations." *American Journal of Sociology* 97:945–69.

Clay, Marie. 1990. "Recovery in the United States: Its Success and Challenges." Speech delivered at the Annual Meeting of the American Educational Research Association, 15–21 April, Boston, MA.

Clegg, Stewart. 1989. *Frameworks of Power.* Newbury Park, CA: Sage.

Clune, William. 1990a. "Introduction." In *Choice and Control in American Education.* Vol. 2, 1–16. See Clune and Witte 1990.

Clune, William. 1990b. "Educational Governance and Student Achievement." In *Choice and Control in American Education.* Vol. 2, 391–424. See Clune and Witte 1990b.

———. 1992a. "The Best Path to Systemic Educational Policy: Standard/centralized or Differentiated/decentralized?" Madison: University of Wisconsin Consortium for Policy Research in Education; Wisconsin Center for Education Research. Mimeo.

———. 1992b. "New Answers to Hard Questions Posed by Rodriguez: Ending the Separation of School Finance and Educational Policy by Bridging the Gap Between Wrong and Remedy." *Connecticut Law Review* 24:721–56.

Clune, William, and Mark Van Pelt. 1984. "A Political Method of Evaluating 94–142 and the Several Gaps in Gap Analysis." *Law and Contemporary Problems* 48:7–62.

Clune, William, and John Witte, eds. 1990a. *Choice and Control in American Education.* Vol. 1, *The Theory of Choice and Control in Education.* New York: Falmer Press.

———. 1990b. *Choice and Control in American Education.* Vol. 2, *The Practice of Choice, Decentralization and School Restructuring.* New York: Falmer Press.

Coe, Pamela, and Patricia Kannapel. 1992. "Rural Responses to Kentucky's Education Reform Act." In *Empowering Teachers and Parents.* See Hess 1992.

Cohen, David. 1990. "Governance and Instruction: The Promise of Decentralization and Choice." In *Choice and Control in American Education.* Vol. 1, 337–86. See Clune and Witte 1990a.

Cohen, Joshua, and Joel Rogers. 1992. "Secondary Associations and Democratic Governance." *Politics and Society* 20:393–472.

Cohen, Michael. 1990. "Diversity Amidst Standardization: State Differential Treatment of Districts, Commentary." In *Choice and Control in American Education.* Vol. 2, 283–88. See Clune and Witte 1990b.

Coleman, James. 1990. "Preface: Choice, Community and Future Schools." In *Choice and Control in American Education.* Vol. 1, 283–88. See Clune and Witte 1990a.

———. 1991. "A Federal Report on Parental Involvement in Education." *Education Digest* 57:3–6.

Consortium on Chicago School Research. 1992. *Charting Reform: The Principals' Perspective.* Report on a Survey of Chicago School Principals.

———. 1993. *A View from the Elementary Schools: The State of Reform in Chicago.* Report of the Steering Committee.

Coons, John. 1992. "Schools and Simple Justice: Toward Dignity of Choice." *Current* 343:30–38.

Coons, John, and Stephen Sugarman. 1992. *Scholarships for Children.* Berkeley: University of California Institute of Governmental Studies Press.

Cowley, John. 1986. "The Limitations and Potential of Housing Organizing." In *Critical Perspectives on Housing,* 399–404. See Bratt, Hartman, and Meyerson 1986.

Dahrendorf, Ralf. 1988. *The Modern Social Conflict.* New York: Weidenfeld and Nicolson.

DeHoog, Ruth. 1990. "Competition, Negotiation, or Cooperation: 3 Models for Service Contracting." *Administration and Society* 22: 317–40.

Delgado, Richard, Chris Dunn, Pamela Brown, Helena Lee, and David Hubert. 1985. "Fairness and Formality: Minimizing the Risk of Prejudice in Alternative Dispute Resolution." *Wisconsin Law Review* 1985:1359–1404.

Derthick, Martha, and Paul Quirk. 1985. *The Politics of Deregulation*. Washington, DC: Brookings Institution.

DiMaggio, Paul, and Walter Powell. 1991. "Introduction." In *The New Institutionalism in Organizational Analysis*, ed. Walter Powell and Paul DiMaggio, 1–38. Chicago: University of Chicago Press.

Dobrof, R. 1989. "Staff and Families: Partners in Caring for the Institutionalized Aged." In *Principles and Practices of Nursing Home Care*, ed. P. R. Katz and E. Calkins. New York: Springer Publishing Co.

Donahue, John. 1989. *The Privatization Decision: Public Ends, Private Means*. New York: Basic Books.

Doty, Pamela, and E. Sullivan. 1983. "Community Involvement in Combatting Abuse and Mistreatment in Nursing Homes." *Milbank Memorial Fund Quarterly/Health and Society* 61:222–51.

Douglas, James. 1987. "Political Theories of Nonprofit Organizations." In *The NonProfit Sector: A Research Handbook*, ed. Walter Powell, 43–54. New Haven, CT: Yale University Press.

Easton, John, and Sandra Storey. 1994. "The Development of Local School Councils." *Education and Urban Society* 26:220–37.

Edelman, Lauren. 1990. "Legal Environments and Oganizational Governance: The Expansion of Due Process in the American Workplace." *American Journal of Sociology* 95:1401–40.

Edelman, Murray. 1971. *Politics as Symbolic Action: Mass Arousal and Quiescence*. Chicago: Markham Publishing Co.

———. 1988. *Constructing the Political Spectacle*. Chicago: University of Chicago Press.

Edelson, Jacqueline Singer, and Walter H. Lyons. 1985. *Institutional Care of the Mentally Impaired Elderly*. New York: Van Nostrand Reinhold Co.

Elazar, Daniel. 1990. "Opening the Third Century of American Federalism: Issues and Prospects." *ANNALS, AAPSS* 509:11–21.

Elmore, Richard. 1978. "Organizational Models of Social Program Implementation." *Public Policy* 26:185–228.

———. 1979–80. "Backward Mapping: Implementation Research and Policy Decisions." *Political Science Quarterly* 94:601–16.

———. 1990a. "Choice as an Instrument of Public Policy: Evidence from Education and Health Care." In *Choice and Control in American Education*. Vol. 1, 285–318. See Clune and Witte 1990a.

———. 1990b. *Working Models of Choice in Public Education*. Center for Policy Research in Education Report Series RR-018. Madison: University of Wisconsin.

———. 1991a. "Public School Choice as a Policy Issue." In *Privatization and Its Alternatives*, ed. William Gormley, Jr. Madison: University of Wisconsin Press.

———. 1991b. Review of *Politics, Markets, and America's Schools* by John

Chubb and Terry Moe. *Journal of Policy Analysis and Management* 10: 687.

Elmore, Richard. 1993. "School Decentralization: Who Gains? Who Loses?" In *Decentralization and School Improvement: Can We Fulfill the Promise?* ed. Jane Hannaway and Martin Carnoy, 33–54. San Francisco: Jossey-Bass.

Engel, David. 1993. "Origin Myths: Narratives of Authority, Resistance, Disability, and Law." *Law and Society Review* 27:785–26.

Etheridge, Carol, and Thomas Collins. 1992. "Conflict in Restructuring the Principal-Teacher Relationship in Memphis." In *Empowering Teachers and Parents*. See Hess 1992.

Ewick, Patricia, and Susan Silbey. 1992. "Conformity, Contestation, and Resistance: An Account of Legal Consciousness. *New England Law Review* 26: 73.

Farber, Daniel. 1992. "Politics and Procedure in Environmental Law." *Journal of Law, Economics, and Organization* 8:59–81.

Farber, Daniel, and Philip Frickey. 1987. "The Jurisprudence of Public Choice." *Texas Law Review* 65:873–928.

Farber, Stephen. 1989. "Federalism and State-Local Relations." In *A Decade of Devolution: Perspectives on State-Local Relations*, ed. E. Blaine Liner, 27–50. Washington, DC: Urban Institute.

Feeley, Malcolm. 1991. "The Privatization of Punishment in Historical Perspective." In *Privatization and Its Alternatives*. See Gormley 1991a.

Felstiner, William, Richard Abel and Austin Sarat. 1980–81. "The Emergence and Transformation of Disputes: Naming, Blaming, Claiming . . ." *Law and Society Review* 15:631–54.

Fiorina, Morris. 1986. "Legislator Uncertainty, Legislative Control, and the Delegation of Legislative Power." *Journal of Law, Economics, and Organizations* 2:33–51.

Fliegel, Seymour. 1990. "Creative Non-Compliance." In *Choice and Control in American Education*. Vol. 2, 199–216. See Clune and Witte 1990b.

Forbath, William. 1991. *Law and the Shaping of the American Labor Movement*. Cambridge, MA: Harvard University Press.

Fowler, Robert. 1991. *The Dance with Community: The Contemporary Debate in American Political Thought*. Lawrence: University of Kansas Press.

Freire, Paulo. 1985. *Pedagogy of the Oppressed*. New York: Continuum.

Friedland, Roger, and Robert Alford. 1991. "Bringing Society Back In: Symbols, Practices, and Institutional Contradictions." In *The New Institutionalism in Organizational Analysis*, ed. Walter Powell and Paul DiMaggio, 232–63. Chicago: University of Chicago Press.

Fuhrman, Susan, ed. 1993. *Designing Coherent Education Policy: Improving the System*. San Francisco: Jossey-Bass.

Fuhrman, Susan, with Patti Fry. 1990. "Diversity Admidst Standardization: State Differential Treatment of Districts." In *Choice and Control in American Education*. Vol. 2, 251–82. Clune and Witte 1990b.

Gamson, William. 1968. *Power and Discontent*. Homeward, IL: Dorsey Press.

Gaventa, John. 1980. *Power and Powerlessness: Quiescence and Rebellion in an Appalachian Valley*. Urbana: University of Illinois Press.

Gilbert, Neil. 1983. *Capitalism and the Welfare State*. New Haven: Yale University Press.

———. n.d. "The Commercialization of Social Welfare." Mimeo. Available through Joel Handler.

Glenn, Charles. 1992. "Do Parents Get the Schools They Choose?" *Equity and Choice* 9:47–49.

Gordon, Linda. 1988. *Heroes of Their Own Lives: The Politics and History of Family Violence—Boston, 1880–1960*. New York: Viking.

Gore, Albert. 1993. *The National Performance Review, Creating a Government that Works Better and Costs Less*. Office of the Vice President, Accompanying Report of the National Performance Review: Improving Regulatory Systems. Washington, DC: Government Printing Office.

Gormley, William, Jr., ed. 1991a. *Privatization and Its Alternatives*. Madison: University of Wisconsin Press.

———. 1991b. "Two Cheers for Privatization." In *Privatization and Its Alternatives*. See Gormley 1991a.

———. 1991c. "The Privatization Controversy." In *Privatization and Its Alternatives*. See Gormley 1991a.

Gramsci, Antonio. 1971. *Selections from the Prison Notebooks*, trans. Q. Hoare and G. Smith. New York: International Publishers.

Gray, Wayne, and John Scholz. 1993. "Does Regulatory Enforcement Work? A Panel Analysis of OSHA Enforcement." *Law and Society Review* 27:177–214.

Gronbjerg, Kristen. 1987. "Nonprofit Responses to Reductions in Federal Support of Health and Human Services." Mimeo. Available through Joel Handler.

———. 1992. "Nonprofit Human Service Organizations: Funding Strategies and Patterns of Adaptation." In *Human Services as Complex Organizations*, ed. Yeheskel Hasenfeld, 73–97. Newbury Park, CA: Sage.

Gruber, Judith, and Edison Trickett. 1987. "Can We Empower Others? The Paradox of Empowerment in the Governing of an Alternative Public School." *American Journal of Community Psychology* 15:353–71.

Gurin, Arnold. 1989. "Governmental Responsibility and Privatization: Examples from Four Social Services." In *Privatization and the Welfare State*, 179–205. See Kamerman and Kahn 1989b.

Hahn, Robert, and Gordon Hester. 1989. "Where Did All the Markets Go? Analysis of EPA's Emissions Trading Program." *Yale Journal on Regulation* 6:109–54.

Hahn, Robert, and Robert Stavins. 1991. "Incentive-Based Environmental Regulation: A New Era from an Old Idea?" *Ecology Law Quarterly* 18:1–42.

Hall, John. 1989. "State-Local Relations in Arizona: Change, Within Limits." In *A Decade of Devolution* 133–60. See Liner 1989.

Handler, Joel. 1986. *The Conditions of Discretion: Autonomy, Community, Bureaucracy*. New York: Russell Sage Foundation.

———. 1990a. "Constructing the Political Spectacle: The Interpretation of Entitlements, Legalization, and Obligations in Social Welfare History." *Brooklyn Law Review*" 56:899–974.

———. 1990b. *Law and the Search for Community*. Philadelphia: University of Pennsylvania Press.

Handler, Joel. 1992. "Postmodernism, Protest, and the New Social Movements." *Law and Society Review* 26:697–732, 819–24.

———. 1995. *The Poverty of Welfare Reform*. New Haven, CT: Yale University Press.

Handler, Joel, and Yeheskel Hasenfeld. 1991. *The Moral Construction of Poverty: American Welfare Reform*. Newbury Park, CA: Sage.

Handler, Joel, and Julie Zatz, eds. 1982. *Neither Angels Nor Thieves: Studies in Deinstitutionalization of Status Offenders*. Washington, DC: National Academy Press.

Hannaway, Jane. 1993. "Decentralization in Two School Districts: Challenging the Standard Paradigm." In *Decentralization and School Improvement*, 135–62. See Hannaway and Carnoy 1993.

Hannaway, Jane, and Martin Carnoy. 1993. *Decentralization and School Improvement: Can We Fulfill the Promise?* San Francisco: Jossey-Bass.

Hansmann, Henry. 1987. "Economic Theories of Nonprofit Organizations." In *The NonProfit Sector*, 27–42. See Powell 1987.

Hanson, Marjorie, Don Morris, and Robert Collins. 1992. "Empowerment of Teachers in Dade County's School-Based Management Pilot." In *Empowering Teachers and Parents*. See Hess 1992.

Hardina, Donna. 1990. "The Effect of Funding Sources on Client Access to Services." *Administration in Social Work* 14:33–46.

Harrington, Diane, and Peter Cookson, Jr. 1992. "School Reform in East Harlem: Alternative Schools vs. Schools of Choice." In *Empowering Teachers and Parents*. See Hess 1992.

Hartmann, Heidi. 1987. "Changes in Women's Economic and Family Roles in Post–World War II United States." In *Women, Households, and the Economy*, ed. Lourdes Beneria and Catharine Stimpson, 33–64. New Brunswick, NJ: Rutgers University Press.

Hasenfeld, Yeheskel. 1992a. "Theoretical Approaches to Human Service Organizations." In *Human Services as Complex Organizations*, 24–44. See Hasenfeld 1992.

———. 1992b. "The Nature of Human Service Oganizations." In *Human Services as Complex Organizations*, 3–23. See Hasenfeld 1992.

———. ed. 1992. *Human Services as Complex Organizations*. Newbury Park, CA: Sage.

Hasenfeld, Yeheskel, and Benjamin Gidron. 1993. "Self-Help Groups and Human Services Organizations: An Interorganizational Perspective." *Social Service Review* 67:217–36.

Hasenfeld, Yeheskel, and Richard Hoefer. 1986. "Is There a Crisis in Personal Social Services? The U.S. Case." Available through Joel Handler.

Hawkins, Keith. 1984. *Environment and Enforcement: Regulation and the Social Definition of Pollution*. Oxford: The Clarendon Press.

Heller, Kirby, Wayne Holtzman, and Samuel Messick, eds. 1992. *Placing Children in Special Education: A Strategy for Equity*. Washington, DC: National Academy.

Henig, Jeffery. 1989–90. "Privatization in the United States: Theory and Practice." *Political Science Quarterly* 104:649–70.

Heskin, Alan. 1991. *The Struggle for Community*. Boulder, CO: Westview Press.

Hess, G. Alfred, Jr. 1991. *School Restructuring Chicago Style*. Newbury Park, CA: Corwin Press.

———. 1992a. "Introduction: Examining School Restructuring Efforts." In *Empowering Teachers and Parents*. See Hess 1992.

———. 1992b. "Through the Eyes of Anthropologists." In *Empowering Teachers and Parents*. See Hess 1992.

———. 1993a. "Race and the Liberal Perspective in Chicago School Reform." In *The New Politics of Race and Gender*, ed. Catherine Marshall, 85–96. New York: Falmer Press.

———. 1993b. "Decentralization and Community Control." In *Reforming Education: The Emerging Systemic Approach*, ed. Stephen Jacobson and Robert Berne, 66. Newbury Park, CA: Corwin Press.

———. 1994a. "Introduction: School-Based Management as a Vehicle for School Reform." *Education and Urban Society* 26: 203–19.

———. 1994b. "The Changing Role of Teachers: Moving Form Interested Spectators to Engaged Planners." *Education and Urban Society* 26:248–63.

———. n.d. "Using School Based Management to Restructure Schools: The Chicago Experience." Chicago Panel on School Policy.

———, ed., 1992. *Empowering Teachers and Parents: School Restructuring Through the Eyes of Anthropologists*. Westport CT: Bergin and Garvey.

Hess, G. Alfred, Jr., and John Easton. 1992. "Who's Making What Decisions: Monitoring Authority Shifts in Chicago School Reform." In *Empowering Teachers and Parents*. See Hess 1992.

Hess, G. Alfred, Jr., Susan Flinspach, and Susan Ryan. 1993. "Case Studies of Chicago Schools Under Reform." In *Evaluating Chicago School Reform*, ed. Richard Niemiec and Herbert Walberg. San Francisco: Jossey-Bass.

Honneth, Axel. 1991. *The Critique of Power: Reflective Stages in a Critical Social Theory*. Cambridge, MA: MIT Press.

Hubbard, Pamela, Perla Werner, Jiska Cohen-Mansfield, and Rochelle Shusterman. 1992. "Seniors for Justice: A Political and Social Action Group for Nursing Home Residents." *The Gerontologist* 32:856–58.

Hula, Richard. 1991. "Alternative Management Strategies in Public Housing." In *Privatization and Its Alternatives*. See Gormley 1991a.

Jepperson, Ronald, and John Meyer. 1991. "The Public Order and the Construction of Formal Organizations." In *The New Institutionalism in Organizational Analysis*, 204–31. See Powell and DiMaggio 1991.

Johnson, Colleen L., and Leslie A. Grant. 1985. *The Nursing Home in American Society*. Baltimore, MD: Johns Hopkins University Press.

Johnson, Susan. 1990. "Teachers, Power, and School Change." In *Choice and Control in American Education*. Vol. 2, 343–70. See Clune and Witte 1990b.

Kamerman, Sheila, and Alfred Kahn. 1989a. "Child Care and Privatization under Reagan." In *Privatization and the Welfare State*, 235–59. See Kamerman and Kahn 1989b.

Kamerman, Sheila, and Alfred Kahn, eds. 1989b. *Privatization and the Welfare State*. Princeton: Princeton University Press.

Kane, Rosalind. 1991. "Personal Autonomy for Residents in Long-Term Care:

Concepts and Issues of Measurement." In *The Concept and Measurement of Quality of Life in the Frail Elderly*, ed. James E. Birren, James E. Lubben, Janice Cichowlas Rowe, and Donna E. Deutchman, 316–34. New York: Academic Press.

Kantor, Rosabeth, and David Summers. 1987. "Doing Well While Doing Good: Dilemmas of Performance Measurement in Nonprofit Organizations and the Need of Multiple-Constituency Approach." In *The NonProfit Sector*, 154–66. See Powell 1987.

Katz, Michael. 1986. *In the Shadow of the Poorhouse*. New York: Basic Books.

Kautzer, Kathleen. 1988. "Empowering Nursing Home Residents: A Case Study of 'Living Is For the Elderly,' An Activist Nursing Home Organization." In *Qualitative Gerontology*, ed. Shulamit Reinharz and Graham Rowles, 163–83. New York: Springer Publishing Co.

Keiffer, Charles. 1984. "Citizen Empowerment: A Developmental Perspective." *Prevention in Human Services* 3:9–36.

Kessler-Harris, Alice. 1982. *Out To Work: A History of Wage-earning Women in the United States*. London: Oxford University Press.

Kincaid, John. 1990. "From Cooperative to Coercive Federalism." *ANNALS, AAPSS* 509:139–52.

Kingsley, G. Thomas. 1991. "Housing Vouchers and America's Changing Housing Problems." In *Privatization and Its Alternatives*. See Gormley 1991a.

Kolodny, Robert. 1986. "The Emergence of Self-Help as a Housing Strategy for the Urban Poor." In *Critical Perspectives on Housing*, 447–62. See Bratt, Hartman, Meyerson 1986.

Kramer, Ralph. 1987. "Voluntary Agencies and the Personal Social Services." In *The NonProfit Sector*, 240–57. See Powell 1987.

———. 1994. "Voluntary Agencies and the Contract Culture: 'Dream or Nightmare?'" *Social Service Review* 68:33–60.

Kramer, Ralph, and Bart Grossman. 1987. "Contracting for Social Services: Process Management and Resource Dependencies." *Social Service Review* 61:32–55.

Krier, James. 1992. "The Tragedy of the Commons, Part Two." *Harvard Journal of Law and Public Policy* 15:325–47.

Kweit, Mary G., and Robert Kweit. 1981. *Implementing Citizen Participation in a Bureaucratic Society*. New York: Praeger.

Leavitt, Jacquiline, and Susan Saegert. 1990. *From Abandonment to Hope*. New York: Columbia University Press.

Lee, Dwight. 1991. "Vouchers—the Key to Meaningful Reform." In *Privatization and Its Alternatives*. See Gormley 1991a.

Lee, Valerie, Robert Dedrick, and Julia Smith. 1991. "The Effect of the Social Organization of Schools on Teachers' Efficacy and Satisfaction." *Sociology of Education* 64:190–208.

Lee, Valerie, Linda Winfield, and Thomas Wilson. 1991. "Academic Behaviors among High-Achieving African-American Students." *Education and Urban Society* 24:65–86.

LeGrand, Julian, and Ray Robinson eds. 1984. Privatization and the Welfare State. London. George Allen & Unwin.

Levin, Henry. 1986. *Educational Reform for Disadvantaged Students: An Emerging Crisis*. Washington, DC: National Education Association.

———. 1990. "The Theory of Choice Applied to Education." In *Choice and Control in American Education*. Vol. 1, 247–84. See Clune and Witte 1990a.

———. 1991. "Accelerating the Progress of All Students." *Rockefeller Institute Special Report No. 31*. New York: State University of New York.

Levin, Henry, and Wendy Hopfenberg. 1991. "Accelerated Schools for At-Risk Students." *The Education Digest* 56:47–51.

Lewis, Dan. 1993. "Deinstitutionalization and School Decentralization: Making the Same Mistake Twice." In *Decentralization and School Improvement*, 84–101. See Hannaway and Carnoy 1993.

Lewis, Dan, and Kathryn Nakagawa. 1992. *Parental Participation and Urban School Reform*. Working paper. Evanston, IL: Center for Urban Affairs and Policy Research, Northwestern University.

Liner, E. Blaine, ed. 1989. *A Decade of Devolution: Perspectives on State-Local Relations*. Washington, DC: Urban Institute.

Lipsky, Michael. 1980. *Street-level Bureaucracy: Dilemmas of the Individual in Public Services*. New York: Russell Sage Foundation.

Lipsky, Michael, and Marc Thibodeau. 1990. "Domestic Food Policy in the United States." *Journal of Health Politics, Policy, and Law* 15:319–39.

Litwak, Eugene, and Rose Dobrof. 1977. *Maintenance of Family Ties of Long-Term Care Patients*. Rockville, MD: U.S. Public Health Service.

Louis, Karen. 1990. "Teachers, Power, and School Change, Commentary." In *Choice and Control in American Education*. Vol. 2, 381–90. See Clune and Witte 1990b.

Lowi, Theodore. 1969. *The End of Liberalism*. New York: Norton.

Luhmann, Niklas. 1985. "The Self-Reproduction of Law and Its Limits." In *Dilemmas of Law in the Welfare State*, ed. Gunther Teubner, 111–27. Berlin: Walter de Gruyter.

Lukes, Steven. 1974. *Power: A Radical View*. London: Macmillan.

———, ed. 1986. *Power*. New York: New York University Press.

Macey, Jonathan. 1992. "Organizational Design and Political Control of Administrative Agencies." *Journal of Law, Economics, and Organizations* 8:93–110.

MacLennan, Carol. 1985. "Comment." In *Regulatory Policy and the Social Sciences*. California Series on Social Choice and Political Economy, no. 5, ed. Roger G. Noll, 160–71. Berkeley: University of California Press.

MacManus, Susan. 1990. "Financing Federal, State, and Local Governments in the 1990s." *ANNALS, AAPSS* 509:22–35.

Malen, Betty, Rodney Ogawa, and Jennifer Kranz. 1990. "What Do We Know about School-Based Management? A Case Study of the Literature—a Call for Research." In *Choice and Control in American Education*. Vol. 2, 289–342. See Clune and Witte 1990b.

Malka, Shalom. 1990. "Contracting for Human Services: The Case of Pennsylvania's Subsidized Child Day Care Program—Policy Limitations and Prospects." *Administration in Social Work* 14:31–46.

Mansbridge, Jane. 1980. *Beyond Adversary Democracy*. New York: Basic Books.

Marmor, Theodore, Mark Schlesinger, and Richard Smithey. 1987. "Nonprofit

Organizations and Health Care." In *The NonProfit Sector*, 221–39. See Powell 1987.

Marrett, Cora. 1990. "School Organization and the Quest for Community, Commentary." In *Choice and Control in American Education*. Vol. 1, 235–40. See Clune and Witte 1990a.

May, Maurice I., Edvardas Kaminskas, Jack Kasten, with David A. Levine. 1991. *Managing Institutional Long-Term Care for the Elderly*. Gaithersburg, MD: Aspen Publishers.

Mayer, J.W., and B. Rowan. 1977. "Institutionalized Organizations: Formal Structure as Myth and Ceremony." *American Journal of Sociology* 83:340–63.

McCann, Michael. 1994. *Rights at Work*. Chicago: University of Chicago Press.

McCubbins, Matthew, Roger Noll, and Barry Weingast. 1989. "Structure and Process, Politics and Policy: Administrative Arrangements and the Political Control of Agencies." *Virginia Law Review* 75:431–82.

Mead, Lawrence. 1986. *Beyond Entitlement: The Social Obligations of Citizenship*. New York: Free Press.

Menell, Peter. 1992. "Institutional Fantasylands: From Scientific Management to Free Market Environmentalism." *Harvard Journal of Law and Public Policy* 15:489–510.

Merelman, Richard. 1990. "Knowledge, Educational Organization and Choice, Commentary." In *Choice and Control in American Education*. Vol. 1, 79–85. See Clune and Witte 1990a.

Merry, Sally. 1986. "Everyday Understandings of the Law in Working Class America." *American Ethnologist*. 13:254–70.

Metz, Mary. 1990. "Potentialities and Problems of Choice in Desegregation Plans, Commentaries." In *Choice and Control in American Education*. Vol. 2, 111–18. See Clune and Witte 1990b.

Meyer, John, and Brian Rowan. 1991. "Institutionalized Organizations: Formal Structure as Myth and Ceremony." In *The New Institutionalism in Organizational Analysis*, 41–62. See Powell and DiMaggio 1991.

Middleton, Melissa. 1987. "Nonprofit Boards of Directors: Beyond the Governance Function." In *The NonProfit Sector*, 141–53. See Powell 1987.

Milofsky, Carl. 1987. "Neighborhood-Based Organizations: A Market Analogy." In *The NonProfit Sector*, 277–95. See Powell 1987.

Moe, Terry. 1989. "The Politics of Bureaucratic Structure." In *Can the Government Govern?*, ed. John Chubb and Paul Peterson, 267–330. Washington, DC: Brookings Institution.

———. 1990. "Political Institutions: The Neglected Side of the Story." *Journal of Law, Economics, and Organizations*, special issue 6:213–54.

Molotch, Harvey, and Deirdre Boden. 1985. "Talking Social Structures: Discourse, Domination and the Watergate Hearings." *American Sociological Review* 50:273–88.

Monk, Abraham, Leonard Kaye, and Howard Litwin. 1984. *Resolving Grievances in Nursing Homes: A Study of Ombudsman Programs*. New York: Columbia University Press.

Montgomery, R. 1983. "Staff-Family relations and Institutional Care Policies." *Journal of Gerontological Social Work* 6:25–37.

Moore, Donald. 1990. "Voice and Choice in Chicago." In *Choice and Control in American Education*. Vol. 2, 153–98. See Clune and Witte 1990b.

———. 1992. "The Case for Parent and Community Involvement." In *Empowering Teachers and Parents*. See Hess 1992.

Moore, Donald, and Abha Pandya. 1992. "Restructuring Urban Schools: Chicago's Reform Strategy." *Illinois Schools Journal* 71:22–39.

Morone, James. 1990. *The Democratic Wish: Popular Participation and the Limits of American Government*. New York: Basic Books.

Muncey, Donna, and Patrick McQuillan. 1992. "The Dangers of Assuming a Consensus for Change: Some Examples from the Coalition of Essential Schools." In *Empowering Teachers and Parents*. See Hess 1992.

Nader, Laura, and Claire Nader. 1985. "A Wide Angle on Regulation: An Anthropological Perspective." In *Regulatory Policy and the Social Sciences*, ed. Roger G. Noll. California Series on Social Choice and Political Economy, no. 5, 141–60. Berkeley: University of California Press.

Nathan, Joe, and James Ysseldyke. 1994. "What Minnesota Has Learned About School Choice." *Phi Delta Kappa* 75:682–89.

Nathan, Richard, and John Lago. 1990. "Intergovernmental Fiscal Roles and Relations." *ANNALS, AAPSS* 509:36–47.

National Commission on Excellence in Education. 1983. *The Nation at Risk: The Imperative for Educational Reform*. Washington, DC: National Commission on Excellence in Education.

Newmann, Fred. 1990. "The Prospects for Communal School Organization, Commentary." In Choice and Control in American Education. Vol. 1, 241–46. See Clune and Witte 1990a.

Noll, Roger, ed. 1985. *Regulatory Policy and the Social Sciences*. Berkeley: University of California Press.

O'Higgins, Michael. 1989. "Social Welfare and Privatization: The British Experience." In *Privatization and the Welfare State*, 157–77. See Kamerman and Kahn 1989a.

Osborne, David. 1989. "They Can't Stop Us Now." *Washington Post*, Sunday, 30 July.

Osborne, David, and Ted Gaebler. 1992. *Reinventing Government*. Reading, MA: Addison-Wesley Publishing Company.

Ostrander, Susan. 1989. "Private Social Services: Obstacles to the Welfare State?" *Nonprofit and Voluntary Sector Quarterly* 18:25–45.

Pack, Janet. 1991. "The Opportunities and Constraints of Privatization." In *Privatization and Its Alternatives. See Gormley 1991a*.

Parsons, Talcott. 1986. "Power and the Social System." In *Power*, ed. Steven Lukes, 94–. New York: New York University Press.

Peterson, Paul. 1990. "Monopoly and Competition in American Education." In Choice and Control in American Education. Vol. 1, 47–78. See Clune and Witte 1990a.

———. 1990–91. "The Rise and Fall of Special Interest Politics." *Political Science Quarterly* 105:539–56.

Polsby, Nelson. 1963. *Community Power and Political Theory*. New Haven, CT: Yale University Press.

Pogrow, Stanley. 1987. "Developing Higher Order Thinking Skills: The HOTS Program." *Computing Teacher* 15:11–15.

Powell, Walter. 1991. "Expanding the Scope of Institutional Analysis." In *The New Institutionalism in Organizational Analysis*, 183–203. See Powell and DiMaggio 1991.

———. ed. 1987. *The NonProfit Sector: A Research Handbook*. New Haven, CT: Yale University Press.

Powell, Walter, and Paul DiMaggio. eds. 1991. *The New Institutionalism in Organizational Analysis*. Chicago: University of Chicago Press.

Powell, Walter, and Rebecca Friedkin. 1987. "Organizational Change in Non-profit Organizations." In *The NonProfit Sector*, 180–92. See Powell 1987.

Purkey, Stewart. 1990. "School-Based Management: More and Less than Meets the Eye, Commentary." In *Choice and Control in American Education*. Vol. 2, 371–80. See Clune and Witte 1990b.

Rabin, Robert. 1986. "Federal Regulation in Historical Perspective." *Stanford Law Review* 38:1189–1326.

Rappaport, Julian. 1992. "The Death and Resurrection of a Community Mental Health Movement." In *The Present and Future of Prevention: In Honor of George W. Albee*, ed. Marc Kessler, Stephen E. Goldston, and Justin M. Joffe, 78–98. Newbury Park, CA: Sage.

Rees, Joseph. 1988. *Reforming the Workplace: A Study of Self-Regulation in Occupational Safety*. Philadelphia: University of Pennsylvannia Press.

Rein, Martin. 1989. "The Social Structure of Institutions: Neither Public Nor Private." In *Privatization and the Welfare State*, 49–71. See Kamerman and Kahn 1989a.

Rivlin, Alice. 1992. *Reviving the American Dream: The Economy, the States, and the Federal Government*. Washington, DC: Brookings Institution.

Rodin, Judith. 1989. "Sense of Control: Potentials for Intervention." *ANNALS, AAPSS* 503:29–42.

Rose-Ackerman, Susan. 1988. "Progressive Law and Economics—and the New Administrative Law." *Yale Law Journal* 98:341–68.

———. 1990. "Deregulation and Reregulation: Rhetoric and Reality." *Journal of Law and Politics* 6:287–310.

———. 1994a. "Consensus versus Incentives: A Skeptical Look at Regulatory Negotiation." *Duke Law Journal* 43:1206–20.

———. 1994b. "American Administrative Law under Siege: Is Germany a Model?" *Harvard Law Review* 107:1279–1302.

Rosenkranz, Todd. 1994. "Reallocating Resources: Discretionary Funds Provide Engine for Change." *Education and Urban Society* 26:264–84.

Rudney, Gabriel. 1987. "The Scope and Dimensions of Nonprofit Activity." In *The NonProfit Sector*, 55–64. See Powell 1987.

Sabatier, Paul, and Daniel Mazmanian. 1981. "Relationships between Governing Boards and Professional Staff: Role Orientations and Influence on the California Coastal Commissions." *Administration and Society* 13:207–48.

Safford, F. 1989. "If You Don't Like the Care, Why Don't You Take Your Mother Home? Obstacles to Family/Staff Partnerships in the Institutional Care of the Aged." *Journal of Gerontological Social Work* 13:1–7.

Salamon, Lester. 1987. "Partners in Public Service: The Scope and Theory of Government-Nonprofit Relations." In *The NonProfit Sector*, 99–117. See Powell 1987.

Sarat, Austin. 1990. ". . . The Law Is All Over: Power, Resistance, and the Legal Consciousness of the Welfare Poor." *Yale Journal of Law and Humanities* 2:243.

Scharlach, Andrew. 1988. "Peer Counselor Training for Nursing Home Residents." *The Gerontologist* 28:499–502.

Schlesinger, Mark, and Robert Dorwart. 1984. "Ownership and Mental-Health Services: A Reappraisal of the Shift toward Privately Owned Facilities." *New England Journal of Medicine* 311:959–65.

Schlesinger, Mark, Robert Dorwart, and Richard Pulice. 1986. "Competitive Bidding and States' Purchase of Services: The Case of Mental Health Care in Massachusetts." *Journal of Public Analysis and Management* 5:245–63.

Scholz, John, Jime Twombly, and Barbard Headrick. 1991. "Street-Level Political Controls Over Federal Bureaucracy." *American Political Science Review* 85:829–50.

Scott, W. Richard. 1985. "Comment." In *Regulatory Policy and the Social Sciences*. California Series on Social Choice and Political Economy, no. 5, ed. Roger G. Noll, 304–11. Berkeley: University of California Press.

———. 1991. "Unpacking Institutional Arguments." In *The New Institutionalism in Organizational Analysis*, 164–203. See Powell and DiMaggio 1991.

Scott, W. Richard, and John Meyer. 1991. "The Organization of Societal Sectors: Propositions and Early Evidence." In *The New Institutionalism in Organizational Analysis*, 108–42. See Powell and DiMaggio 1991.

Selznick, Philip. 1985. "Focusing Organizational Research on Regulation." In *Regulatory Policy and the Social Sciences*. California Series on Social Choice and Political Economy, no. 5, ed. Roger G. Noll, 363–67. Berkeley: University of California Press.

———. 1992. *The Moral Commonwealth: Social Theory and the Promise of Community*. Berkeley: University of California Press.

Shapiro, Martin. 1983. "Administrative Discretion: The Next Stage." *Yale Law Journal* 92:1487–1522.

Shapiro, Sidney, and Robert Glicksman. 1988. "Congress, the Supreme Court, and the Quiet Revolution in Administrative Law." *Duke Law Journal* (1988): 819–78.

Shapiro, Sidney, and Thomas McGarity. 1989. "Reorienting OSHA: Regulatory Alternatives and Legislative Reform." *Yale Journal on Regulation* 6:1–63.

Shepsle, Kenneth. 1989. "The Changing Textbook Congress." In *Can the Government Govern?* ed. John Chubb and Paul Peterson, 238–66. Washington, DC: Brookings Institution.

Silver, Hilary. 1991. "The Privatization of Public Housing in Great Britain." In *Privatization and Its Alternatives*. See Gormley 1991a.

Slavin, Robert. 1991. *Success for All*. Washington, DC: U.S. Department of Education.

Smith, K., and V. Bengston. 1979. "Positive Consequences of Institutionalization:

Solidarity between Elderly Parents and Their Middle-Aged Children." *The Gerontologist* 19:438–47.

Smith, Steven. 1987. "Privatization and the Politics of Social Welfare Spending." Paper presented at the Ninth Annual Research Conference of the Association of Public Policy Analysis and Management, Bethesda, MD.

Smith, Steven, and Michael Lipsky. 1992. *Nonprofits for Hire: The Welfare State in the Age of Contracting.* Cambridge, MA: Harvard University Press.

Sosin, Michael. 1986. *Private Benefits: Material Assistance in the Private Sector.* New York: Academic Press.

———. 1990. "Decentralizing the Social Service System: A Reassessment." *Social Service Review* 64:617–36.

Spiller, Pablo, and John Ferejohn. 1992. "The Economics and Politics of Administrative Law and Procedures: An Introduction." *Journal of Law, Economics, and Organizations* 8:1–7.

Starr, Paul. 1988. "The Meaning of Privatization." *Yale Law and Policy Review* 6:6–41.

———. 1991. "The Case for Skepticism." In *Privatization and Its Alternatives,* 25. See Gormley 1991a.

Steinberg, Richard. 1987. "Nonprofit Organizations and the Market." In *The NonProfit Sector,* 118–38. See Powell 1987.

Stewart, Richard. 1986. "Reconstitutive Law." *Maryland Law Review* 46:86–114.

———. 1990. "Madison's Nightmare." *University of Chicago Law Review* 57:335–56.

———. 1992. "Models for Environmental Regulation: Central Planning Versus Market-Based Approaches." *Boston College Environmental Affairs Law Review* 19:547–62.

Stinchcombe, Arthur L. 1990. *Information and Organizations.* Berkeley: University of California Press.

Streeck, Wolfgang, and Phillippe Schmitter. 1985. "Community, Market, State—and Associations?" In *Private Interest Government: Beyond Market and State,* ed. Wolfgang Streeck and Phillippe Schmitter. Newbury Park, CA: Sage.

Sunstein, Cass. 1990. *After the Rights Revolution: Reconceiving the Regulatory State.* Cambridge, MA: Harvard University Press.

Sviridoff, Mitchell. 1989. "The Local Initiatives Support Corporation: A Private Initiative for a Public Problem." In *Privatization and the Welfare State,* 207–33. See Kamerman and Kahn 1989a.

Tarrow, Sidney. 1989. *Struggle, Politics, and Reform: Collective Action, Social Movements, and Cycles of Protest.* Ithaca, NY: Cornell University Press.

Tatel, David. 1992–93. "Desegregation Versus School Reform: Resolving the Conflict." *Stanford Law and Policy Review* (Winter): 61–72.

Testa, Mark. 1992. "Racial Variation in the Early Life Course of Adolescent Welfare Mothers." In *Early Parenthood and Coming of Age in the 1990's,* ed. Margaret Rosenheim and Mark Testa, 1–29. New Brunswick, NJ: Rutgers University Press.

Thomas, Robert. 1990. "National-Local Relations and the City's Dilemma." *ANNALS, AAPSS* 509:106–17.

Touminen, Mary. 1991. "Caring for Profit: The Social, Economic, and Political Significance of For-Profit Child Care." *Social Service Review* 65:450–67.

Tyack, David. 1990. "'Restructuring' in Historical Perspective: Tinkering toward Utopia." *Teachers College Record* 92:170–91.

———. 1991. "Public School Reform: Policy Talk and Institutional Practice." *American Journal of Education* 100:1–19.

———. 1992. "Can We Build a System of Choice That Is Not Just a 'Sorting Machine' or a Market-Based 'Free-for-All?'" *Equity and Choice* 9:13–17.

———. 1993. "School Governance in the United States: Historical Puzzles and Anomalies." In *Decentralization and School Improvement*, 1–32. See Hannaway and Carnoy 1993.

U.S. Congress. House. 1991. Select Committee on Aging.

Van Horn, Carl. 1991. "The Myths and Realities of Privatization." In *Privatization and Its Alternatives*. See Gormley 1991a.

Walker, Alan. 1984. "The Political Economy of Privatisation." In *Privatization and the Welfare State*, ed. Julian LeGrand and Ray Robinson, 19–44. London: George Allen & Unwin.

Walker, Jack. 1983. "The Origins and Maintenance of Interest Groups in America." *American Political Science Review* 77:390–406.

Weiler, Hans. 1993. "Control versus Legitimation: The Politics of Ambivalence." In *Decentralization and School Improvement*, 55–83. See Hannaway and Carnoy 1993.

Weiss, Janet. 1990. "Control in School Organizations: Theoretical Perspectives." In *Choice and Control in American Education*. Vol. 1, 91–134. See Clune and Witte 1990a.

Wells, Lilian, and Carolyn Singer. 1988. "Quality of Life in Institutions for the Elderly: Maximizing Well-Being." *The Gerontologist* 28:266–69.

Wetle, Terrie. 1991. "Resident Decision Making and Quality of Life in the Frail Elderly." In *The Concept and Measurement of Quality of Life in the Frail Elderly*, ed. James E. Birren, James E. Lubben, Janice Cichowlas Rowe, and Donna E. Deutchman, 279–96. New York: Academic Press.

White, Lucie. 1990. "Subordination, Rhetorical Survival Skills, and Sunday Shoes: Notes on the Hearing of Mrs. G." *Buffalo Law Review* 38:1.

Willey, Zach. 1992. "Behind Schedule and Over Budget: The Case of Markets, Water, and Environment." *Harvard Journal of Law and Public Policy* 15:391–426.

Witte, John. 1990a. "Introduction." In *Choice and Control in American Education*. Vol. 1, 1–10. See Clune and Witte 1990a.

Witte, John. 1990b. "Choice and Control: An Analytical Overview." In *Choice and Control in American Education*. Vol. 1, 11–46. See Clune and Witte 1990a.

Wright, Dell. 1990. "Policy Shifts in the Politics and Administration of Intergovernmental Relations, 1930s–1990s." *ANNALS, AAPSS* 509:60–72.

York, J., and R. Calsyn. 1977. "Family Involvement in Nursing Homes." *Gerontologist* 17:500–505.

Young, Dennis. 1987. "Executive Leadership in Nonprofit Organizations." In *The NonProfit Sector*, 167–69. See Powell 1987.

Zald, Mayer. 1980. "The Federal Impact on the Deinstitutionalization of Status Offenders: A Framework." Working paper, commissioned by the Panel on Deinstitutionalization of Children and Youth, Assembly of Behavioral and Social Sciences, National Research Council, Washington, DC.

Zimmerman, Joseph. 1990. "Regulating Intergovernmental Relations in the 1990s" *ANNALS, AAPSS* 509:48–59.

Zimmerman, Marc. 1993. "Empowerment Theory: Psychological, Organizational and Community Levels of Analysis." In *Handbook of Community Psychology*, ed. J. Rappaport and E. Seidman. New York: Plenum.

Zimmerman, Marc, and J. Rappaport. 1988. "Citizen Participation, Perceived Control, and Psychological Empowerment." *American Journal of Community Psychology* 16:725–50.

Zucker, Lynne. 1991. "The Role of Institutionalization in Cultural Persistence." In *The New Institutionalism in Organizational Analysis*, 83–107. See Powell and DiMaggio 1991.

CASES

Abbott v. Burke, NJ 1994.
Adarand Construction, Inc. v. Pena, 115 S. Ct. 2097 (1995).
Missouri v. Jenkins, 115 S. Ct. 2038 (1995).

MISCELLANEOUS

Lower Income Rental Assistance Program, Housing and Community Development Act of 1974

INDEX

38, 39; regulatory design and, 34–36; schools and, 26–27; work/training programs and, 27–28

pollution regulations, 50, 54, 55, 60, 218, 241

post-structuralist view of power, 119–20, 121

poverty: social welfare codes and, 42–43, 47; tenant organizations and, 159

power: adversary vs. unitary democracy and, 232–33; bargaining and, 131–32; conflict management and, 117–18; defining, 9–10, 116n; in human service agencies, 123–30; three dimensions of, 116–23, 128–30. *See also* empowerment

Power: A Radical View (Lukes), 117

powerlessness: countering, 122, 166–68, 217–18, 241; as loss of control, 122

practice ideologies, 124, 127

preemption, federal, 64–65

principals, school: school reform leadership by, 202, 206, 210, 234–35; site-based management by, 227

Priority Boards, 163

private schools: autonomy of, 182–83; voucher programs and, 56, 181–82

private sector, and social services, 7–8

privatization: arguments for, 79–80; conflict management and, 78; decentralization and, 19, 78; defining, 6–7, 78; efficiency and, 83–85, 86; government contracting and, 7, 78–93; local control and, 4–5; political interests and, 87–88; reallocation of power and, 8–9; regulation and, 56; taxpayer's revolt and, 3; vouchers and, 78, 80–81, 108–10

process of empowerment, 122–23, 217–18, 228–42

professional community, 206–7, 209

professional control, 174

Professional Personnel Advisory Committee (PPAC), 200

professionals, in nonprofit agencies, 101

professional safety movement, 136

Progressive Era, social welfare programs during, 43–44

property taxes, school funding through, 173

Proposition 13 (California), 64

public education: democratic localism in, 198–214; failure of, 170, 182; five kinds of control in, 174–76; governmental responsibility for, 69; local government

and, 72–76; school choice and, 181–94, 221–22; standardization requirements in, 170–71; total institution approach to, 194–97. *See also* education; public schools; school reform

public goods theory, 78–79

public housing, tenant empowerment in, 156–62

public policy, and privatization, 7

public programs, implementing, 36–39. *See also* social services; welfare programs

Public School Education Act of 1975 (New Jersey), 73

public schools: accountability in, 169–71, 177; controlled choice in, 186–93; democratic localism and, 198–214; empowerment process in, 228–42; as organizations, 173–77; political influences on, 26–27; state financing of, 72–74, 75; as total institutions, 194–97; voucher programs for, 56. *See also* Chicago public school system; public education; school reform

Quality Assurance Unit (QAU), 61

quiescence, 239–40

racial issues: local control and, 75; magnet schools and, 186, 190–94; school reform and, 170, 172–73; social welfare programs and, 42, 46–47; tenant organizations and, 159. *See also* desegregation; segregation

rational-legal model, 19–20

Reading Recovery Program, 197

Reagan administration: decentralization movement and, 8; devolution during, 63–67; privatization strategies of, 80, 90; regulatory enforcement by, 59

reciprocity, and cooperative regulation, 60–61

redistribution: school financing and, 73, 75; school reform and, 172

Rees, Joseph, 134–39

reflexive process, empowerment as, 133, 166, 219

regulation, government: command-and-control, 49–56; cooperative, 56–63, 132, 134–55; delegation of, 64–65; in human services, 139–55; politics of designing, 32–36; privatization and, 56; worker safety and, 134–39

About the Author

JOEL F. HANDLER is Richard C. Maxwell Professor of Law at the University of California at Los Angeles. He is the author of *The Poverty of Welfare Reform* and of *Law and the Search for Community*.